THE DASH

SHORT CIRCUITS

Mladen Dolar, Alenka Zupančič, and Slavoj Žižek, editors

THE DASH—THE OTHER SIDE OF ABSOLUTE KNOWING

Rebecca Comay and Frank Ruda

THE MIT PRESS   CAMBRIDGE, MASSACHUSETTS   LONDON, ENGLAND

This book was set in Joanna MT Pro by Toppan Best-set Premedia Limited.

Library of Congress Cataloging-in-Publication Data is available.

ISBN: 978-0-262-53535-9

CONTENTS

A short circuit occurs when there is a faulty connection in the network—
faulty, of course, from the standpoint of the network's smooth functioning.
Is not the shock of short-circuiting, therefore, one of the best metaphors
for a critical reading? Is not one of the most effective critical procedures to
cross wires that do not usually touch: to take a major classic (text, author,
notion) and read it in a short-circuiting way, through the lens of a "minor"
author, text, or conceptual apparatus ("minor" should be understood here
in Deleuze's sense: not "of lesser quality," but marginalized, disavowed by
the hegemonic ideology, or dealing with a "lower," less dignified topic)? If
the minor reference is well chosen, such a procedure can lead to insights
which completely shatter and undermine our common perceptions. This is
what Marx, among others, did with philosophy and religion (short-circuiting philosophical speculation through the lens of political economy, that
is to say, economic speculation); this is what Freud and Nietzsche did with
morality (short-circuiting the highest ethical notions through the lens of the
unconscious libidinal economy). What such a reading achieves is not a simple
"desublimation," a reduction of the higher intellectual content to its lower
economic or libidinal cause; the aim of such an approach is, rather, the inherent decentering of the interpreted text, which brings to light its "unthought,"
its disavowed presuppositions and consequences.

And this is what "Short Circuits" wants to do, again and again. The underlying premise of the series is that Lacanian psychoanalysis is a privileged
instrument of such an approach, whose purpose is to illuminate a standard text or ideological formation, making it readable in a totally new way—
the long history of Lacanian interventions in philosophy, religion, the arts
(from the visual arts to the cinema, music, and literature), ideology, and politics justifies this premise. This, then, is not a new series of books on psychoanalysis, but a series of "connections in the Freudian field"—of short

Lacanian interventions in art, philosophy, theology, and ideology. "Short Circuits" intends to revive a practice of reading which confronts a classic text, author, or notion with its own hidden presuppositions, and thus reveals its disavowed truth. The basic criterion for the texts that will be published is that they effectuate such a theoretical short circuit. After reading a book in this series, the reader should not simply have learned something new: the point is, rather, to make him or her aware of another—disturbing—side of something he or she knew all the time.

Slavoj Žižek

This book works with a set of basic propositions that are all interrelated.

First: If you want to modernize Hegel—to retrieve Hegel as a postcritical, profane thinker (that is, someone not only alert to the contingencies of social and historical existence but equipped and motivated to intervene in these)— you sooner or later have to face the monster. You've got to take seriously the most embarrassingly grandiose moment in the system, the point at which it's all too tempting to start skimming, start apologizing, or simply put the book down: absolute knowing.

Hegel's critics, from Kierkegaard onward, have never stopped reviling Hegel's absolute idealism as a philosophy of identity (or of narcissism, if you wish): it swallows contingencies, it smothers singularities, it cancels out time, it consigns historical suffering to the slaughter bench of history. The climax of the system is thus the moment of its most terrible regression: absolute knowing is an updated form of Stoicism—an ultimate indifference to the concrete world. Such indifference is expressed by philosophy's principled disengagement from political life in the wake of the French Revolution and its subsequent sequestration as a "priesthood apart"[1]—the resignation crystallized in the infamous image of the owl of Minerva. Hegel tellingly ends the *Phenomenology* with the religious gesture of sacrifice: we learn in the end that we have to let things go. Hegel might have been the one philosopher who explicitly did not tell us how to change the world. He promulgated no agenda; he refused to "give instruction as to what the world ought to be."[2] The avowed aim of his philosophy was to grasp its own time in thought.

Jean Hyppolite remarked on the shift that occurs with the move into the sphere of religion in the *Phenomenology*: we leave all phenomena behind and the phenomenology turns into a noumenology, a revelation of what lies behind and beyond appearances.[3] The *Science of Logic* is explicitly defined as the "exposition of *God as he is in his eternal essence before the creation of nature and of* a *finite spirit*"[4]—an exposition of a moment before time, a timeless pastness of all the categories constitutive of the world and thought. Hegel thus performs a megalomaniac transgression of Kant's prohibition: he presents us with everything needed to think everything that is, was, and will ever be. We are invited to think what God thought before he created the world—we become privy to a world without us—a privilege that, however, only forces us to give up any idea of changing the world we do have (for we could not but rely on the categories that are permanently constitutive of this world and that establish its necessity). But this form of absolute knowing, as Schelling objected, gives a monstrous precedence to logic, not only over the workings of human history, but also over nature, even over the nature that unconsciously works inside all of us (a point Kierkegaard will also emphasize). This is an abbreviated balance sheet of the conceit that stands at the center of Hegel's thought—a claim so exaggeratedly absolute it seems irredeemable for any form of contemporary thinking.

Given this historical consensus, the contemporary state of Hegel's reception is peculiar. For the generalized disparagement of absolute knowing no longer entails a dismissal of Hegel's thought altogether, as it did for most of the last two centuries.[5] The current situation rather bears curious similarities with the situation described by Friedrich Engels, who wrote apropos of Feuerbach's intervention in the immediate post-Hegelian aftermath that "everyone became instantly a Feuerbachian."[6] Hegel surprisingly seems to have become the Feuerbach of the twenty-first century. Today, ignoring the absolute bone in the throat of knowledge, everyone has become a Hegelian. Having been cured of his metaphysical sickness, Hegel has suddenly become compatible with an unexpected variety of contemporary philosophical projects. From radical theology to Anglo-American pragmatism, from liberal democratic theory to radical anarchism, from speculative realism to psychoanalysis, a plethora of diverging positions have set out to prove that Hegel was actually not so bad. He was less teleological, less totality-obsessed, less reactionary, less nationalist, less patriarchal, less warmongering, less monarchical, less contradiction-fetishizing, less sublation-crazy—and not even always off the wall in his logical deduction of the number of existing planets (seven!) in the solar system.[7] Even Hegel's un-owl-of-Minerva-ish geopolitical prophecies have proved to be not so outlandish (for example, his description of the impending global hegemony of the United States) ...

Is this book another such rescue attempt? Yes and no. Here's our gamble: the only way to provide a rigorously nonmetaphysical rendering of Hegel is by affirming what is normally taken to be Hegel's most moribund metaphysical baggage. What is usually regarded as the "mystical shell" of the Hegelian system turns out to be its most rational kernel. Instead of reining in the Hegelian enterprise—whether by retreating to a critical-transcendental (broadly epistemological) standpoint or by embracing his all-round friendliness as a theorist of recognition, his compatibility with liberal democracy, his contributions to human rights, or his attunement to singularity and alterity—our intention is rather to push Hegel's project to its limits. One must unapologetically exaggerate what seems most irredeemable: it is at the extremities of Hegel's system that the points of resistance are found. We take Hegel's radicalism to be located at the point where his thought is usually taken to regress most. Far from serving up a sophisticated recycling of some version of precritical rationalist metaphysics, it's precisely the concept of absolute knowing that establishes Hegel's contemporary credentials. To locate this kernel is to retrieve a countercurrent that will redeem the speculative promise of pragmatism against its most vocal proponents—that is, praxis itself.

Second (and this directly follows): you can't sever the *Phenomenology of Spirit* from the *Science of Logic*. The infamous *Abgeschloßenheit* of the *Phenomenology*, its closure or completion, is not only sustained and elucidated by the passage to the *Logic* but also opens it up in startling directions. Unlike standard attempts to link the *Phenomenology* to the *Logic* (or to uncouple them), our starting point is the following: the *Logic* does not so much stabilize, authorize, or ground the *Phenomenology*, although it elucidates or illuminates it. Its function is not to provide the *Phenomenology* with some kind of rational scaffolding or to supply the hermeneutic key to its interpretation. And for this reason, among others, it cannot be harnessed either to a neo-Kantian agenda (for example, as an explication of the transcendental rules governing our historically evolving epistemic practices) or to a neopragmatist one (a clarification or "making explicit" of the implicit commitments sustaining our ongoing language games). These last two agendas, the neo-Kantian and the neopragmatist, are surprisingly compatible and have even come to coalesce in recent Hegel scholarship. Nor does the *Logic* represent an unfortunate regression from the "thoroughgoing skepticism"[8] of the *Phenomenology* to a precritical, dogmatic metaphysics. It does not speak of or from the perspective of an ontotheological plenum where thought coagulates or copulates with being. It cannot be peeled away from the *Phenomenology* like mystical flotsam or relegated to the basement of a long-discarded tradition. And so too conversely: the *Phenomenology* cannot be jettisoned from the *Logic* as some kind of positivist or historical excrescence or set aside as a propaedeutic protocol that can be discontinued once one has arrived at a place called absolute knowing.

A traditional view of Hegel's *Logic* (usually presented as a criticism) is that Hegel is not only expounding the eternal laws of reality but thereby trying to prove the omnipresence and omnipotence of reason. Contemporary critics of this grandiose vision sometimes attempt to rehabilitate his *Logic*—to rescue the *Logic* from its own "metaphysical" carapace—by arguing instead that the book establishes Hegel's more modest credentials as a philosopher of social practice: the *Logic* unfolds the specific constraints of our historical forms of life. Rather than elaborating the unchangeable laws of being, the *Science of Logic* describes the ever-evolving protocols of rational discursive activity.

Despite their manifest differences, both these readings rely on a similar account of the relationship between these two monumental texts. The standard argument is that the move from the *Phenomenology* to the *Logic* is a move from the examination of inherited assumptions to the elucidation of the structure of rationality. This move can be understood in two different ways: on the one hand, as a Platonizing move from illusion to reality, from appearance to being; on the other hand, as a Kantian move from experience to its transcendental conditions. In other words, the *Science of Logic* is read either as a disquisition in dogmatic rational metaphysics or as an exercise in critical philosophy.

Our approach is different. If the passage to the *Logic* is essential to the *Phenomenology*, this is precisely because it exposes experience to its own impossibility. If there is a final push beyond experience, this is not because thinking has arrived in a realm of noumenal otherworldliness where the subject is finally able to actively think its thoughts instead of passively undergoing them. Absolute knowing rather marks the point where experience turns into an experience of the impossibility of experience. The "beyond" of experience is strictly immanent to experience.

Mindedness somehow seems too pallid a term to capture the upheaval at work. Rather, we have reached a moment of radical destitution where all the coordinates of subjectivity have been taken apart. We have been brought to a point beyond consciousness, beyond self-consciousness, beyond the collective self-consciousness of every community. All given structures and all structured givenness of experience have been relinquished. Not only have the established forms of objectivity been systematically dismantled but the form of subjectivity itself has been undone. At the limits of experience, something happens that completely reshuffles the cards—not only of substance but equally of subject. Hegel hints of such destitution in the closing pages of the *Phenomenology* when he describes the final kenosis of spirit and its release into the domain of "free contingent happening."[9] This is the moment when something like a decision is at stake. Hegel speaks of an *Entschluss*, a strange resolve that arises at the point of irresolution between activity and passivity, between the voluntary and the involuntary. A strange kind of freedom.

Third (and this too follows): Reading Hegel can demand a kind of mind-numbing literalism: one must risk triviality to the point of pedantry. But the stakes are high. It will demonstrate the tenacity of the infinite judgment in all its ridiculousness—"Spirit is a bone"[10]—the conjugation of the "highest" and the "lowest," the most grandly universal and the most stupidly particular, the essential and the inessential, the necessary and the contingent, the formal and the material.

In other words, according to Hegel's own protocol, to read speculatively—to read at all—one needs to suspend every advance decision about what is major and what is minor, what is essential and what is inessential. There is no preexisting standard by which to assess what may be significant; you must proceed as if anything and everything is important, as if there is a necessity at work in the most ordinary contingencies of existence. "Even the foam is an expression of essence!" (Lenin).[11] This indiscriminate attentiveness can create the impression of a certain obsessiveness and even paranoia, and it is no doubt in part responsible for the accusations of "panlogicism" that have plagued the reception of Hegel ever since Krug (unreasonably) challenged him to deduce his own pen from the machinery of the concept.[12] But this would misconstrue the nature of the vigilance: it is not that everything is significant, only that anything might be, and you can't know in advance what that might be. Even Hegel describes his encounter with speculative words, for example, as a happy accident (elsewhere he speaks of a "free contingent happening"),[13] a kind of slip or lapsus: he stumbles against the miraculous polysemy of the word *Aufhebung* the way you might stub your toe. "[It] can delight a thinker to fall upon such words and to find the union of opposites naively shown in the dictionary as one word with opposite meanings."[14] The occasion is as unrehearsed and as momentous as the Proustian narrator's stumble in the Guermantes courtyard. A lapse of spirit from which speculative spirit may at any point arise: felix culpa.

Hegel demands of his readers a properly psychoanalytic attitude. The absolute method is the equivalent to the "fundamental rule" of analysis—the annoying obligation to speak "freely"—to communicate whatever comes to or "falls into" the mind, *Einfälle*, without selection, omission, or concern for connection, sequence, propriety, or relevance. Like a passenger on a train (that's Freud's own somewhat Proustian analogy), you're to report the changing mental scenery as it passes by, merely "looking on [*reine Zusehen*],"[15] suspending judgment and leaving understanding and explanation to another day (or person). Our task is simply to "take up *what is there before us* [aufzunehmen, was vorhanden ist]."[16]

Contemporary deflationary readings seek to update Hegel's thought by discarding from his system anything redolent of metaphysics (the term currently functions much as *religion* had functioned for nineteenth-century left-Hegelianism), where the supreme metaphysical hobgoblin is typically crystallized in the category of spirit (the personified agent of universal history) or in the category of the absolute idea (the translucency of rational substance). Such approaches tend to cast aside as insignificant what Hegel himself reckoned to be the weightiest component of his system. We will invert this deflationary gesture by inflating what might seem at first glance to be most trivial. Not only must one unflinchingly affirm the absolute, but this is accessible only in the most mundane minutiae of its material unfolding. "Spirit is a bone." The devil is (in) the detail.[17] "Thought is, after all, the most trenchant epitomist":[18] it cuts into the real, it takes its cue from the miniscule, it discerns in every particle an abbreviation of the totality. As Adorno said of psychoanalysis: the truth lies in the exaggerations.[19] Reading Hegel without presupposition, without eliminating anything in advance or making any prior decision about what is essential and what is inessential, what is living and what is dead, we will attempt to explore Hegel's presentation of the absolute to the letter. This literal approach may at times require going against what would seem to be the spirit of Hegel's own self-interpretation.

Sometimes what seems most obvious can on closer inspection turn out to be the most enigmatic. Hegel defamiliarizes everything we take most for granted, above all our own language.[20] Reading philosophy to the letter is difficult not because its language is especially arcane or complicated (on the contrary, Hegel exhibits a Lutheran commitment to the vernacular[21]) but on the contrary because it appears so banal and trivial that it can seem unworthy of inspection. This is why "individuals who otherwise possess the educational requirement for understanding them" nonetheless complain about the "unintelligibility of philosophical writings."[22] Philosophy is difficult not because it speaks an esoteric idiom or relies on specialized terminology. It is difficult because it does strange things with the language we take most for granted. Hegel took nothing for granted. (Actually, he showed us that we cannot even take "nothing" itself—neither word nor thing—for granted.) If he can be characterized plausibly as an ordinary language philosopher, this is only because he manages to extract weirdness from the most innocuous particles of everyday speech. Rather than plumbing the depths or revealing the mysteries of being, he brings to light what is already on the surface; he exposes what has become invisible through overexposure. One of Hegel's unremembered pupils, Karl Friedrich Ferdinand Sietze, remarked that "every language appeared foreign to him."[23] Hegel invented a "new concept of 'naïveté'"[24] that enabled him not only to "revivify the hidden treasures of language"[25]—but to unleash the uncanny, undead energy of living speech. This is what it means to write and to read speculatively. To read "naively"—to discover in ordinary language the conceptual accomplishment of philosophy—is to stumble on nature's own deviation from itself. Natural language generates its own impediment and spiritual surplus—"a dash [Querstrich] of nature."[26]

The idea for this book originated several years ago in a stupid little observation that kept derailing both of us: Hegel punctuates strangely. There's a peculiarly placed dash in the last sentence of the Phenomenology, and in the opening sentence of the Logic another odd dash appears. Two of the strangest books in the history of philosophy, the *Phenomenology* and the *Logic* ended up being the only books Hegel actually managed to write. Their relationship has puzzled generations of readers. The two books seem to have little enough in common, but they do share a punctuation mark. And this is what we are choosing to focus on? The exercise might seem precious and perverse. Why should there be a grain of significance in a punctuation mark? No one really knew how to punctuate properly in the nineteenth century anyway—and certainly not when it came to dashes (they still don't). Does this not amount to a fetishism of sheer contingency, historical accident, or trivial fact—a category mistake on a par with the Enlightenment reduction of God to the banalities of mere "letters, papers, and copyists"?[27] Had not Hegel famously denounced this kind of positivist enterprise: "so much the worse for the facts!"[28] Why should anyone bother to endow two insignificant strokes of the pen with the dignity of a philosophical investigation?

The German word for "dash" is suggestive. *Gedankenstrich*: the genitive is ambiguous. The stroke points to a pause in thought, a pause for thought, but also to a kind of short-circuiting or cancellation of thought. As a punctuation mark, the dash induces a moment of essential uncertainty in reading. It can mark the beginning of a break, but can also introduce an addition, a digression, a temporary detour; it signals either a continuation or a definitive rupture. This uncertainty connects to the most intractable questions of the whole Hegelian enterprise: totality and closure; continuity and transition; development and progress; identity and difference; beginnings and ends. We will be zooming in on these two particular marks. But as there are dashes of absolute knowing pretty much everywhere in Hegel, we will simultaneously zoom out to unfold their speculative significance. The exercise requires looking through two ends of the telescope at once, which can be disorienting. Only by combining a paranoid microscopism of the detail with a preposterous macroscopism of the system can one stake a claim to the contemporary legacy of Hegel.

This is obviously not a philological claim about the historically correct reading of Hegel. The problem of absolute knowing, a seemingly quaint piece of nineteenth-century ontotheological arcana, resonates surprisingly with contemporary preoccupations extending over an array of fields and engages with some overtly anachronistic approaches, most notably psychoanalysis and Marxism in their various guises.

Our approach is by this token deliberately one-sided. "One-sidedness," *Einseitigkeit*, is, for orthodox Hegelians, a term of abuse: from the perspective of a sovereign *Allseitigkeit*, an imaginary view from nowhere, any particular standpoint unfailingly presents itself as illegitimately partial and blindly partisan. Absolute knowing is usually associated with such a view from nowhere. Our take is the opposite. Absolute knowing is rather the acknowledgment of the partisanship inherent in thought as such; the conceit of "all-sidedness" is a phantasm that obscures the real antagonisms of historical existence. This is not an endorsement of historicism or a plea for immanence, but rather an acknowledgment of the ideological interest of all disinterested universal claims. Only from the blinkered perspective of natural (that is, naturalized) consciousness does knowledge appear as an impartial tribunal—"an eye turned in no particular direction."[29] Absolute knowing dispels this mirage.[30] Or, which amounts to the same, thinking involves a decision. Against every pragmatist commitment constrained by the force of socially authorized reasons, we are attempting to return to what is salvageable of the left-wing Hegelian legacy. This requires engaging Hegel's thinking at the most retrograde of all sites—absolute knowing.

PART I

FIRST TIME AS *PHENOMENOLOGY*, SECOND TIME AS ... *LOGIC*?

CHAPTER 1

"KANT BROUGHT TO HIS SENSES"

In the preface to the first edition of the *Science of Logic*, in 1812, Hegel ana-
lyzes the historical juncture at which he situates his own project: people have
lost interest in the contents and even the form of metaphysics, and this situation is a paradoxical effect of Kant's attempt to inaugurate modern philosophy by bringing rational metaphysics to its completion. Kant had argued
for an active forgetting of all earlier forms of metaphysics, for "extirpating"
them "root and branch,"[1] since they were never anything but "*mental fancies*."[2]
But his attempt to do metaphysics properly by rescuing it from dogmatism
effectively became "the justification … for renouncing (*entsagen*) speculative
thought" altogether.[3] The unwitting outcome of Kant's efforts is a paradoxical *Entsagung*—a renunciation or disavowal. What is disavowed by Kantian philosophy is precisely philosophy itself. Kant had noted in the preface to the
first edition of the *Critique of Pure Reason* that reason cannot be indifferent to
the questions it cannot prevent itself from raising and that necessarily drive it
beyond its own capacities into a swamp of contradiction. But because critical
philosophy was committed to flagging reason's limitations, it was reduced to
endorsing a form of rationally justified belief in abstract ideas that had already
been emptied of any possible imaginable content—a religion unfit for everyday purposes. By hypostatizing the human finite condition, Kant unwittingly
joins forces with the dogmatism he had set out to overcome: in this case, the
stupid empiricism that assumes metaphysical speculation is useless anyhow.[4]

Kantian reason ends up doing the impossible: it succumbs to its own constitutive interestedness in the absolute. Reason is forced to concede that it
will never know what it nonetheless cannot stop desiring to know: "The
world is often a closed book."[5] Reason disavows itself, it abdicates from or
abjures speaking, *sie entsagt sich*.[6] It unsays or undoes what it says and does
in the act of speaking about itself—a "self-renunciation of reason [*Verzicht-
tun der Vernunft auf sich selbst*]."[7] The most reasonable act of reason is to waive

reason altogether—the final act in the "drama of the understanding."[8] Hence Hegel's diagnosis of the Kantian dialectic of enlightenment. This renunciation at the center of critical philosophy produced "the singular spectacle" of a "cultivated people without metaphysics"[9] and a regression to the vulgar pragmatism of everyday life. The demand for "popular practicality" turned the edifice of metaphysics into a profaned temple "without a holy of holies." Kant thereby became an ally of Goethe's Mephistopheles: "All theory, dear friend, is gray." There is no use, only abuse, of metaphysics for life.

With Kant philosophy had died stillborn. And thinking therefore turned away from mortifying metaphysical questions about the absolute and toward "the gospel of everyday thinking."[10] It embraced the vitality of ordinary life— "the bright world of flowers."[11] Faced with the questions that were supposed to have fundamental impact on life and death—God, being, eternity, the infinite—philosophy opted for life without further question. Thinking lurched "without any concept into the wild."[12] It regressed into the "wilderness of the nearly animal consciousness."[13] Yet this choice came with a disavowal of its own; thought abandoned logic by consigning it to the restricted sphere of "formal utility."[14] Avoiding further frustration arising from Kant's empty promises, philosophy tried to act as if nothing had happened. It "ignored"[15] the transformation introduced by the Kantian "Revolution der Denkungsart":[16] reason turned against itself—a literal re-volutio. Philosophy cultivated an indifference to the very thing about which it could be least indifferent. Disavowal was fought with disavowal and yielded another kind of belief, namely in the vibrancy of a life unspoiled by the tedium of endless metaphysical speculation. And the death of metaphysics in this way turned out to be yet another occasion for prolonging life beyond its expiration date. Philosophy "lives on because the moment to realize it was missed."[17]

Hegel thereby situates his own epoch at a peculiar juncture of disavowal and ignorance: philosophy is caught between a deadly formalism that seems to ignore concrete life practices and an artificial liveliness that numbs itself in the repetitive rituals of daily life. Formalism contemplates the limits of the forms of speculative thinking and thereby unwittingly endorses empiricism; empiricism reifies the given forms of existence and thereby lapses into formalism. The choice is thus a forced one: either a deadened life or a falsely vitalized death. The only option is to refuse the choice altogether. To borrow Lenin's verdict: "Both are worse!"[18]

Hegel's response to this impasse is not to neutralize the antinomy. He rather shows that this deadlock can be circumvented only by picking sides. Despite the formal symmetry of the impasse—despite or because of the dialectical reversibility of the two poles—there is no neutral third term that would resolve the contradiction. Hegelian mediation has nothing to do with middle terms or intermediaries: every mediator or middle term has already vanished. Hegel privileges the strange term *Ver-mittlung* as one of his master terms. It is the enigmatic prefix *Ver-* that must be emphasized (we will return to this strange particle)—sheer mediation without mediator or medium. Whenever there is a conflict between competing particular claims to the universal, mediation does not consist in finding a mutually agreeable arrangement whereby each side learns to understand and accommodate the other's position. On the contrary, it is a matter of sharpening the antagonism to the point where the formal framework of the conflict shatters.[19] This introduces a fundamental asymmetry into what would otherwise be a paralyzing impasse.

One cannot choose—and therefore one cannot but choose, and furthermore there is only one choice possible. In the face of an impossible decision (and every true decision is impossible) one must opt for one side only—namely, the side that forces us to completely change the parameters of the original decision.[20] Faced with the choice between formalism and empiricism, one must unequivocally opt for formalism.[21] It is in this sense that one will always have to side with Kant. It is not because Kant represents the lesser evil, or that he can somehow be made less evil, that his formalism can be mitigated (as with so many recent efforts to naturalize or normalize Kant), while empiricism remains forever stupid and intractable.[22] Here, there are no degrees of worseness. Any choice is by definition absolutely the wrong choice. But this does not balance the books or render the two sides commensurable. It does not mean that any choice will do, or that what we are choosing, when we choose, is ultimately just the possibility of choice itself—which would be to endorse either decisionism (a self-affirmation of the will for its own sake) or consumerism (an assertion of the empty right to choose between a heap of indifferent equivalents). There is nothing arbitrary or indifferent about the choice at stake. Both are worse, both are doomed to failure: one must resolve to *fail better*.

Form is therefore not only the better choice, it is the only choice. This choice is multiply paradoxical: it is a choice that offers no choice, on several counts. Not only does one not have the option of not choosing, but there is only one option to choose, and furthermore this option is not really an option: form itself is not a substantive position in a binary opposition. The choice has the initial form of an opposition between "form" and "content" (i.e., between formalism and empiricism) as its two equally unconvincing *contents*. But by opting for form—by endorsing a full-throttled and even exaggerated formalism—we force "form" itself out of its position as a placeholder that would provide the content of one side in a formal binary arrangement. Only by purging form of the last grains of givenness—including every pregiven understanding of form—can one address the form of the choice between form and content. In other words, one must exaggerate form so that form becomes what it is. It is only by shedding its own content (and ultimately by arresting its own ineluctable tendency to become its own content) that form manages to twist out of the givenness of every context, and thus to transform the formal coordinates of the original decision. This is why one must always opt for form and formalism. This is another way of saying that the passage from substance to subject is a one-way street.

Self-avowed Hegelian pragmatism—undoubtedly the most influential form of Hegelianism today—defines rational practice as a normatively imbued endeavor located within a preestablished "space of reasons." Human agents collectively commit to fundamental attitudes and beliefs from which further commitments follow according to an intersubjectively realized and continually renegotiated set of inferential rules. The *space* of reasons in this sense is also always a circumscribed *time* of reasons and a rationalization of time: normative commitments are legitimized within a restricted sphere and regulated historically by the givenness of social context and epoch; the insight into this constitutive normative framework is precisely what makes modernity modern. We self-identify as a community when we understand that within this space we engage with one another as a collective of rational agents committed to continually renegotiating our shared orientations. Practical transformation occurs (inexorably) because we are forced to make our normative commitments explicit and in so doing are inevitably led to modify them.

Historically, Kant is usually taken to have been the first to establish that everything humans know and do is immanently normative: both cognition and action are based in the faculty of judgment. Our concepts are rules, and we take the world to proceed in a lawful fashion: "Everything in nature, both in the lifeless and in the living world, takes place *according to rules*."[23] But Kant took the premises of these normative commitments to be transhistorically, or transcendentally, given. Hegel's innovation was to radicalize Kant's transcendental gesture: he eliminated this residual givenness by embedding all norms within a specific historical framework that is produced and sustained by socially constituted and reciprocally interacting rational agents. Intersubjective practice works both within and on the norms that govern it.

Hegel is here taken to be pragmatism's founding father in that the premise of his system is an acknowledgment of this fundamental practical embeddedness: there is no position external to the normative context into which we are thrown. Normativity defines our specifically human take on the world. We learn from experience that we cannot but commit to what we take in a historically specific situation to be a universally binding norm, and to convey this commitment to others with the expectation that they will in turn endorse it. Conversely, when asked for our reasons for assuming this, we must and therefore can make these reasons explicit, in the course of which we will inevitably come to revise these normative commitments, clarifying and eventually transforming them when we are forced to confront their apparent inconsistencies.

This revisionary procedure is inherently progressive and potentially endless insofar as it commits us to seek ever-increasing explicitness and transparency. In other words, our rationality places us within an essential conversation with others, whereby we reshape and reaffirm both the content of our normative space and our collective commitment to this space. Such a narrative in this regard follows the time-honored practice of identifying Hegel as a philosopher of recognition.

Yet, the one thing that cannot be challenged, in this pragmatist account, is the space of reasons itself—the irreducible fulcrum of history that enables historical modulation and discursive progress. This space can only be tinkered with or *interpreted* differently; it cannot be fundamentally *changed*, let alone refused: the form of rationality remains essentially unchallenged and is even reproduced in efforts to resist it. Having eliminated the vestigial positivity of Kant's transcendental, Hegel seems to have introduced an even more intractable givenness—the inescapable language game that supplies the paradigm and basis of all our intersubjective negotiations and that thus functions as a new transcendental.

Fredric Jameson has aptly characterized such approaches to Hegel as "Habermasian."[24] The "constraint-free force of the better argument"[25] supplies the transcendental condition for a process of hermeneutic negotiation: we are *all* beings of language. If we must justify our individual commitments in the presence of others, this justification functions only because we implicitly recognize each other as partaking of a shared rational capacity. As speaking subjects, we are always already bound by the rules of language (this is the case even when we seem to break these rules, for example in lying, or when we knowingly bend them, for example in poetry). This appeal to a transcendental normativity threatens to reverse the mandatory Hegelian movement from substance to subject by reifying the constitutive conditions of language as always already given. In other words, this neo-Hegelian project reverts to a positivist "myth of the given."

A symptom of this regression is that the only form of change imaginable is a gradual amelioration brought about by a constant adjustment of our discursively negotiated commitments. Unthinkable within such a framework is that some might be excluded from or choose to opt out of the space of reasons: the space is bounded with all exits and entrances sealed. This precludes the possibility of radical dissensus and therefore of drastic change: the terms of rational agency are already determined such that alternative forms of practical rationality are ruled out from the outset as infeasible, ridiculous, violent, dangerous, undemocratic, unreasonable, irrational, inhuman, even prehuman or nonhuman.

Our reading will also emphasize a kind of commitment—we will argue that absolute knowing is essentially a philosophy of commitment, but one whose normative authority is impossible to secure or stabilize. And it will also imply a kind of "linguistic turn": thought and action are fundamentally structured like a language and the (historical) limits of our language are the limits of the world. Yet whereas for the deflationary pragmatist the space of reasons is a consistent totality and thus formally complete (this is what makes it a coherent and localized "space" in the first place), we will argue that there is an incompleteness and ungroundedness inherent in language—a loophole in the normative fabric of the social bond. Language is internally riven by an "other side"[26]—an *inneres Ausland*, an internal foreign territory[27]—that some-times forces us to speak, think, and act differently. Hegel's achievement is to engage this other side by exposing from within the cracks inherent in every transcendental conception of thought and language. This unhinges the quasi-spatialized coordinates of every speaking community and introduces a fundamental dislocation into every speech act. Only from such radical disori-entation does a new form of orientation become thinkable, without any tran-scendental guarantees.

To clarify this point: there are at least two ways to understand the prag-matic dimension of language. The first takes the logical syntax of language as a complete and consistent framework that supplies the basic rules of ratio-nal conduct. Pragmatist readers of Hegel usually take this to be the kernel of Hegel's "holism."[28] The second emphasizes the incompleteness and inconsis-tencies on which this syntax hinges. Discursive practice relies on something that exceeds the grasp of rationality even though it is generated by and only thinkable from within rationality; there is a constitutive exception at the basis of every speech act.[29] The first position assumes a performative model of suc-cessful speech acts: language fundamentally *works*, it "does things," it pro-duces significant effects. This assumes an instrumental and communicative model of language; misunderstanding can eventually be overcome by clarify-ing what we mean to say (and by learning to mean what we actually do say). The second position puts into question the efficacy of language as a symbolic performance and emphasizes language's own unworkability and unworking.

The first model assumes that language practice is essentially an actualiza-tion and activity. Language is not only formed but performed: its contents are actualized within an established normative framework that also prescribes the mode of its own actualization. The second model emphasizes a transfor-mation, not only of content, but of form itself. And as there is no preexisting form or norm of such transformation, it is not a question of moving from one form to another; there is rather a deformation or unforming of every form of language including the form of transformation itself.[30] This "afformative" operation[31] is not a negation of form but rather a working through in which language divests itself of everything external or antecedent to its own self-production—a kind of "strike" in which language completely renegotiates its basic working conditions. This does not mean that language is all there is, or that there is "nothing outside the text" (as vulgar readings of Derrida propose). On the contrary, language is *not-all* there is. There is nothing but language—except that language itself is internally riven: it is marked by an "other side" that can be accessed only through the practice of language itself.[32]

The encounter with this other side of language forces us to reorient ourselves by shaking every natural, historical, or transcendental horizon: something happens that produces the desire to start again without knowing where this might lead. It is no longer a question of constructing rational arguments about objects of the world (either this world or any other). We are rather forced to affirm the existence of something that cannot have previously been known to exist as such (this also holds for revolutions)—a peculiar object that did not exist outside the act of speaking even though it never fully coincides with its own articulation (one always says too much or too little), and whose existence therefore cannot be decided by recourse to any judgment. This is why, for Hegel, the grammatical form of the proposition—subject, predicate—is inapt for articulating speculative truths. This is precisely why it is so difficult to read philosophy. We are forced to devise a form for that which does not yet have a form, a formal revolution in language in which neither the content nor the form of the transformation remains intact. Such a seemingly "subjective" use of language is not (or not only) a *Privatsprache*, not simply a private idiom or personal lyricism, but rather the ultimate form of *Menschheitssprache*. It expresses the convergence of the singular and the cosmopolitan, to invoke Kant's terms.[33]

We are invoking the notion of "material incompleteness" in open reformulation of Gödel: in any consistent formal system one can formulate statements that can neither be proved nor disproved within this system, and the claim about the system's consistency is just such a statement.[34] These statements render incomplete the logical framework that enables them; and precisely because they are at the same time undecidable, they become the site of a possible decision. But the notion of materiality also needs to be explained. Hegel goes beyond the conventional understanding of the correlation between form and matter. It is not simply that matter is matter only through form or that form exists only as the form of an independent matter. It is rather that the very form of the distinction between form and matter disappears when we see that this distinction itself is a purely formal one. There is therefore something like an *immaterial (or formal) matter*, and a *material form*, each emerging through this formal difference between form and matter. But the stakes of this strange materialism need unpacking.

Material incompleteness can be understood in two ways, one emphasizing that matter appears because of discursive incompleteness, the other emphasizing that matter is itself incomplete. Matter presents itself where an existing

KANT BROUGHT TO HIS SENSES"

formal framework appears to be incomplete (and hence capable of being reconstituted and transformed). But matter is not an empirical substance that precedes and resists form as a surd of defiant thingliness. It is brought about by purely formal operations with their accompanying inconsistencies: matter itself is thus immaterial or purely formal. This means that matter, as well as form, is inherently incomplete.[35]

Hegel's radicalization of Kant thus cannot consist simply in thickening the transcendental conditions of experience—for instance, by pluralizing the first person of the "I think" or, which amounts to the same thing, by historicizing its conditions of possibility. This is of course the standard formula: Hegel = Kant + sociability, or Hegel = Kant + history. Our contention is precisely the opposite: Hegel's innovation is to show how the project of transcendental philosophy must culminate in a radical emptying out of the transcendental conditions of subjectivity itself. The point is not to add stuff but rather to *subtract*—to bring formalization to a pitch so as to let matter itself appear in its incompletion and inconsistency. This subtraction does not shrink back from the demands of historicization but rather makes these demands legible. History does not provide a buttress for practice, any more than the fact of pluralization (the "sociability of reason") supplies a filling for the lonely transcendental ego. Hegel divests the first person in all its situatedness and dilation—the "I that is we"—of its last shred of positive substantiality.

This points to a radical emptying out not only of subjectivity but of reality itself. Not only is the subject deprived of consistency and therefore lacking any privileged place within the world: being itself lacks coherence. Hegel is thus more Kantian than Kant: the subtraction he inflicts applies "not only to subject" but "equally to substance" (to flip around the formula). But Hegel does not stop here. He not only voids both substance and subject of their substantiality. In a further step, he goes on to desubstantialize their very relationship: there is no preassigned place for the subject in substance, nor for (even an evacuated or desubstantialized) substance in the subject. This also, incidentally, makes the speculative-realist complaint about the "correlation" or codependence between thought and being beside the point. Any relation between subject and substance is strictly a *nonrelation* (as the term *absolute* suggests).[36]

In other words, rather than offering a corrective to Kant's "empty formalism" Hegel radicalizes the Kantian void. Rather than softening the austerity of the transcendental ego by supplying its material furniture (institutional conditions, social situation, cultural-historical setting, etc.), Hegel shows the incompleteness and inconsistency of materiality itself.[37] Far from providing a stable grounding or coherent framework in which the subject can find a foothold, he shows that every context is riddled by negativity. This points to the inherent limits of every historicist or cultural-studies approach to philosophy that would reduce philosophy to an expression or transcription of its historical situation. When Hegel defines philosophy as "its own time grasped in thoughts"[38] (in the *Philosophy of Right*), or as "comprehended history [*begriffene Geschichte*]"[39] (in the *Phenomenology*), the point is not simply to embed philosophy in its existing conditions but rather to intervene in these conditions. Philosophy thinks what is universal or eternal in every present and hence transforms this present. Its grasp exceeds and thus extends the reach of any given context. This is why it takes off only when day has turned to dusk.

This explains Hegel's insistence on the rationality even of what might appear to be devoid of reason (there is reason in history, for example, or even in nature): his entire philosophy is an *idealism of matter*. Philosophy must therefore be prepared to grasp the truth of what is most negligible, neglected, and seemingly unworthy of inspection, and to linger over things that are worn out, outmoded, and stripped of significance. This is why philosophy can be "a bottomless abyss for personal idiosyncrasies": the concept finds traction in the stupid particularity of daily life. Hence one must always "throw oneself into [philosophy] *à corps perdu* [*sich à corps perdu hineinzustürzen*]"—one must take the plunge, commit to philosophy without reserve, body and mind, without procrastination or premeditation. Hegel emphasizes that by *body* he means "the sum of one's idiosyncrasies."[40] One must not only abandon oneself to one's particular attachments, but must also let go of these attachments—more precisely, one must question one's ideological investments in these attachments by acknowledging their constructedness as second nature.

There is thus a renunciation at the heart of philosophy. "The individual ... *forgets* himself, as the nature of Science implies and requires."[41] This renunciation is not driven by an ascetic conceit of impartial universality, but is rather performed in the awareness that all investments remain parochial and in need of ruthless autocritique (including the investment in universality itself). Autocritique can itself, of course, become another source of self-aggrandizement, which is why the demand for critique remains interminable, and why this interminability is in turn so easily fetishized: critique itself is always on the verge of becoming an exercise in pious self-humiliation, which is ultimately a form of reattachment. This is the kernel of Hegel's attack on the specular narcissism of the beautiful soul, with its endless obsessional rituals of self-purification. To remain faithful to critique requires relinquishing the ego ideal of uncontaminated universality and affirming a commitment to the impurities of idiosyncrasy and partiality: true universality is partisan. Philosophy is in this sense essentially a matter of resolve.

HYPERFORMALISM AND THE HYPEREMPIRICISM OF THE DETAIL

Hegel's volte-face against Kant lies in showing that the latter did not remain faithful to the speculative principle that (despite Kant's own intentions and yet to his everlasting credit) constitutes the novelty and promise of the Kantian project. Although Kant sought to critically investigate reason by means of reason alone—to deduce categories and principles with universal validity[42]—his endeavor culminated in a twofold failure. On one side he emptied out reason and subjectivity of all substantial content, but only to ground these on a transhistorical foundation of existing forms that he took as given[43] (only waiting to be discovered by critical introspection). The problem with Kantian formalism is not that it is "empty," that it lacks content or filling, but rather the converse: by taking specific forms to be transcendentally or transhistorically given, *Kant is not formalist enough.* He did not raise the question of the very constitution of the forms he claims to have excavated: he ultimately took them as a given. The perennial question whether Kant's table of categories is complete or not is a symptom of this. He substantialized the form of form itself and thereby filled it with content—or rather, he collapsed the difference between form and content by turning form itself into its own content. By claiming to have excavated the conditions of possibility of subjectivity, Kant managed to replenish the empty form of the subject with content (inter alia categories). The form of subjectivity itself becomes reified and therefore ceases to be form. Despite or rather because Kant took his philosophy to be the recovery of the originary form of reason, he never managed to reach form proper.

Worse yet, Kant saw these (insufficiently formal) forms as the conditions of possibility for human beings to relate to the empirical world. In other words, he assumed, like the English philosophers before him, that one has to start from what is given. The symptom of Kant's incomplete formalism is thus a disavowed empiricism. The peculiar outcome of his thought was to limit the scope of reason to its formal conditions of possibility, thereby effectively placing it under the aegis of the understanding.

Already the early Hegel had (in his Latin *Habilitation* thesis) criticized Kant for having only developed an "imperfect or incomplete form of skepticism."[44] If German idealism remained trapped in the endless quarrel between skepticism and dogmatism, this is ultimately because it could not see how the very form of that opposition had already congealed into a new positivity: the opposition itself provided thought with an endless reservoir of content. By accepting the received form of this opposition, it unfailingly ended up endorsing a kind of dogmatism.

The way out of this deadlock opens by way of a surprising inversion: Hegel's response is to radicalize skepticism, to turn ordinary skepticism into a "thoroughgoing skepticism"[45]—to push skepticism beyond itself by teaching it to be suspicious of every established form of skepticism. Philosophy must formalize its own procedure to purge every residue of unprocessed content, including the implicit content contained in the very form of its own unquestioned attachment to its own method. This means, paradoxically, that thinking must become more dogmatically skeptical than ever. Skepticism must become hyperdogmatic about its own skepticism if it is to free itself from the dogmas of transcendental skepticism.[46] Kantian skepticism remains insufficiently skeptical about its own position of enunciation. It has not fully formalized its own starting point: it still rests its case on the infallibility of the doubting subject, which functions as a *fundamentum inconcussum* no less for Kant and Fichte than for Descartes. Hegel will push through this performative impasse. The skeptical Kantian philosophers have hitherto only (partially) interpreted formalism; Hegel's point is to realize it.

The devastating outcome of Kant's closet empiricism appears most clearly in the practical realm. The problem with his rigorism is not its "empty formalism" (this is the usual critique of Kantian ethics as a kind of decisionism: it is the purely formal nature of the moral law that opens the floodgates to arbitrariness whenever this law is put into practice; there is always an avalanche of circumstances rushing in to fill the vacuum[47]). The problem is precisely the opposite: Kant is not formalist enough. The law is never empty enough: its emptiness is always thickening into a new positivity, the void keeps on supplying its own filling, absence is forever reifying itself, and this self-substantialization is precisely what blocks every practical engagement with the actually existing world.[48] We can see here a perfect demonstration of the logic of the fetish.[49]

Here also lies the ultimate difference, according to Hegel, between Hegel and Spinoza. Spinoza's "substance does not contain the absolute form" because it fails to give an exposition of its own "determining and informing [*Formieren*]." Even though he had a sense of the coincidence of being and thought, Spinoza was unable to articulate their speculative convergence because he did not make the critical move from substance to subject: he did not see that truth is nothing but its own formalization. In short: "Substance lacks the principle of personality."[50] And one should recall here that already the young Hegel had criticized Kant for still being a Spinozist.

Hegel thus takes Kant's original speculative insight more seriously than did Kant himself: he "outdoes Kant," or rather, he "brings Kant to his senses." *Hegel ist der zu sich selbst gekommene Kant.*[51] Hegel does not shy away from either empiricism or formalism but rather radicalizes both in full acknowledgment of their ultimate convergence. On the one hand, he shows that there is no form outside of the act of formalization. There are no pregiven forms of rationality waiting to be discovered: there is nothing to see behind the curtain except for what we ourselves put there.[52] The forms of thought produce themselves in the process of being formalized. It is in this sense that Hegel describes the *Science of Logic* as the science of the absolute form: the absolute is form and form is absolute in that it is strictly absolved from any relation to every antecedent or external object. On the other hand, "this formality [*dieses Formelle*] ... must have a *content* in it which is adequate to its form."[53]

How to conceive of such a contradictory demand? We are to begin with evacuating the last bit of content from form—this is Hegel's hyperformalism—and yet are nonetheless supposed to find a content adequate to this form. Here we confront the essential paradox of the Hegelian absolute: as absolute, it is absolved from all relation, it is the very epitome of self-relation, like Aristotle's Unmoved Mover it is self-instituting and seems to run on empty; and yet by virtue of this very autoreferentiality it must yield to an intrinsic exteriority that it cannot (consciously) generate or produce. It must expose itself to an outside that is at once its own and yet irredeemably opaque and therefore not its own. Philosophy thus must own up to an irreducible heteronomy at its core. It must "discover" [*finden*] what it "invents" [*erfinden*] and assume responsibility for what it happens to stumble on.[54] This apparent vacillation between autonomy and heteronomy has always invited a chorus of contradictory objections. Hegel is forever being attacked on both sides for being either too idealist or too positivist or both. On the one hand he inflates reason, even behind the back of its agents (the infamous cunning of reason). On the other hand, he renders philosophy servile to its circumstances and the philosopher a lackey to his regime. This intractable ambiguity pervades absolute knowing.

Hegel responds to this paradox when he criticizes the "formal, unsystematic dialectic"[55] that assumes that the absolute is nothing but a form so abstract that nothing can be said about it (which is, of course, just another way of saying something about it, according to the well-rehearsed logic of the Kantian limit or *Schranke*). Rather the absolute form is the form of the absolute: the absolute is nothing but its own exposition[56] or self-interpretation (*Auslegung*). *Auslegung* is not the revelation of an essence that would preexist its own exposition; it is not the expression of an inner meaning, the excavation of a buried treasure, or the extraction of a hidden content. It rather undoes the very distinction between surface and depth, outer and inner, explicit and implicit: "It does not externalize itself for it is the identity of inner and outer."[57] *Auslegung* is therefore neither a *Grundlegung* nor an *Äußerung*: it does not lay a foundation or bring a latency to the surface. It rather produces itself in arranging itself; it lays itself out and displays itself; it points to itself (*sich zeigen*)[58] as its own "absolute content." *Auslegung* shines light on what is hidden in broad daylight. Working at the surface, it exposes what has become invisible through overexposure, like the purloined letter.

Kleist's description of the gradual (*allmähliche*) production or preparation (*Verfertigung*) of thought while speaking is suggestive here.[59] Thought produces itself "gradually," bit by bit, stepwise, by discrete degrees. It proceeds haltingly rather than flowing forth as a stream of consciousness or as a deductive syllogistic sequence. Despite the apparent progression of the "steps" or "stages" (as in Hegel's unfortunate image of the "ladder"), thinking does not proceed in an unbroken progressive linear fashion. Like the nineteenth-century revolutions that Marx praises in the *Eighteenth Brumaire*, thought moves episodically and retrogressively, constantly revisiting and reformulating its premises, at each step revising everything that has gone before. Thinking is *all-mählich*—it is "all in parts." Each new moment reconfigures the whole by simultaneously completing and "incompleting" everything that has preceded: it brings together what is still unfinished and keeps undoing or unfinishing what it has already finished (*verfertigt*). It supplies meaning and direction to what has preceded even as it opens itself onto a disorienting array of new possibilities. Thinking therefore finds itself in a state of "absolute dismemberment"—Hegel's answer both to the Romantic fragment and to Goethe's living form. This is what it means to "stare the negative in the face."

It is in this sense that the "absolute becomes... what it already is."[60] *Auslegung* is sheer surface without depth—pure externalization without anything to externalize.[61] Spirit's "depth is only as deep as it dares to spread out and lose itself in its exposition."[62] *Auslegung* is the process in which the absolute takes form and discovers this form as its own content—a "self-bearing movement."[63] This circularity is not the self-relation of a hermeneutic circle (where every interpretation revises its own prejudices and therefore turns into yet another object of interpretation), if only because there is no preexisting formal framework or context for the movement of *Auslegung*.

This distinguishes Hegel's method from every hermeneutics of suspicion and accounts for its disorienting effect: the activity of *Auslegung* concerns not only the content but equally the form of its own practice.[64] Form itself resists its own complete formalization. *Auslegung* is not an explicitation of the implicit but rather a demonstration of the latter's persistence—a making explicit of the necessity of implicitness itself. Depth itself gets you nowhere, as Brecht remarked.[65] Meaning is not an inner latency waiting to be extracted: it is what obscures itself in full view. There is an irreducible opacity at the kernel of the self-conscious subject: the secrets of the absolute are secrets for the absolute itself.[66] This is why it is not a question of excavating a buried depth or revealing an ungraspable thing in itself (or even a transcendental subject) lying beyond, before, or beneath appearances. Thinking does not ground, justify, recover, or consolidate itself in an act of transcendental return-to-self. It rather "loses itself": it relinquishes the certainty of its own agency and even of the agent underpinning this agency as it circles around the abyssal foundation of its own practice.

This is why Hegel writes, at the very end of the *Phenomenology*, that "to know one's limit is to know how to sacrifice oneself." The sacrifice is absolute in that it relinquishes the residual theological apparatus of sacrifice itself (together with the instrumental reason that has always secretly sustained this). This renunciation signals philosophy's final escape from the dialectic of enlightenment. To "know how to"—and to know that one must—sacrifice oneself, to sacrifice absolutely, is to relinquish the coordinates within which this act could even be considered a sacrifice. The sacrifice is not for anything or anyone; there is nothing for the sake of which such sacrifice is productive or meaningful. It is moreover unclear what exactly has been sacrificed or even who is performing the sacrifice: the sacrifice retroactively dissolves the substantiality of both the sacrificial subject and object.

Hegel describes this sacrifice as an "externalization in which Spirit displays the process of becoming Spirit in the form of free contingent happening."[67] The Logic formalizes this externalization in an act of abyssal resolve—a strange decision (we will return to this) that will have learned to abandon the volitional capacity of the self-willing subject.[68] Relinquishing all foundations and every transcendental guarantee, including even the power of its own conviction, thinking abandons itself to the contingency of its own unfolding. Auslegung is Hegel's name for this "Napoleonic" pragmatism: "On s'engage, puis on voit."[69] Doing precedes knowing.[70]

Absolute form is therefore the "self-bearing movement [selbst tragende Bewegung]" that "begins from itself and arrives at itself."[71] The absolute delivers itself to itself—it gestates, supports, and gives birth to itself—in an incessant movement of self-parturition and self-parting that is precisely the opposite of spontaneous or autochthonous self-generation. One should not be misled by Hegel's vitalist-sounding formulations or by the traditional sounding "organicism" of his depiction of form (holism, self-organization, autopoiesis, and so on). Absolute form must be distinguished from its eighteenth-century biological counterparts—for example, the nisus formativus in Blumenbach,[72] the morphology of life processes in Goethe,[73] or the entelechy of the organic in Kant. All these inherited vitalisms erode the fundamental distinction between "the life of nature" and "life in the idea."[74] This also puts pressure on recent efforts to enlist Hegel's thought for a "new materialism"—ultimately a neo-Spinozism—that would bask in the vibrant liveliness of all things.

Hegel was always reluctant to model thinking on any preestablished template—in this case on the self-organizing structure of biological life. By modeling its own reflexivity on the (hypothetical) autopoiesis of organic nature, thought would relinquish the very quality it sought to claim for itself, namely autopoiesis. The life of spirit is rather a denaturalized life that comes to know itself as such;[75] spirit must prove that life itself will always already have been unnatural.[76] Purely natural life is not really life; it does not live properly. This is why the transition from the biological order of merely living creatures to the life of the human spirit is marked by malfunction of the organism, by failure of the organs, sickness and death. Life is alive only when it breaks down and encounters its own limits.

And death must be similarly denaturalized: spirit must also discover a death proper to spirit.[77] The *Phenomenology* describes a repeated effort to register death as a properly *spiritual* problem—to transform natural death into a "done" or performed death,[78] to reclaim a biological "happening" as a historical product—to transform *ein Geschehenes* into *die Geschichte*. This is why Hegel's narrative is essentially structured as a sequence of unnatural acts of dying: heroic struggles to the death, mortifying penitential rituals, knightly sacrifices, obstinate mourning rites, revolutionary decapitations, romantic suicides, Christian transfigurations.

The *Logic* completes the project of the *Phenomenology* by showing that "spirit" must not only be denaturalized but also despiritualized. The very movement from nature to spirit must be stripped of its fixity as second nature. The historical institutions and practices that have worked to sublimate natural life will have to be divested of their artificial vitality along with the deadly mechanism on which such liveliness relies. The *Logic* elaborates a life that belongs neither to nature nor to second nature; it shows that the relation between these two natures must be denaturalized. The opposition between nature and spirit is neither natural nor spiritual. There is no (substantial) relation between nature and culture if only because neither nature nor culture is substantial. Logical life is situated at the interstice of nature and spirit and is thus neither.[79] Formalization exceeds and undermines the life of both nature and spirit by undoing the opposition between life and death as such. It is in this sense that we must reconsider Hegel's invectives against "dead formalism"—the "monotonous"[80] and "monochromatic"[81] procedures that keep reducing the living work of philosophy to a "skeleton," a "lifeless schema."[82] The problem with previous formalisms is not that they are too dead but rather that they are not dead enough. Hegel's response, in the *Logic*, is to offer an undead formalism.

The *Logic* depicts a state before the creation of nature. Radical formalization brings into view a "pure life" that precedes the opposition between nature and spirit, and that thus precedes both the natural and the spiritual distinction between life and death as such.[83] Such a purely logical form of life is not simply the negation of natural life through spiritual freedom (as in the master/slave dialectic). It is precisely the negation of spiritual negation. It emerges "between two deaths"—between the biological death of the living organism and the spiritual death of a culture that has congealed into second nature. In exposing the non-relation between nature and culture, logical life presents us with a constitutive "surplus of life" that goes beyond what either natural or spiritual life can bear.[84]

"The method is the absolute form, the concept that knows itself and everything as concept."[85] These kinds of statements (and they are of course everywhere) are usually cited as evidence of Hegel's panlogicism. The concept knows everything as concept. But Hegel's statement actually points in the opposite direction. For this conversion of the immediate into a mediated beginning (the essential Hegelian operation) reshuffles the coordinates of existence and inexistence and therefore sidesteps the terms of the dogmatism-skepticism debate. While the absolute method does not presuppose any prior givenness, it does not simply generate its own content or convert idea into existence in the manner of a Cartesian God. It rather grasps the object "immediately as [the object] presents itself."[86] It merely "looks on."[87]

If absolute form is not attached to any preexisting content, this is not because it simply lacks an object or that it conjures up its object out of thin air. Rather, it is *not without* object. *Ce n'est pas sans objet*, to use Lacan's pointed qualification of anxiety: the object is "passing"—*un passant objet, un objet passant*.[88] Heidegger will later stress the nonintentional character of anxiety: unlike fear, which is "always in the face of this or that"[89] (tigers, spiders), anxiety is not directed at a determinate object. When I am anxious, the whole world slips away and I am left with … nothing. Nothing but myself, that is— and of course (the) Nothing. This is why anxiety is the fundamental mood in *Being and Time*. But Lacan's qualification is important: anxiety is not simply *without* an object (which would condemn the subject to a "frictionless spinning"); it is rather a relation to a *nonobject*—a passing object, something that passes, that takes place (*se passe*) without taking up space or occupying a fixed position.

Anxiety is the fundamental mood for Hegel too, and for precisely the same reason. Although anxiety is triggered by a specific event and tethered to a specific occasion, it always assumes a free-floating and therefore universal dimension. Hegel stresses that the slave is not trembling before "this or that" object or at "this or that moment."[90] The slave trembles not only before his human master but ultimately before "the absolute master"—namely death itself. Anxiety is an affective "infinite judgment"—a short circuit between universal and particular where the shaking body establishes its own philosophical credentials. Absolute knowing brings no release from anxiety. On the contrary, it brings anxiety to an unprecedented pitch.

Kant was anxious: he had anxiety about the object—"Angst vor dem Objekt"—and herein lies his great insight.[91] His contribution was to officially introduce anxiety into modern philosophy by pointing to the forever problematic character of the object. But Kant was ultimately not anxious enough. His anxiety eventually found an object: he placed himself before a permanently inaccessible object, the *Ding an sich*, about which he could rest secure in the knowledge that this object would remain safely quarantined in a realm beyond human cognition. Kant defended himself against his own anxiety by clinging to the reassuring presence (in absence) of the lost object. He thus assuaged his own anxiety by dodging behind the protective shield of human limitation. Kant's skepticism was therefore not "thoroughgoing." Like every preceding skeptic, he domesticated his own anxiety by parading it as a cautious "fear of error," behind which Hegel detects a secret "fear of truth."[92]

Philosophy has always nourished itself on small doses of anxiety but has hitherto lacked the "will and courage"[93] to endure this. We must purge these concepts—will and courage—of all heroism and moral virtuousness. The *Logic* registers an anxiety that goes beyond the slave's terror in the face of death. It presents anxiety as a strictly logical affect.

Absolute knowing is a passing encounter with a passing object. Hegel writes that the "course of the method... is the course of the object itself [*der Gang dieser Methode ... ist der Gang der Sache selbst*]."[94] Thinking confronts not *die Sache selbst*—not the thing itself and not the thing-in-itself—but rather the thing's "going" and even "downgoing." In exposing itself to its own movement the subject registers the passing of its object (including the passing of the subject itself as this turns into its own lost object). The significance of this speculative encounter with transience is hard to grasp; logical movement must be distinguished from both the perpetual transience of nature and the mobility of spirit.[95]

This might also shed light on some of Hegel's more disreputable moves, most notably his infamous description of the state as the *Gang des Gottes*, for decades mistranslated as the "march of God," a phrase that inspired decades of misreadings of Hegel as a totalitarian theocratic thinker. The *Gang* marks not the triumph of God but rather his passing; the state is the place where the evacuation of divinity is institutionalized by a religion that has explicitly relinquished its claims over civic life. Hegel describes art's obsolescence in similar terms: art is, notoriously, "a thing of the past"—*ein Vergangenes*.[96] It is gone. There is an ephemerality installed at the highest reaches of absolute spirit.

"Si fractus illabatur orbis, impavidum ferient ruinae."[97] Hegel quotes Horace at the beginning of the *Logic*: "If the world were to fall into pieces, the ruins will hit (even) the fearless."[98] Thinking begins with the catastrophic scenario of a world in which every stable achievement has been systematically dismantled. All that is solid has melted into air: was it not the ultimate task of the *Phenomenology* to "spiritualize" all nature, to vaporize every substantial shape of natural and naturalized experience? The final act of spirit would be to denaturalize its own plastic power of transformation—to spiritualize spiritualization itself. What better image for this vaporization than the image of *vanitas*? Tellingly, the *Phenomenology* ends with an image not of rubble but of foam: "From the chalice of this realm of spirits foams forth for [spirit] its own infinitude."[99] The devastation accomplished by the *Phenomenology* does not produce a tabula rasa for heroic reinvention or a landscape for Romantic ruingazing; the subject finds no consolation either in its own powers of self-positing or in the contemplation of its own limits. The slate is never clean. Despite or because of the radicality of the destruction, there is always a residue—intangible and yet material, as insubstantial and yet as sticky as foam. Foam marks both the effervescence and the putrescence of absolute spirit.

If philosophical method ultimately coincides with philosophical object—this is Hegel's (self-avowed) repetition of Aristotle's *noesis noeseos*[100]—this is not because thought finally returns to itself in a moment of transparent self-coincidence. At its moment of self-realization, thinking rather grasps that there is something that eludes the grip of the *Begriff*. The object passes, it *goes*, without indicating a direction, sense, or meaning—the *pas sans* is simultaneously a *pas sens* in every sense. This is, of course, the very description of the Lacanian *objet petit a*. The subject circles around itself, forever missing itself, as its own lost object. *Pas sans*: Is this double negativity not the perfect expression of the negation of the negation? Hegel's readers are right, up to a point, when they associate absolute knowing with a kind of mourning.

This is why the philosopher must take up not only what is given but what barely seems even to appear as such: all the deficiencies, refuse, and remnants of the world of appearances—the *Abhub der Erscheinungswelt*, "the dregs of the phenomenal world."[101] Once more we can see the similarity between the speculative method and the "fundamental rule" of psychoanalysis: it is only by attending to the most meaningless details that one can identify the constitutive cracks in rationality and thereby lay a claim to rationality. Hegel's infamous statement "The true is the whole"[102] is just the injunction to identify and acknowledge the cracks on which totality itself hinges. The true is the (w)hole. Totality includes and depends on what is not-all; it must incorporate what it structurally excludes. One encounters a form of the Liar's Paradox, on par with all the other self-referential koans often associated with Hegel. "Everything is dialectical"[103]—an apparently undialectical statement which immediately proves, by this token, to be once more dialectical.[104] Fidelity to this paradox requires a combination of the most austere formalization with the most undiscriminating attentiveness to the trivial: at once absolutely stupid rigidity and absolutely rigid stupidity.[105]

This produces peculiar reading protocols. On the one hand, Hegel's writing performs a constant reduction to the formal and even formulaic (the slogans erupting everywhere, the constant drive toward abbreviation and condensation). On the other hand, there is no preassigned distinction between the formal and the empirical, between the rule and the example. Every formula is a trivialization, but every scrap of trivia harbors the force of the universal.[106]

Hegel wrote only two books. But it seems as if even this scanty production had already generated at least one book too many. For the two books do not quite form a couple, and they do not exactly add up. At least in Hegel's case, two seems to be an odd number. He produced an odd couple, even a "pseudocouple."[1] This oddness is not easily evened out and will produce some unsettling results.

Even these two books had already proved multiply unwritable—the one exploding beyond all reasonable limits, the other imploding under the pressure of its own initiative. The first, written under impossible personal conditions,[2] had proved impossible to contain or finish properly, while the second, written under only marginally more auspicious circumstances, seemed impossible even to begin.[3] The one had set out to consume the world and had swollen into a monstrous conglomeration of indigestible material; the other, attempting to deduce ex nihilo the logic of the entire creation, had consumed itself in a vortex of self-commentary. The one was praised (but also attacked) as "an unpalatable, even uncanny work,"[4] inducing nausea with its relentless inversions of familiar assumptions; the other was simply pronounced "indigestible."[5] The one had expanded so far beyond its initial agenda that the book seemed to have lost all integrity and direction; when Hegel applied the "torturous rigor [Spanische Stiefel] of the method"[6] the Spanish boots had ended up hobbling all movement and momentum.[7] The other had collapsed into a black hole of abstraction, turning into "a book of the most abstruse content."[8] The one, bursting wide open, had ended up contracting to an infinitesimal "point" of self-enclosure.[9] The other, rotating around itself in self-imposed isolation,[10] had ended up exploding in an uncontainable paroxysm of "discharge [Entlassen]."[11] If this sounds like bad sex, we will see soon enough why this is so: the coupling exhibits all the dysfunctional features of the "non-rapport sexuel."[12]

The first book had turned outward to embrace a world of seemingly uncontrollable historical contingency; the second had fallen inward toward an abyss of reflection.[13] On his deathbed Hegel was still going over the revisions for the second edition of the *Science of Logic*,[14] a revision that remained less than half-finished after almost two decades.[15] He wrote that the work would have to be rewritten "seventy-seven times over"[16] if it were ever to reach completion, pointing out that this oddly precise figure amounts to exactly eleven times the number of revisions it had taken Plato to complete the *Republic* (and neglecting to mention that even this hyperbolic sum was far less than the incalculably large number of times—seven times seventy—that Jesus had declared necessary to grant unconditional forgiveness …).[17]

After the publication of the two volumes of the *Science of Logic* (in 1812 and 1816), Hegel never wrote another book. All the publications that were to follow, during the remaining two decades of his life, were either essays or teaching material: the four textbooks published within his own lifetime (the three volumes of the *Encyclopaedia* as well as *Elements of the Philosophy of Right*) and the avalanche of student transcripts of the lecture cycles at Heidelberg and Berlin (nineteen volumes in total) that would form the literary corpse or corpus of the posthumous *Corpus Hegelianum* that was published shortly after Hegel's death by the "society of the friends of the deceased" (after having been partially redacted by Hegel's widow, who personally selected "what the world shall receive and what not").[18] Although the volumes of the *Encyclopaedia* and the *Philosophy of Right* were all signed by Hegel, and published during his lifetime, they are not books strictly speaking: they are explicitly *Grundrisse* and *Grundlinien*—a set of shorthand notes, outlines, or sketches assembled to guide students through the accompanying oral lectures.[19] They are not intended for readers, but are rather tools for auditors—*zum Gebrauch seiner Vorlesungen*.[20] Hegel's outlines were supplemented in the later editions by his own annotations, and eventually, after his death, by further additions by his students based on his oral remarks in class (these latter additions were often treated as if they had flowed directly from Hegel's head). All this pedagogical material represents "discourse of the university" in every sense—that is, works pronounced from the perspective of a neutral and anonymous knowledge that has learned to efface even the trace of its own drive to mastery. Part of this effacement involved erasing the idiosyncratic signature of the author.[21] In the university lecture hall, knowledge was to flow without impediment from speaker and auditor to produce a perpetual writing machine— "one speaking mouth and very many ears with half as many writing hands."[22] This stream of knowledge passed effortlessly between the students sitting at Hegel's feet, three in a row, who took turns taking dictation as they assembled the official corpus we know today as the *Vorlesungen*. Despite their derivative textual status, it was precisely the *Enzyklopädie* and the accompanying lectures that were for a long time taken to be the heart of Hegel's system, especially in Germany.[23]

It had not been part of Hegel's original plan to stop nearly so soon. He had announced his official writing project as early as 1802 as he geared up for the (still distant) publication of the *Phenomenology*.[24] The *Phenomenology* was to be the introduction or "ladder" (but also, mysteriously, the "first part") of the System of Science (of which the *Logic* itself was also, even more confusingly, said to be not only the "first part"[25] but also the introduction: "Only the *Logic* can serve as an introduction to philosophy"[26]). There is thus almost from the beginning a deadlock, not only between two competing "first parts" but also between two competing "introductions." The beginning has immediately stalled and fissured and thus ceased to be a beginning. There are two first parts, and there are two introductions. The beginning splits in two, twice over, before it even gets started.

Hegel had begun one of his first courses at Jena University, in 1801, titled *Introductio in philosophiam*, by declaring that "philosophy as science neither needs nor tolerates an introduction." One must "not turn philosophy into an introduction or take introducing for philosophy."[27] Hegel will never stop writing prefaces insisting on the uselessness of all prefaces: it will have been necessary to write them if only to demonstrate their futility.[28] The paradox pervades Hegel's philosophy. Nothing will prove more difficult than to begin, not because it is hard to find a good reason for doing so, but because there are so many ways not to begin. That this is a real philosophical problem becomes apparent if one raises the simple question as to what Hegel's system of philosophy actually begins with.

In his published announcement (*Selbstanzeige*) for the *Phenomenology*, in 1807, Hegel describes the book as the first of two volumes; its sequel was to be a single three-part volume containing the "system" of logic, nature, and spirit.[29] Within this second volume, the *Logic* (*systema reflexionis*[30] or *metaphysica generalis*[31]) was to be completed by a two-part *Realphilosophie* (roughly corresponding to the remaining two parts of *metaphysica specialis*—to invoke the scholastic classification still in place in Hegel's day[32]). The remaining two parts of the second volume never saw the light of day. Instead, what was to be the first part of this three-part volume, the *Logic*, ended up filling about a thousand printed pages and required a separate volume (actually, three separate volumes) of its own.[33] In other words, Hegel never got beyond the introduction and the first part—or more precisely, beyond the endless oscillation between one "introduction" and another "introduction," and between one "first part" and another "first part"—of his final system.

The tripartite system itself would appear only in truncated form, as the *Encyclopaedia* textbook. By this point the *Phenomenology* itself will have apparently ceased to function as an introduction to the system and will instead have been incorporated in miniature as a chapter within the third volume of the abbreviated trilogy, where it will occupy a circumscribed moment within the section devoted to subjective spirit.[34] The first volume of the Encyclopaedia is an abridged (often thought to be a more user friendly) version of the Logic, the so-called "shorter" or "little" Logic that now appears to perform the introductory task previously assigned to the Phenomenology.[35] So instead of being continued by a book-length philosophy of nature, as the last pages of the Logic lead us to expect, and that would in turn be followed by a book-length philosophy of spirit, the Logic is immediately followed by … a second Logic. The original volume is thus followed by a miniaturized replica of itself. Repetition and abbreviation take the place of development and expansion.

Neither the encyclopedic Phenomenology nor the encyclopedic Logic exactly replicates its eponymous predecessor. The miniaturization is not a case of scale reduction but rather involves a fundamental distortion and displacement. Rather than reproducing the original, each replica proceeds in its own mutant fashion. Hegel begins the Encyclopaedia Logic by offering a clear-cut definition of what lies ahead: "Logic is the science of the pure idea, that is, of the idea in the abstract element of thinking."[36] This is precisely what the Science of Logic had pronounced impossible: there is no way to know in advance what the peculiar subject matter is to be. No sooner have we entered the precinct of the Encyclopaedia than we are ejected from the domain of philosophy proper. We begin the "little" Logic by being reminded that we are excluded, as readers, from the immanent self-determination of the concept: we are students, there is the teacher, we will be instructed every step of the way. From the beginning the reader needs to be told what the endeavor is all about. When we move from the Science of Logic[37] to its encyclopedic homonym a shift of perspective takes place: we move from the subjective generation of truth to the objectification of this truth in the form of knowledge. We are no longer "doing" logic but being told about logic as an object of transmittable knowledge. We are no longer "learning to philosophize" but "learning philosophy" (to recall Kant's famous distinction).[38] In other words we are on the verge of retreating to a precritical dogmatism. Between the "big" and the "little" Logic there is no longer a family resemblance but a similarity in name or title only.[39]

A symptom of this shift is that in the Encyclopaedia Logic the argument is broken down into discrete numbered paragraphs: the student is given a roadmap in advance of all the destinations to be visited, while the conceptual transitions and transitional concepts that had been elaborated in the Science of Logic are almost entirely absent. Someone always already knows where we are, how we got there, and where we will be going.[40] We proceed from paragraph to paragraph following the predictable sequence of natural numbers. This order is one that we presuppose (and do not discover or investigate), even though the arrangement seems to give an inexplicable privilege to the givenness of numerical order, and despite the fact that according to the argument of the *Logic* itself, quantity itself is a derivative category (a successor to the category of quality).

Whereas Hegel insists (and demonstrates) throughout the *Science of Logic* on the coimbrication of form and content, throughout the *Encyclopaedia* we are invited to rely on an external framework that Hegel himself depicts (like nature itself) as essentially arbitrary and unreliable. The chain of natural numbers supplies an unquestioned and yet capricious background that constrains what nonetheless presents itself as the free movement of thinking. Thinking itself is thus stripped of both freedom and necessity: you cannot count on what is simply given by counting. Hegel's repudiation of Spinoza's *more geometrico* as the expression of an unacknowledged dualism does not prevent him from embracing an unembellished arithmetic arrangement for his own mature enterprise.[41] The recourse to number also introduces the specter of the bad infinite of endless serial progression. There is no philosophical significance to the fact that the final volume of the *Encyclopaedia* happens to end at §577, nor that the first volume of the *Encyclopaedia* ends at §244. The number series continues implacably from one volume of the *Encyclopaedia* to the next, with no signpost to mark the break or to indicate that we have entered an entirely new conceptual sphere.[42]

But there are also crucial thematic truncations of the *Logic* in its encyclopedic rendering, some of which are philosophically telling. A couple of brief examples will suffice. Hegel not only shrinks the first book (the doctrine of being) to half of its size but drastically reorganizes the material. The "greater" *Logic* moves from quality to quantity to measure, each of which unfolds through a web of subcategories. We are presented with the same sequence of categories in the *Encyclopaedia Logic*, but all subcategories of the final category on measure are omitted: 150 pages are here condensed into six. In a similar abridgement Hegel obliterates the conceptual transition from the doctrine of being to the doctrine of essence: there is no "becoming of essence" in the *Encyclopaedia Logic*. "Being" and "essence" are here merely externally related, succeeding one another like elements in a series of natural numbers. A similar truncation can be found at the beginning of the *Encyclopaedia* doctrine of essence. Although both the longer and the shorter texts describe the same basic sequence—from "essence" via "appearance" to "actuality" (*Wirklichkeit*)—the encyclopedic version elides the entire first chapter of essence that was devoted in the *Science of Logic* to the concept of semblance (*Schein*). The transition from "being" to "essence" is thus cut off at both ends: the former section ends as abruptly as the latter section begins, with all semblance of a relation dropped.[43] What was mediated in the *Science of Logic* is now only externally aggregated.[44] Suspending conceptual mediation, the *Encyclopaedia* thus resembles what Hegel had denigrated as the "latest compendiums of logic": its contribution "consists mostly of omissions [*Weglassungen*]."[45]

Whereas the *Logic* accounts for the emergence of relation and presents "reality" in *statu nascendi*, the *Encyclopaedia* takes this reality to be already established and organized according to the givenness of natural numbers. The later work thus presupposes what it exposes. The *Encyclopaedia* moves along as if it does not know what it does. Like the nature it describes as (only) one of its components, it exhibits a agglutination of substantial thought objects evacuated of thinking subjectivity.[46] Is this what Hegel had meant, at the end of the *Science of Logic*, when he wrote that the absolute idea was to release itself into nature?[47] The *Encyclopaedia* seems oddly to fulfill this promise, but only by regressing to a renaturalization of thought. Before we can encounter nature as the object of encyclopedic understanding we must divest thought itself of its vital organicity and mobility. We must refashion logic in nature's image before we can proceed to dissect nature according to the reified categories of logic.

There is an even more drastic difference between the *Phenomenology of Spirit* and its encyclopedic homonym. The latter, sandwiched between the Anthropology and the Psychology subsections of "Subjective Spirit" in the *Encyclopaedia Philosophy of Spirit*, offers a massively abridged summary of the genesis and stages of consciousness. Not only is the "little" *Phenomenology* presented in the same bureaucratic shorthand as the rest of the *Encyclopaedia* but its thematic scope is similarly truncated. While the first two sections more or less correspond to the opening chapters of the 1806 *Phenomenology* (from sense-certainty through to the end of the "Lord and Bondsman" episode), Hegel abruptly cuts off the discussion just before it starts veering into social-cultural-historical territory. After a highly condensed section on reason, the phenomenological enterprise comes to a sudden halt.[48] Phenomenology is now followed by a distinctly new section on psychology before we make the transition to the social and political terrain (here construed as "objective spirit)."[49] The scope of phenomenology is thus cut back from its original dimensions. It no longer functions as the first part or even as the ladder to the system.[50] Quarantined from the contingencies of history, phenomenology has been reduced to a small component of an encyclopedic enterprise that has finally managed to dispense with introductions and is now running on empty.

This means that the encyclopedic vision of philosophy—the idea of a total work, expressing the totality of being, and articulated immanently as a self-developing "circle of circles"—is reduced from the outset to a ruin or torso. University discourse is the "royal road" to philosophy: we know about philosophy without practicing philosophy; we learn about swimming without getting into the water;[51] we read "reviews, prefaces and first paragraphs"[52] without attending to the thing itself. Science in its encyclopedic version is knowledge without desire—"wisdom" without "love of wisdom." Is this what Hegel had in mind when he spoke of the need to "bring philosophy closer to the form of science"—to let it finally cast off its old name of "'love of knowing' and become *actual* knowing"?[53] Reduced to pure theory, science now attends to past things and becomes itself a thing of the past: it is already worked over, predigested, prestructured, instantly available for teaching and transmission, having already been subjected to a kind of secondary revision—like what we recall on waking from a dream. Under the pressure of academic life and discourse the system turns into a textbook. This self-inflicted dismemberment is the first of many mutilations that Hegel's thought will suffer over the centuries.

Why did Hegel stop writing? The sheer grind of the academic routine is not quite sufficient as an explanation, although Hegel was busy and broke. Virtually his last written words, sent the day before he died, were a note to his printer, asking him to add a Latin epigraph from Cicero to the title page of the forthcoming second edition of the *Science of Logic*:[54] "Est enim philosophia paucis contenta judicibus, multitudinem consulto ipsa fugiens, eique suspecta et invisa [For philosophy is content with few judges. With fixed purpose it avoids, for its part, the multitude, which in turn views it as an object of suspicion and dislike]."[55] Hegel's last wishes seem to have been disregarded, perhaps because the antisocial sentiment seemed un-Hegelian, perhaps for more pedestrian reasons. With the exception of the posthumous second edition of the second book (the doctrine of essence) of the *Science of Logic* (1834), the motto is absent from almost all editions to this day. Where did it go?[56] Cicero might seem a surprising choice of epigraphs, but this is actually not the first time Hegel will have cited this passage. He had already quoted it in the preface to the third (1830) edition of the *Encyclopaedia* to deflect critics who had, he claimed, attacked "some fantastic empty image of philosophy."[57] Carl Friedrich Göschel, an orthodox Christian reader, had immediately reproached Hegel for the evident elitism, also suggesting that he took criticism too personally and that his impulse to withdraw from the world was idiosyncratic.[58] And then—as an answer to this criticism?—Hegel decided to move Cicero to an even more prominent position: to the very front of the *Science of Logic*.[59]

Not only must the encyclopedic digest be protected from incompetent readers: it needs the apparatus of the university if one is to understand it at all. The textbook on its own, without the elucidation of the accompanying lectures, has no pedagogical value. But the "book" (in the strict sense) is even more vulnerable to abuse. Orphaned from its author and lacking the support of the classroom, with no professor to speak for it and no lecture to amplify the reading, the book is at constant risk of falling into incomprehension. Without any *Vorlesung*, without any expository prereading, without the possibility of reading before, or in front of, an audience, we are left only with an infinity of rereading. One can speak of the book only when one has worked through it. The *Logic*, like the *Phenomenology*, is a book for all and none.

It might be tempting to explain Hegel's decision to stop writing by turning him into a Romantic. Had the sublime incompleteness of his first two books already preempted both the possibility and the necessity of any sequel?[60] Why write another book when a lifetime is not long enough to plumb the depths of the two books on hand? From this perspective it is puzzling why Hegel even would have ventured beyond the *Phenomenology* in the first place. Why should he have bothered to write two unfinishable books: is one fragment not fragmentary enough? This Romantic approach misunderstands the logic of unfinishedness at work in both books and also misconstrues the relationship between the two works. There cannot be a single concept of unfinishedness, for the simple reason that unfinishedness itself must remain unfinished.

The *Logic* and the *Phenomenology* are incomplete in opposite ways: one is infinitely revisable, the other too broken to repair. Whereas the one demands an infinity of rewriting, the other is so fractured it prevents any revision from taking hold. At the end of his life, contemplating the possibility of a second edition of his "peculiar early work," Hegel recoiled from the idea of any revision to the *Phenomenology*: "Do not rework."[61] If the *Phenomenology* is incorrigible, if it can tolerate no tampering, this is not because its perfection should be embalmed intact. On the contrary, the work is marked indelibly by its own historicity and it is precisely this historical index that must be set in stone. Even as it performs the universal task of system-building, the *Phenomenology* is stamped by the singular circumstances of its origin, the "then-time [*damalige*] of its composition."[62] Every blemish, every defect must be preserved, even or especially where these imperfections take the form of bald-faced error. Hegel alludes to the prevailing atmosphere of abstraction that had ruined the reception of his early work and thus disfigured the work itself. The book was marred by the constraints of its time, and must forever display this damage like a specimen under glass: "The *abstract absolute* reigned back then."[63] It is precisely this (abstract) universality that makes Hegel's first book irredeemably particular and therefore incorrigible. There can never be the introduction to the system when every possible introduction is marred by distortions that are stamped as indelibly as the printer's marks on the title page. Bamberg, 1807: History itself makes the *Phenomenology* unfinished—and therefore unfinishable. Its irreducible contingency makes it impossible to revise.

The *Logic* is afflicted by a different type of unfinishedness. Speaking from the impossible perspective of God before the creation, it cannot but de-create what has been created to begin the world anew. It must subtract the last grain of established finitude; it must take back all that has been said and done so as to generate the categories necessary to think at all. Finitude is part of the creation and not a prior condition. Yet this purification comes with a price:

the very act of clearing away the order of creation generates an interminability of its own.

On the one hand, we confront the *permanent* unfinishedness of thought in its historical embeddedness as it gropes toward the conditions of its own universality. The *Phenomenology* presents a permanent archive of all the failures necessary to attain conceptual transparency and truth. On the other hand, we witness the *ongoing* unfinishedness of thought as it overtakes and draws in everything that is not yet part of its own movement. By ceaselessly showing all obstacles to be obstacles of thought, the *Logic* does away with any external limit to thinking, and demonstrates the irrepressible pulsation of the drive to thinking as such.[64]

Strangely, the *Phenomenology* commits to permanence while the *Logic* refuses to stand still: history freezes while eternity becomes flux. Hegel's concrete universal displays itself as an endless shuttling between the two competing poles of *concrete* universality and concrete *universality*. He unfinishes unfinishedness by unfinishing in two different ways. Hegel, the philosopher of the end, ended by leaving some unfinished business—twice. The immediate outcome was that Hegel's readers tried to settle things once and for all as they sought to complete his project and repair what might never have needed fixing in the first place.

To paraphrase Marx: the history of all hitherto existing attempts to account for the relation between the *Phenomenology* and the *Science of Logic* has been the history of (interpretive) struggles. Readers have typically given precedence either to one book or the other and have emphasized either a continuity or a discontinuity between the two texts. The options to date can be formalized by a logical square of oppositions: the first position gives precedence to the *Phenomenology* and assumes it stands in continuity with the *Logic*; the second gives precedence to the *Phenomenology* and emphasizes a discontinuity with the *Logic*; the third gives precedence to the *Logic* and supposes a continuity between the two books; and the fourth gives precedence to the *Logic* but assumes a discontinuity between them.

We will introduce a fifth option, namely that *there is* no relationship between the two books (with the emphasis on the "there is" and along the lines of Lacan's "il n'y a pas de rapport sexuelle …")—and that one must therefore give precedence to both.

The first position takes the *Phenomenology* to be the core of Hegel's project and the *Science of Logic* as an explicitation of the logic implicit in this earlier work. It assumes that the dialectical movement driving both books is essentially the same. This ultimately undermines the autonomy of the *Logic* and makes it conceptually redundant: with the *Phenomenology* everything is always already developed, at least in *nuce*, and the very continuity of the dialectical movement from one book to the other renders the *Logic* superfluous. While the former provides a concretion or condensation of universal history,[65] the latter presents its inessential afterthought—a "realm of shadows."[66]

The second position also prefers the *Phenomenology* because of its wealth of detail and historical substance. Such empirical profusion invalidates in advance any logical scaffolding that would lie beneath or beyond it in an otherworldly ether. Despite his own self-estimation, Hegel was truly Hegel only when he wrote the introduction to his system; the *Logic* (together with the subsequent encyclopedic apparatus it unleashes) only betrays the living historical dynamics that gave rise to it.[67] Once again, but now for opposite reasons, the *Phenomenology* stands alone: its account of historical "mobilism"[68] overpowers the eternalizing machinery of the *Logic* and shows the latter aspiration to be untenable. The project of the *Logic* presents a mortifying—transcendental—step back behind what Hegel had already accomplished in his earlier book. Such a reading opens the floodgates to a historical relativism that not only cuts off the *Logic* from the *Phenomenology* but also excises the final chapter of the *Phenomenology* on absolute knowing: the preceding chapters will have already invalidated any claim to such knowledge. This position inadvertently endorses a self-refuting form of eclecticism: it cannot but isolate (in Freud's sense) specific shapes of spirit and turn them into decontextualized and transhistorical paradigms of experience. (This is of course the contradiction of every historical relativism.) Detached parts of the *Phenomenology*, and thus the book as a whole, turn into the very thing the *Phenomenology* itself had just demonstrated to be impossible: everything becomes a frozen fragment of the *Logic*.

The third position avoids such inadvertent endorsement of the *Logic* by embracing the latter's necessity head on. It explicitly declares the later book to be the essential one and the earlier book to be merely its contingent application (unabashedly particularistic and even Eurocentric)[69] whose method and categories are legible and legitimated only through the book that follows. This reading is a mirror inversion of the first: the *Logic* makes explicit what is implicit in the *Phenomenology*, but this continuity now diminishes the latter's significance. There is ultimately just one book, articulated in both a pure and applied form—a kind of bilingual edition corresponding to a parallel universe whose laws one can either read in translation or decipher in the original language. For the literate reader, a single reading, a single book will suffice. And the task of accounting for the relation between the two books immediately dissolves.

The fourth and (almost) final position takes literally Hegel's unfortunate description of the *Phenomenology* as the "ladder" needed to gain entrance to the system.[70] Once one reaches the top of the ladder one must throw it away in Wittgensteinian fashion.[71] The *Phenomenology* must eventually remove itself from the picture so that the *Logic* can begin afresh on its own terms, unimpeded by the burden of historical contingency. In the end, there is only the *Science of Logic*—the truly presuppositionless science. The *Phenomenology* maps out the arduous historical itinerary that must be traversed to reach the absolute standpoint. Yet once this standpoint is reached it becomes clear that this itinerary had relied on the pure structures depicted in the *Logic*. The ultimate point of the *Phenomenology* will have been to make itself redundant. This is a mirror inversion of the second reading and displays a similar performative contradiction. The historical necessity of the *Phenomenology* implies its own superfluity.

All these readings systematically elide the "almost insoluble problem" they seek to address.[72] Every attempt to account for the relation between the two books misses the count; we can no longer count to two or count two as two. The two books become one. But this only defers the problem. The question shifts from whether the *Phenomenology* or the *Logic* is the "book of all books"[73] to whether either can be said to be "a 'book' at all."[74] For the antinomy keeps reproducing itself. The tension between the two books keeps resurfacing at the interior of each, as witnessed by the constant attempts to prune, to divide, to dissect, to demarcate, to siphon off what is essential and what is inessential, what is relevant and what is irrelevant, in each book. Everyone always asks: just how much of this book do we actually have to swallow? Can we stop reading here, or here, or must we also read this chapter? I can go along with Hegel only to this point; yet what follows is really just too much, I have to skip the section on this (it's too empirical), or this bit (is it meant historically or structurally, anyhow?), or this (it's so boring and technical) … No one really believes you actually have to get through the whole thing (something similar happens with the three volumes—and three more were planned—of *Capital*[75]).

It might seem like a trivial gesture to dismiss Hegel's megalomaniac category of totality. But without some version of this category, how do we draw the line between what is living and what is dead, what is metaphysical and what is nonmetaphysical, what is contemporary and what is merely historical, what is timely and what is simply outdated and irrelevant? But these choices are forced. The very compulsion to dissect, to divide between the living and the dead parts of Hegel's system, would seem to succumb to the mortifying logic of the understanding. Or is the splitting generative and productive—a kind of cell division? Can we tell the difference between the reproduction of the living organism and the dismemberment of the corpse, between the multiplication of life and the replication of death? Can one split the difference between these two kinds of splitting? To paraphrase the old Maoist slogan: Two fuse into One, yet (each) One constantly divides into Two again.[76]

This might account for the confusion that has always vexed readers of the *Phenomenology*, namely the relationship between the empirical and the formal:

the split inherent in phenomenology itself between the things themselves (the phenomena) and the *logos* of their unfolding. One of the abiding puzzles and irritations of the *Phenomenology* arises from the tension between the more recognizably philosophical problematic of the first part of the book (the opening three or four chapters raise standard philosophical problems: empiricism, idealism, skepticism, the problem of other minds) and the historically drenched discussions of the later chapters (the later chapters are citation laden, moody, bursting with cultural references and historical allusions).[77] The second half of the *Phenomenology* is often relegated to history of science, social history, or cultural studies, the obsessive accumulation of details sometimes attributed to Hegel's lingering positivism or to the distracting force of circumstances. Theodor Haering described the book as a mass of "improvisation."[78] The world spirit was riding around on horseback and it could be hard to concentrate.

Confusion had set in even while the book was still in production. The plan had been to conclude the "Science of the Experience of Consciousness" with a chapter called simply "The Science."[79] But Hegel changed his mind. "It was impossible to restrict the quest to the mere form of consciousness" without including "the development of the *content*," a decision that eventually ended up clogging the work with buckets of empirical detail. Material belonging to the later system (the *Realphilosophie*) was "prematurely dragged into the introduction,"[80] while "the science" itself seemed perpetually put off beyond the book's outer limits. Does the second part of the *Phenomenology* belong to the *Science of the Experience of Consciousness* or had it been pushed onto the ladder without belonging there? Halfway through printing, Hegel's publisher refused to pay the first installment of the author's fee, which had been due on submission of half the manuscript. That halfway mark seemed to be perpetually receding. Confronting the mounting pile of pages and the ever-growing sprawl of topics, the publisher wrote Hegel "that he would first have to have the entire manuscript in hand before he could decide how much half of it was."[81]

The division within the *Phenomenology* between the first and second halves (in some respects reminiscent of the bifurcation of *Being and Time* into separate "divisions") broadly anticipates the division between the *Phenomenology* and the *Logic* themselves, and similar divisions are repeated within every chapter of the *Phenomenology*. Fichte's son, Immanuel Hermann Fichte, saw these endless internal divisions as the expression of an irreconcilable conflict between "real philosophy" (the positive sciences) and epistemology (the logic of their articulation), a contradiction that ended up making "something half out of both [*etwas Halbes aus beiden*]." Even if we take only one book at a time, we end up with only half a book, while that half refuses to stay only a half, simultaneously diminishing and expanding into "monstrous dimensions."[82] Rudolf

Haym saw the *Phenomenology* as a "palimpsest" of two disparate texts.[83] Friedrich Köppen, another contemporary of Hegel's, saw the lack of a coherent structure as symptomatic of Hegel's "battle with his old philosophical self"[84] (he is thinking specifically of the undigested remnants of Schelling that continue to clog the text). The book "makes war upon itself"—as Hegel once described the activity of spirit in general.[85]

Hegel's apparent indecision even about how to name the book (for a time there were two distinct titles running concurrently: the *Science of the Experience of Consciousness* and the *Phenomenology of Spirit*) reflected this sense of fracture.[86] There is also a discrepancy at an organizational level: whereas the text presents eight consecutive chapters, the table of contents announces six sections, while in his advertisement for the book, Hegel compounds the confusion by describing seven stages.[87]

Whatever the count, the finish line seems clear: "Consciousness will arrive at a point [Punkt] at which ... its exposition will coincide with the authentic Science of Spirit."[88] Otto Pöggeler remarks aptly that "the point of the authentic science of spirit is not a point at which we could point a finger":[89] it is not an objective endpoint or starting point, although it is a tipping point, a point of no return, and herein lies its properly revolutionary significance. Hegel will famously hail Napoleon's arrival in Berlin as just such a punctuation of history: "It is indeed a wonderful sensation to see such an individual, who, concentrated here at a single point, astride a horse, reaches out over the world and masters it."[90] The question is thus continually repeated: What (and where) is the final point? And as it seems impossible to answer, everyone draws a line, dividing and cutting the book into pieces. Within a century of its publication Wilhelm Windelband, a pupil of Hegel's pupil Kuno Fischer, had observed that "the generation that was able to understand Hegel's *Phenomenology* is about to die out. Even now, one can count those who have read it from beginning to end."[91]

One can observe a similar bifurcation in the *Logic*, which may contribute to its equally piecemeal reception. Hegel complained after a bad review: "My poor innocent *Logic* and I are being pilloried."[92] It might seem less mutilating to cut into this work than into the *Phenomenology*, since here we are dealing only with the "dead bones"[93] of abstraction, but the effect of this dissection is no less disorienting. Readers again draw the line in different places. The opening sentences of the *Logic* seem to have an immediate contemporary resonance (being and nothing can be grasped only from the perspective of becoming, that is, from a historically specific perspective), but this appeal vanishes by the time you get to the climactic description of the absolute idea that cavorts with itself and finally releases nature from its own loins. Just about everyone loves the "determinations of reflection"—with their relentless reversals and undermining of hierarchies they have proved useful for ideology-busting—but almost everyone stalls by the time they reach the "Himalayan" peaks of the third book (on the "concept").[94] Others recoil at the point when Hegel defines the absolute idea as an activity of pure self-determination. At this point the work seems to have immunized itself against all commentary; any critique can only be an autocritique that cannot but rely on Hegel's toolkit if only to refute him (this predicament tormented anti-Hegelianism throughout the twentieth century). Others take leave where Hegel links the forms of syllogism to seemingly empirical categories. The categories themselves seem to be continually invaded by extralogical matter: How do terms like *mechanism, chemism, life,* and *love* become specifically *logical* operators?[95] It is as if the *Logic* has signed off prematurely, collapsing into the empirical sciences before its own project is completed, its final moments invaded by the nature that should arrive only later.

This puts pressure on the notion of totality. It also points to an uncertainty about the status of the logical categories. The challenge is not only dealing with the morass of examples from now mostly forgotten eighteenth-century mathematics or physics. The issue is to clarify the logic of exemplarity itself. What is the relationship between a concept and its application? Does Hegel's *Logic* inherit the ambiguities of the Kantian project of transcendental logic? In his critique of the Kantian table of categories, Hegel had reproached Kant for having uncritically blurred the line between the logical and the empirical,[96] just as Kant himself had criticized the Aristotelian catalogue of categories for being "rhapsodic."[97] If the task is to adumbrate the concepts of possible objects of experience, are these concepts indelibly tainted by the contingency of their potential referent? This dilemma had pervaded the transcendental deduction and gave rise to the still ongoing debates about the relative ranking of concepts and intuitions. If the concept is fully emancipated from the empirical realm, how can it establish its validity within this realm? And yet if it relinquishes its purity by entering into a relationship with the empirical, does critical philosophy not risk losing its transcendental status and regressing to a kind of anthropology? Kant had tried to resolve this dilemma by introducing the unifying activity of an originary "I think." Yet for Hegel this solution only perpetuates the problem. The connection between the form and content of the categories remains formal, which again begs the question of how form and content ultimately are related.

This is where we must again underscore the key difference between Hegel and Kant. Hegel is not talking about conditions of possibility. What is at stake is neither the content nor the form of possible experience but rather "the categories of the absolute"[98]—the impossible "exposition of God before the creation."[99] We are being forced to think from the standpoint of the *impossibility* of experience without finding refuge in a realm beyond experience—whether as supersensible substratum or noumenal background. Hegel is not retrieving the transcendental conditions of cognition that we may have forgotten or overlooked. The *Phenomenology* had released the subject of its dependence on all substantial content, including the forms of experience that are continually congealing into a new content. Hyppolite aptly describes the phenomenological itinerary as a "working through" of experience: the subject learns to mourn the loss of the coordinates of subjectivity itself.[100] Detached from its moorings, the disoriented subject is forced to turn the page on everything it has known, including the self who is doing the page-turning. The *Logic* is thus freed to explore a subjective movement prior to all given forms of subjectivity. It depicts an event—the creation of a world.

We must finally consider a fifth possible way of relating the *Phenomenology* and the *Logic*—namely that there is no relationship between the two books. The punctuation is indispensable: there is an active (or absolute) non-relation between the two works. This formulation[101] can help us unpack a formula of the young Hegel: "the conjunction of conjunction and nonconjunction"[102]— literally, the binding of binding and unbinding (die *Verbindung der Verbindung und der Nichtverbindung*). Between the two bound volumes there is an infinitely binding unbinding that rips off the bindings of each book and forces a passage between them. This passage is cluttered by the profusion of transitional paratextual material that we can see piling up in the interstitial border zone between the two books—the strange hiatus after the one book has ended but before the other has properly begun—a blank space, a concluding epigraph, two book covers, a title page, a table of contents, an introduction, another introduction, some general classificatory remarks, another preparatory section on how to begin. The *Ver-bindung* unbinds what it binds. It cuts all ties between one volume and another even as it inextricably knots them together. After the *Phenomenology* nothing can continue as before, all familiar coordinates have been relinquished, we have learned to forget everything we have learned: we must start again from scratch—literally, ex nihilo (or with being, which will turn out to be the same).

There is a fundamental uncertainty when we pass from one book to the other. Is anything getting through? Is there a functioning communication or do we have a bad connection or even the wrong number—*falsch verbunden*? Are we left with the endless monologue of spirit talking to itself without even a self to talk to? Is this what God was doing before he created the world? This uncertainty ruins the possibility of any common measure that would allow us to compare the books as two of a kind. Bookkeeping becomes impossible. That the two books share nothing simultaneously stitches them together and tears (each of) them apart.

One must therefore read the two books in tandem. This is different from reading them as complementary counterparts or as two halves of a whole. And while we are emphasizing their heterogeneity, this disparity cannot be understood simply as the nuclear fallout of "dualisms not overcome."[103] Philosophy is not only a split science but a science of the split—a twofold science of the twofold. Heidegger remarks that for Hegel "science … develops [entfaltet] to the full in two [zwiefach] directions":[104] it unfolds by splitting. Adorno sees this as Hegel's core insight: "the greatness of Hegel's philosophy lies in the moment of splitting [Entzweiung]."[105] There is a reason why Hegel always begins twice: the *Phenomenology* and the *Logic*, "being" and "nothing."

Hegel's "absolute method" immediately complicates any reading that would try to rank the two works, to divide them into major and minor, essential and inessential, or to see either as the other's foundation, culmination, or destination. This seems intuitively obvious, if only because both the *Logic* and the *Phenomenology* work so hard to problematize at a thematic level all the ways we customarily deal with things that arrive in pairs—inside and outside, cause and effect, ground and consequence, essence and appearance, form and content (and at least by implication, prior and posterior, minor and major, primary and secondary, prequel and sequel, and so on). The relentless reshuffling of dichotomies in the second book of the *Logic* has implications for reading the *Science of Logic* as a whole. It prompts us to think not only about the book's own internal bipartition, but also about its mysterious relationship to its companion text.

However you try to connect the two books, the *Logic* brings into the foreground the problematic status of their conjugation. It explicitly raises two-someness itself to the dignity of a philosophical problem,[106] and it does so precisely by dissolving the specular bond we usually take for granted whenever we try to count in pairs.[107] If two are not to be fused into one, reduced to two of a kind, or positioned as two poles of a dyad, one must not assume that one even knows how to count. This is not to suggest that the *Logic* has a privileged perspective on coupledom: the *Phenomenology* had already dismantled every natural attitude toward pairs: to have traversed the pathway of despair is to have punctured the bubble of the imaginary (in this respect it is correct to describe the *Phenomenology* as a kind of ideology critique). It has exploded the double consciousness that superstitiously equips itself with "two sorts of eyes, two sorts of ears, speaks with two voices."[108]

This accounts for the privilege of "despair" as a philosophical attitude (which would otherwise register simply as some kind of post-Reformation or proto-existentialist pathos).[109] When Hegel speaks, in the introduction to the *Phenomenology*, of the need to pass from skeptical doubt, *Zweifel*, to full-throttled despair, *Verzweiflung*, he is talking about a transformation of the very idea of twoness. Both *Zweifel* and *Verzweiflung*, and for that matter the English words *two* and *doubt*, hinge on a sense of twinning, *Zweiheit*—see also *twig*, *twine*, *twain*, *twist*, *dual*, *duo*—but the sharp difference between the two words can easily be overlooked. The passage from ordinary to "thoroughgoing skepticism" is essentially from *Zweifel* as a regulated vacillation between secured binary polarities to an unbound *Verzweiflung* that problematizes any measure by which one could even count the two as two in the first place. The *fel* of *Zweifel* etymologically suggests that two are *folded* into one. Ordinary doubt appears when it seems certain that we have only one option, namely that we must pick from two comparable alternatives. Even when seeming to doubt everything, we still cling to the unquestioned certainty that there are two sides between which to choose.

Despair, *Verzweiflung*, casts doubt on the certainty of this folding: it unfolds what was securely folded together in the act of doubt, and twists together what had seemed most cleanly separated. We move from doubt to despair, from *Zweifel* to *Verzweiflung*, precisely when we are forced to question the opposition that doubt takes most for granted. A doubt more hyperbolic than Descartes's hyperbolic doubt, *Verzweiflung* raises doubt to the second power. It puts doubt into doubt—*Zweifel am Zweifel*. The opaque prefix *Ver-* also appears as an inconspicuous token in the German words for both reason and understanding: *Vernunft* and *Verstand*, and we have already just encountered it in *Verbindung*, "union" or "binding." (This particle does similar work in the Freudian vocabulary of *Verdrängung* and *Verneinung*, and also in the Heideggerian *Verwindung*.[110]) This prefix is matched in its difficulty only by the equally strange *Ent-* that we will later be examining in *Entschluß* and that we have just encountered in *Entzweiung*. The *Ver-* distorts, deforms, twists out of shape, but at the same time shows the two elements of the pair to be inseparably entwined. The pair is in disrepair and dis-pair.[111]

If the two books come as a package, this is not a function of their mutual complementarity or by virtue of some kind of mystical unity of opposites, and there is no third term, no further synthesis to bind the two books together within the space of a single volume. Every mediator has vanished. The two texts coexist rather in an uneasy relationship of supplementarity, where each functions as the shadow side of the other, simultaneously superfluous and indispensable. Despite or because of the impossibility of crossing from one side to another, each side has already passed over into the other side, as on a kind of Moebius strip. This spatial model complicates any stable assignment of borders, frontiers, and divisions: there is no clearly established line of demarcation, no (Kantian) *Schranke*, separating the two territories, even while the distance between them remains impassable. The passage from recto to verso is more complicated than turning a page. We can never be certain which side we are on, and it is impossible to mark the precise moment that we pass from one side to another—we can only mark this crossing once we have already crossed over. Whatever disorientation may result in the passage from one side to the other, the fact that *there is* another side emerges with unshakable certainty, signaling that "there is no relationship" between one side and the other. It is impossible to keep going without ending up on the other side. Lacan will argue that anxiety signals the irruption of the other side into the immanence of this side. It is in this sense that anxiety is indubitable; it never deceives.[112]

This model also complicates any Kantian reading that would split the *Phenomenology* and the *Logic* along the axes of intuition and concept (or, more broadly, along the axes of necessity and freedom). That Kantian approach often assumes an implicit decision regarding the textual status of the transcendental deduction (consider the ongoing debates around the ranking of the A and B editions). Does the concept swallow up intuition, does form overwhelm content, or must we acknowledge the priority of a pre- or nonconceptual matter in every judgment? Does the *Logic* engulf the *Phenomenology* or does the *Phenomenology* exert an irreducible pressure of historicity into the Logic's transhistorical procedure? And if we are to take Kant at his word when he imagines a "common, but to us unknown root"[113] between concept and intuition, is this root "unknown" because it exists at the level of the noumenal substratum or because it emerges from a preconceptual sensuous opacity? It is always tempting to reify the split between *Phenomenology* and *Logic*—to turn the gap itself into the ultimate transcendental (this is Adorno's suggestion of how to read the transition from Kant to Hegel[114])—but this again turns Hegel into another avatar of transcendental philosophy.

Mathematicians describe the Moebius strip as a "nonorientable two-(dimensional) manifold." Its topology is that of a plane and not that of a line; it is nonorientable because the path it opens up brings us back to our starting point, except that everything is in reverse, as in a mirror. (The return is thus different than when a traveler comes home to the same place after circumnavigating the globe.) The two sides of the Moebius strip are *verschränkt*: they are knotted into one another; each side has already crossed over into the other even while the two sides remain unbridgeable. The *Phenomenology* and the *Logic* are in *Verschränkung*: there is no synthesis that binds them and yet the border that separates them is continually breached. We are caught at every point in a "multi-sided and ambiguous tangling [*vielseitige und vieldeutige Verschränkung*]"[115] that complicates not only the transition between the two books but equally every transition at each stage within both works. This is how Hegel had described the impeded movement of the *Phenomenology* in a rueful letter to Schelling in 1807: the whole thing is "a tangle of cross-references going back and forth [*verschränktes Herüber-und Hinübergehen*]."[116] Thinking is constantly crossing back and forth over an uncertain border.[117] Hence Hegel's famous image of the circle of circles: every end takes us back to the beginning and any point on the circle can be the beginning.

This topology allows us to see how Hegel's philosophy explodes the coordinates of the critical turn. Kant had reified the limitation of human cognition by attempting to banish every thought of the beyond (*Jenseits*): we will always remain on "this side" (*diesseits*)[118] of the boundary. We will never be able to reach the other side and therefore it is our duty to refuse all attempts to do so. We cannot, so we must not. But Kant's prohibition of what is already impossible did not exorcise the outside but only reified it as an unattainable beyond. Kant "remained afflicted by the very object he avoided."[119] The driving motive and outcome of critical philosophy is an "anxiety before the object [*Angst vor dem Objekt*]."[120]

Kant's greatness lies in unveiling the fundamental topology of thinking and its ultimate object. But unable to countenance the anxiety unleashed by his own insight, he disavows the *Ver-* in *Verschränkung*, straightens out the twisted coil of the Moebius strip, and ends up with a reified *Schranke*, a stable boundary separating one side from the other. He flattens the "orography of anxiety."[121] Heidegger remarks that Kant "places [*schiebt*] anxiety before the object": he shoves anxiety in front of the object as a protective wall. He thus deflects the impact of anxiety by reconstituting anxiety itself as "an imaginary or constructed [*eingebildete*] anxiety before the *subject*."[122] Kant in one blow conceals what he reveals. He prematurely identifies the object of thought with the subject in such a way as to elide the essential cause of anxiety itself. He thus fundamentally misconstrues his own genuine anxiety before the object. This anxiety is only partially explicated in being attributed to the reflexive activity of the anxious subject (which is just another way of objectifying it). The point is not simply that I am the one that makes myself anxious, that thinking torments itself in its reflexive scrutiny. Anxiety arises rather because there is something in me that exceeds my grasp: there is another side of thought within thought itself—not an unknowable absolute but a secret or unknown knowing at the heart of knowing. Absolute knowing is the articulation of this immanent exteriority of thinking in its starkest form.

Hegel once complained that writing a logic while teaching theology (the same problem applies to writing a logic while writing a phenomenology)— is "like being a whitewasher and a chimney sweep at the same time."[123] This doubletasking is necessary because one is forced to speak two incompatible languages simultaneously—both the representational language of natural consciousness and the conceptual language of pure thinking—and the difficulty is that there is no objective criterion for distinguishing these two idioms. There is no way to identify from a position external to the discourse which is the language of the chimney sweep and which the language of the whitewasher. Hegel's avowedly Lutheran decision to use ordinary language, his stated ambition to "teach philosophy to speak German,"[124] is premised on this fundamental ambiguity.[125]

Even if we get "used to breathing" the "pure mountain-air"[126] of speculative thinking, the words we use are continually dragging us back down to earth. The contamination arises not simply from the fact that our language is historically constituted, that words fluctuate between literal and figurative usage, that we for the most part have to obey the ordinary rules of grammar, and therefore that residues of natural language inevitably keep resurfacing in the formal language of pure logic, although this is all crucial. Hegel himself points out, for example, that the word *Dasein*, literally being-there, contains an indelible spatial reminder,[127] while the word for essence (*Wesen*, from *gewesen*, the past participle of *Sein*) conveys a sense of "timeless pastness,"[128] and "ground" (*Grund*) is always on the verge of disintegration or "running aground" (*zugrunde gehen*). The more abstract and conceptual the words, the more forcefully Hegel keeps reminding us of their sensuous associations. Nowhere is this phenomenological remainder more palpable than where philosophy sets out to demarcate the limits of the phenomenal. Nowhere does Kant himself show himself to be more entangled in worldly experience than when he announces the (spatialized) limits of experience—when he tries to draw the uncrossable barrier that separates us from the "other side."

But Hegel's point is not etymological. He is pointing to the constitutive regressiveness of rationality as such. The upward movement of *aufheben* is always accompanied and enabled by intervals of seemingly nondialectical decline. This tendency to "perennial relapse"[129] (*Rückfall*: literally a falling backward) is neither an accident nor a simple failure of reason, but is immanent to the process of speculative unfolding. In the introduction to the *Phenomenology*, Hegel describes an ineradicable inertia of thinking: not only does thinking cling to whatever position it happens to finds itself in, but it is constantly retreating to standpoints that have already proved untenable and should have been superseded long ago. This regressiveness applies not only to natural consciousness but to logical thinking at its most refined.[130]

Thought therefore keeps on breaking off prematurely to go nowhere. A given position "has been sublated in vain";[131] it has been superseded for no reason and with no consequence—in other words, it has been sublated without being sublated. Yet what is dead can develop a life of its own and can linger on long after it should have vanished. A vain sublation is at once a sublation and not a sublation. It is in this sense that Hegel presents the entire movement of the *Logic* as an ever-ramifying rearticulation of its own beginning. On this path it cannot but constantly regress.[132] This methodological regression is captured by Hegel's image of the circle of circles. But we must distinguish between two kinds of regression, one reactionary, the other generative. The first is an empty repetition where *nothing* moves; the second works through this emptiness by showing that nothing *moves*. In the first case, repetition coincides with structure and can only serve to consolidate a preexisting content. This is basically Hegel's critique of "empty formalism": it is never empty enough; it is always subservient to the givenness of extant conditions. In the second case, repetition works to generate an expanding universe of ever new determinations.

This generative regression coincides with a peculiar movement of anticipation—which is another way of saying that each book exerts a secret pressure on the other. The *Phenomenology* begins from the premise that "the absolute is already with us [*bei uns*]":[133] it is literally beside us, at our side, lodged within us, the very point of our endeavor, even when it seems most beside the point and pointless. We cannot but anticipate the absolute even though we do not hold it before us as a destination or yearn for it as an unreachable regulative ideal. The absolute is always working silently alongside us, forcing us at every step to revise what we took to be our unshakable foundations and to adjust what we thought to be our ultimate aim. It intrudes into our mental space and defamiliarizes our habitual undertakings. What seemed merely adjacent to us turns out to be what is most our own, and what is most familiar becomes untenable and opaque.

The *Logic* begins by registering a different kind of sideways pressure. We must "set aside all reflection"—we must put away, place beside us, out of reach, every representation, every opinion, every habitual position and posture. Or more precisely: *there is nothing* to be done other than a deliberate "setting aside" (*Beiseitsetzung*) of every critical position so that we can take up what is simply lying there before us: "Ist nichts zu tun, als zu betrachten oder vielmehr mit Beiseitsetzung aller Reflexionen, aller Meinungen, die man sonst hat, nur aufzunehmen, *was vorhanden ist*."[134] The anonymity of this action is crucial. There is no longer even a designated agent of thinking—only the impersonal agency of a thinking that has given up all presuppositions, including the presupposition that there is an agent performing the giving up. We must actively forget everything we have taken to be self-evident, including the self-evidence of the "we" who are to do the forgetting.

This marks the difference between the method of the *Phenomenology* and the method of the *Logic*, despite the superficial similarity of their initial protocols. Both the *Phenomenology* and the *Logic* are engaged in a continuous project of self-purging. Both are engaged in cleaning activities—chimneysweeping and whitewashing (although it is hard to say which is which). Both are involved in tasks of Herculean proportions: both are clearing out the Augean stables of tradition—scrubbing philosophy of the debris of accumulated prejudice and presupposition. Both set out from an attitude of methodical skeptical epoché; both suspend the assumptions of the natural attitude, including every preconception about the apparent givenness of the naturalized coordinates of time and space. But there is a fundamental difference between the logical and the phenomenological epoché. The *Phenomenology* brings us to the point of doubting the very thing that doubt takes for granted—namely that there is a consistent subject who doubts.

This is what marks the trajectory of spirit as a labor of mourning and ultimately of self-mourning. "To know one's limit is to know how to sacrifice oneself."[135] The Phenomenology ends with a gesture of radical erasure: "Spirit starts afresh ... as if, for it all that preceded were lost and it had learned nothing."[136] Thinking pushes itself to the point of producing its own collapse, and thereby ensures its own continuation. The beginning of the Logic is for this reason a second beginning: it is the deletion of a deletion, the repetition of a repetition. To erase, one must have already erased, and one must have also erased the memory of this erasure. To forget, one must forget that one has already forgotten. One must wash away the dirt left behind by the chimneysweep even while this whitewashing only adds further detritus to be cleared away.

In repeating this gesture of effacement, the Science of Logic both remembers and forgets the Phenomenology. It remembers precisely in forgetting—and, of course, vice versa. To do away with all presuppositions we must do away with everything learned on the highway of experience, including the final lesson of experience—namely that one must forget experience. It is therefore at once necessary and therefore impossible to begin without the Phenomenology. The beginning of the Science of Logic is thus marked by a fundamental impasse. The Phenomenology has always already launched into the project it is supposed only to introduce: it prematurely keeps assuming a task that should begin only after its end will have been secured. The Logic is constantly sliding back into a domain it has already superseded, repeating its moves all over again, if only to keep on going forward. Badiou describes the procedure of the Logic as involving two intertwined and constantly repeated operations: there is first a dialectical explicitation of a point whose existence one takes for granted, then after reaching an impasse, there is a retroactive maneuver that transforms the coordinates of this starting point; the process begins anew, aiming at overcoming its own unavoidable regression.[137]

We can now reconsider Hegel's description of the Logic as a presentation of the mind of God before the creation of the world. It is the fantasy of being the spectator of a world without us. The end of the Phenomenology presents us with the catastrophe of a world from which we will have erased ourselves from the picture. The Logic is working through this fantasy. One book is working through the constitutive illusions of experience, deconstructing the ideological constructions underpinning our relation to what we take to be the real. The other book explores what it might mean to have traversed this fantasy. We do not simply pierce through the curtain of illusions to reach an "other side" unfettered by the obfuscations of natural consciousness; rather we encounter reality as the objective truth of these illusions. There is nothing beyond the curtain of appearances except for what we put there.[138] This is the essential difference between the Kantian and Hegelian dialectic. For Hegel, the antinomies produced "nothing beyond tortuous antitheses."[139]

In moving from the *Phenomenology* to the *Logic* Hegel does not simply violate the Kantian prohibition: we do not simply step away from appearance to reality, from the phenomena to the things themselves. We rather learn that our propensity to illusion does not derive simply from the deficiencies of natural consciousness but is inscribed in the act of thinking—and therefore in being—as such. We move from the illusion that there is something real beyond illusion to the real of this illusion. We become disillusioned with the illusion of the dichotomy of truth and illusion.

This is what happens when we reach the "*point at which* [consciousness] *gets rid of its semblance of being burdened with something alien...a point where appearance becomes identical with essence.... This point* [coincides] with the authentic Science of Spirit."[140] This point is the *punctum saliens* of the *Phenomenology*—literally its jumping point, *der springende Punkt*,[141] the turning point where the phenomenological project leaps toward its logical successor. Hegel repeats the word *point* three times in this single climactic sentence in the introduction to the *Phenomenology*: he names a literal elision. And in line with this, at the beginning of the *Logic*, Hegel will go on to quote Horace's apocalyptic motto: "*Si fractus illabatur orbis, impavidum ferient ruinae* [If the world were to fall to pieces, the ruins would strike (or sustain) the fearless]."[142]

We thus begin the *Logic* with the scenario of an ultimate erasure. Yet this forces us to acknowledge that even before the creation of the world there is still thinking. There is a world "*before the creation of nature and of a finite spirit*,"[143] a world in which one can speak neither of spirit nor even of the absence of spirit—in short, there is no nature as such. This might be why Hegel never wrote the philosophy of nature in speculative or book form; nature itself can appear only in the abbreviated and naturalized form of the *Encyclopaedia*. There can be no philosophy of nature strictly speaking. As soon as we reach the end of the *Logic*, the absolute idea releases itself into nature, but the labor of the *Phenomenology* has to begin again if only so as to undo the naturalization that is depicted and inflicted in the *Encyclopaedia*. We are stuck in the first day of creation.

CHAPTER 3

THE DASH, OR HOW TO DO THINGS WITH SIGNS

Now for the pedantry. There's a strange punctuation mark that crops up at two key moments in both of Hegel's books. The mark appears once at the end of the *Phenomenology* and then again at the beginning of the *Logic*. It can be easy to miss, especially if one is working with the (until recently standard) published English translations, because each time the translator decided to leave it out.[1] It should have been the easiest thing to translate. It did not even need to be translated: strictly speaking, all the translator needed to do was simply to transcribe the mark without further alteration. A punctuation mark does not seem to belong to any particular language; like the black page or the squiggle in *Tristram Shandy*, it would seem to be a job for the typesetter rather than the task of the translator. Curiously, both times, the translator, A. V. Miller, deletes the punctuation mark as if it were inconsequential. He strikes it out. The erasure is telling. Miller's decision seems to confirm Walter Benjamin's point, in the "Task of the Translator," that what is most untranslatable in every language—the "navel" of the translation, so to speak—is not the *je ne sais quoi* of the "poetic," not the sonorities of the acoustic, not the idiosyncrasies of idiom or authorial style, but rather the uncertain point where translation itself has always already occurred. What proves to be the greatest obstacle to translation is precisely what makes it possible. It is *translatability* that blocks the possibility of translation.[2]

The rest of this book will be focused on a pair of seemingly trivial details. Hegel punctuates strangely. He ends the *Phenomenology of Spirit* with a dash. He suddenly breaks off his complex, winding, final sentence, inserts a dash and then a paragraph space, and abruptly appends as an apparent epigraph to the book a subtly altered quotation from a poem by Schiller. And he begins the *Logic* with a dash. After about eighty pages of throat clearing (two prefaces, an introduction, a supplementary elaboration on why it is so difficult to begin), Hegel finally writes down his famous opening sentence, a sentence that is grammatically speaking only a sentence fragment. There is no verb, no definite article, only a repetition, followed by a punctuation mark—actually two marks: a comma and then a dash—which forces the reader to return to the beginning and start again.

Here are the two sentences we will be exploring. The first sentence is verbose and convoluted and reads as follows:

> Their preservation, regarded from the side of their free existence appearing in the form of contingency, is history; but regarded from the side of their [philosophically] comprehended organization, it is the science of knowing in the sphere of appearance; the two together, comprehended history, form alike the inwardizing and the calvary of absolute Spirit, the actuality, truth, and certainty of its throne, without which it would be lifeless and alone. Only—
>
> from the chalice of this realm of spirits
> foams forth for it its own infinitude.[3]

The second sentence is much shorter:

> Being, pure being,—without any further determination.[4]

The contrast between the two sentences could not be starker. Both sentences are equally bewildering, but for precisely opposite reasons. The first meanders, a sprawling network of syntactic and grammatical connections, ending with a flurry of metaphors as it reaches its conceptual climax. The second is barely a sentence in its tautological brevity[5]—there is no verb, no definite article, no adjective, no action or predication—and the phrase itself is devoid of both sensuous and conceptual content. All we are given is the repetition of the most abstract and uninformative word—"being"—to which Hegel adds the equally uninformative qualifiers "pure" and "without any further determination."

The dash in the closing sentence of the *Phenomenology* points in two opposing directions: it retrospectively confirms the preceding phenomenological trajectory even as it turns its back on the phenomenological horizon by pointing forward to a new (purely logical) beginning. Even as the volume closes in on itself, returning to its beginning and supplying a retrospective commentary on its own method, it points beyond its own terminus, opening to a sequel that will suspend the framework of the original book. The dash in this way functions simultaneously as a minus sign and an underlining: it interrupts, subtracts, and cancels out the project of phenomenology even while emphasizing the latter's most fundamental claims. It concedes to the persistence of appearances even as it suspends their coercive grip. It marks the ending of the *Phenomenology* as both a break and an interminable repetition.

The dash in the opening sentence of the *Logic* also points in two directions. The punctuation forces the reader to return to what has just been left behind—the stammering opening words, the accumulation of prefatory material, and finally the *Phenomenology* itself as presupposition and precursor text. And it underscores the incompleteness of the first three words—it interrupts the sentence before it has the chance to complete itself—and promises a supplement that in itself, however, will end up adding nothing new.

The German word for "dash" is suggestively ambiguous—*Gedankenstrich*. The double genitive points to a pause both in and for thought—a moment of hesitation where thinking draws back from its customary engagement with the world. One might speak of a phenomenological epoché, a temporary suspension or bracketing of the natural attitude, although, strictly speaking, this suspension does not take place within the confines of phenomenology. The act is not internal to phenomenology but is rather the suspension of phenomenology. It signals the point where phenomenology calls into question its most fundamental commitment—namely its commitment to the persistence and foundational priority of consciousness itself. But the word also points to a short-circuiting or striking out of thought: a cancellation that may also involve a kind of effacement and concealment.

The English word *dash* is even more ambiguous: it condenses into one efficient monosyllable a pile of divergent meanings—speed (a dash to the finish line), violence, destruction, improvisation (to dash off an article), erasure, unmeasurable minimality or brevity (a dash of salt), superficiality, and even fashion (a dash of style). If you listen hard enough the word even contains a faint echo of blasphemy. The quaintness of the euphemism points not only to the stirrings of an archaic taboo but to the disappearance of this taboo—a negation of the negation that seems oddly appropriate to the disenchanted territory in which we've finally arrived.

But the ultimate ambiguity of the dash is not semantic but pragmatic. The peculiarity of the mark is not primarily a function of the names we assign to it, but is rather embedded in its performative impact. Every dash introduces a moment of uncertainty in reading. As a punctuation mark, the dash displays a puzzling temporal and syntactic ambiguity. Its orientation is simultaneously retrospective and prospective. It also displays a fundamental uncertainty in number. Unlike the period, which arrives just once in every sentence, and unlike parentheses or quotation marks, which come only in pairs, the dash can either stand alone or in tandem. As such, it can signal a definitive breaking off, a temporary digression, or an emphatic clarification. Does the punctuation mark a break, an interruption, a continuation, a detour, a hesitation, a prolongation, a premature termination? The dash combines hesitation and acceleration: it both holds back and propels. It both suspends speech and drives it forward. It scatters and connects. It corrects and confirms. It generates non sequiturs and announces explanations. It points to dead ends and to the most incisive conclusions. It points in all possible directions: continuation, detour, deviation—but also simply random, meaningless termination. Is there a better way to begin and end a couple of books that aggravate the meaning of both ending and beginning?

The ambiguity of the mark is similar to that which Hegel elsewhere attributes to "speculative words" and "speculative sentences." Hegel was delighted to discover, in his own mother tongue, a treasury of words bearing heterogeneous and even antithetical meanings: "It can delight thought to stumble upon in the lexicon as one word that union of opposites which ... to the understanding is nonsensical."[6] The famously untranslatable *Aufhebung*, of course, is Hegel's most celebrated example, and we will return to this (and even propose a new translation), but a host of other words also come to mind: *Er-innerung* (remembrance/interiorization), *Entschluss* (resolve/unclosing/non-syllogism), *Urteil* (judgment/primal division), *Bedingung* (condition, "be-thinging").

A speculative word is literally a contra-diction: it speaks against what it seems to be saying. Some speculative words have a *Doppelsinn*,[7] a double meaning; some contain *Mehrfachsinn*, multiple meanings; some even bring together opposing meanings (*entgegengesetzte*[8] *Bedeutungen*). Like the primal words (*Urworte*) in which Freud discovered a confluence of opposite meanings (*Gegensinn*),[9] a speculative word condenses different meanings into a single signifier without any common denominator that unites these meanings under a unifying conceptual rubric. Its heterogeneous meanings are tied together contingently through an arbitrary "quilting point" that brings the utterance into momentary focus.

Even while it brings all the pleasures of a chance discovery—we trip on such words inadvertently and without premeditation—the encounter is nonetheless the "result of speculative thinking."[10] We can only recognize the conceptual richness of such words if we approach language with a rigorous philosophical commitment. To read speculatively is to take up what is contingent as if it were necessary—to discern rational connection in what would otherwise present itself as nonsensical concatenation. "To him who looks upon the world rationally, the world in its turn looks back in a rational way."[11] To read philosophically is to suspend every prior judgment as to which words have conceptual density and which are meaningless—in other words, to entertain the possibility that any word might be speculative (or not) at any moment.[12] Like Oedipus, we become responsible for what befalls us and for what we fall on. This is what it means to posit the presupposition.

Hegel had also insisted on the importance of speculative grammar. He showed the propositional form of the sentence to be thoroughly overdetermined. Every sentence must be parsed in at least two ways. It can be read the habitual way, according to the linear sequence of metaphysical "picture think-ing." S is P. Or it can be read philosophically, according to the recursive and self-interrupting rhythm of speculative thought. The speculative proposition both is and is not a proposition, and this is why there is a moment of error built into every act of reading. Objectively, there is nothing to distinguish a speculative from an ordinary proposition.[13] When we first encounter any given sentence, we expect this sentence to behave as normal sentences do: we "believe that the usual subject-predicate relation obtains."[14] This expecta-tion is unavoidable. Only by way of a preliminary misreading is it possible to achieve a speculative reading; truth arises only in the experience of a failure that shatters our most basic cognitive assumptions. In other words: misrecog-nition and repetition are constitutive of reading. This is why the speculative sentence is the "paradigm of the whole movement of spirit"[15]—and indeed the paradigm of the Idea itself.

This produces some paradoxes for reading. A couple of years after the pub-lication of the *Phenomenology*, Hegel posted an advertisement for the book in the *Bamberger Zeitung*, where he was then working as editor (his academic career having temporarily fizzled in the wake of Napoleon's invasion). Apolo-gizing preemptively for the scattershot appearance of the book, Hegel warns potential readers that the book will make no sense upon first reading. Only the second time around will the work have any meaning. Only in rereading is it possible even to begin reading.[16]

If, at first, one reads a speculative as an ordinary proposition, its move-ment "destroys" the standard representational framework in which we usu-ally describe the world. We find this "irksome" or "burdensome" (*lästig*),[17] because we are forced to see that there is "meant something other than we meant to mean [*die Meinung erfährt, dass es anders gemeint war, als sie meinte*]."[18] Philosophy means differently, or more precisely, it aims at something else than meaning, "and this correction of our meaning compels our knowing to go back to the proposition."[19] Philosophy is in this sense the compulsion to repeat. Our thinking is impeded by a burden that weighs down our ordinary movement forcing us to stumble and to go back to the beginning. The coun-terthrust[20] we experience in our encounter with speculative grammar is the analogue to our stumbling encounter with speculative words.

We begin with the grammatical subject as the stable basis of the proposi-tion and wait for a predicate to be assigned to it. But we find that the sub-ject only repeats itself in this predicate: when S *is* P, an identity is expressed such that the subject disappears into the predicate. "The passive subject" of the proposition in this way "perishes."[21] We are forced to revise our prior assumptions about both subject and predicate, and therefore also about their relation. Tellingly, in Hegel's paradigmatic example of the speculative proposi-tion, "Gott ist das Sein" ("God is being")[22] it is both the subject and the verb that are repeated in the predicate. "Being" is the nominalized infinitive of the copula that binds together subject and predicate; it manages to condense all the elements of the sentence into a single compact syllable.

The relation between S and P is in this way logically syncopated,[23] which causes thought itself to short-circuit: thinking expects to move but it does not end up where it had expected. Thinking finds itself inhibited: it "suffers, as we might put it, a counterthrust (*Gegenstoß*)" that returns us to the starting point that we thought we had left behind.[24] The *Gegenstoß* is not the Fichtean *Anstoß* (we are not led to posit anything as our starting point). It is rather an interruption that triggers further repetition—a progression through regression.[25] "The advancing [*Fortgehen*] to a result is thus as well the return [*Rückgehen*] into itself, the counterthrust against itself."[26]

Picture thinking thus faces a logical abyss: it seeks to flee this impasse but does not know where. This inhibition, as in Freud, is both the occasion and the defining feature of anxiety. Seeking to return to a safe haven, we find upon return that our starting point is empty: there is only an empty space where we had previously assumed the subject to reside. Where substance was, now appears only the void of subjectivization. This throws us back again to the predicate in which this desubstantialized subject finds itself expressed. We are thrown back and forth according to the "immanent rhythm of the Notion."[27] Thought repetitively moves in circles until this rotary movement eventually becomes the essential content and form of thinking—the "drive [*Trieb*] to truth."[28] This presents both an impasse and opportunity. Freed from the metaphysical assumptions of ordinary thinking, the subject finds a kind of freedom in its own stuckness. "Truth is its own self-movement."[29]

"Philosophical knowledge is indeed quite different in kind from the knowledge that we are used to."[30] Philosophy is peculiar not because it concerns itself with the unknowable or because it worries whether things are unknowable in themselves or only for us. It does not direct itself toward what is occult, opaque, buried, or accessible only to the initiated. "Science is open and equally accessible to everyone."[31] The absolute is out there in the open, it requires no arcane language, no secret talent or expertise; we encounter it in the most ordinary utterances of daily life. We give voice to it every time we speak. Philosophy brings us to see what is invisible in plain sight: it teaches us to stumble. We need to learn how to take up what is right there before our eyes. Philosophy is nothing more than the activation of a knowledge that we did not know we had, an "unknown known" (as in Žižek's variation on Donald Rumsfeld)[32]—which is precisely, of course, how Freud defines the unconscious.

So there are speculative words and speculative sentences. But the speculative work of language also takes place at a more inconspicuous and even micrological level—a level that is both deeper and more superficial than either semantics or grammar, at once more hidden and more exposed. There is also such a thing as a speculative punctuation mark. Hegel's idiosyncratic punctuation is illuminating for a number of reasons, not least because it forces us to revise the standard account of his so-called phonocentrism. This still prevalent view, which feeds into the general impression of Hegel as a metaphysician of presence, has been largely encouraged by a (selective) reading of Derrida's critique of Hegel's privileging of speech over writing. It is not our point here to refute these charges, or to propose a different reading of the notorious passages in the *Encyclopaedia* where Hegel (orally and problematically) denigrates the mortifying externalities of ideographic writing systems (Chinese, Egyptian, the Leibnizian *characteristica universalis*) in favor of the living self-presence of alphabetic script.[33] In forcing the reader's attention to the graphic capacities of language, Hegel not only confirms Derrida's claim that, despite appearances, "the place of semiology is really at the center, and not in the margins or the appendix, of Hegel's *Logic*."[34] He also proves himself to be, as Derrida is also the first to acknowledge, "the first thinker of writing."[35]

But we are dealing here with another kind of writing altogether. The punctuation mark is neither alphabetic nor ideographic. It is bound neither to speech nor to writing but operates at the extremities of both. It introduces phrasing into the sentence and is thus even closer to the voice than a letter of the alphabet: it tells us to breathe. It remains an unpronounceable mark and is thus even closer to writing than a logographic sign: it forces us to look. At once pure writing and pure voice, punctuation points to another region of language.

The dash forces us to turn the gaze to ever-smaller units. Everything is growing smaller as we shift our attention from the sentence to the word to the punctuation mark. We seem to have reached a limit point of abbreviation. It is tempting to consider the dash a linguistic atom: a minimal, nonanalyzable unit in which is crystallized the compacted energy of the system—a kind of linguistic monad. But this would be misleading. The dash is not an atomic unit: it does not represent a zero degree of shrinkage, if only because there is no limit to the differential movement of language, only an endless fissuring that in turn calls for an interminable analysis. The dash marks the splitting of the logical atom.

But what are the atoms, philosophically speaking, that we take the dash to split? Ancient atomists, from Leucippus and Democritus onward, took atoms to be the indivisible units of which all matter is composed. But to account for the emergence of matter they needed to introduce another principle, namely the void that lies between the atoms and opens up the space for them to move. There is a split between atoms and the void. Atoms seem to fall on the side of being, the void on the side of nonbeing; the void names "the nothingness that is between the atoms."[36] But if the atoms are the components of matter, they must precede the formation of matter. And so, as the story goes, they have fallen in straight lines in the void, until there was a clinamen, a contingent swerve, a cosmogenic parapraxis that caused them to collide. What are the atoms and the void before their deviation, if neither the atoms nor the void are defined as material beings?[37]

Lucretius proposed a striking analogy between atoms and letters:[38]

Are many letters common to many words,
But yet you must admit that words and lines
Differ in meaning and the sounds they make.
Such power have letters through mere change of order;
But atoms bring more factors into play
To create all things in their variety.[39]

Like atoms, letters have a specific power that appears "through mere change of order."[40] Matter (and meaning) is constituted through the singular encounters occasioned by the collision of the atoms (the shifting of the letters). But this means that there is no straight fall of the atoms prior to their deviation, and no letters prior to their slippage.

Hegel notes that atomism is, in truth, an idealism of a "higher" order.[41] The atoms are not material entities (already Democritus had referred to them as *atomoi ideai*[42]) since "the principle of [the atom] is fully ideal."[43] But if atoms are not the minimal material unit, and if they do not precede their own collision, what are they? How can matter (and meaning) emerge from the deviation of something purely ideal? Mladen Dolar argues that to answer this question "Democritus enigmatically introduced precisely something that wouldn't fall on either side of the divide between the one and the void. He coined a term, den ..."[44] Den, Democritus's name for the atom, points to a peculiar kind of negativity. The neologism itself exhibits the structure it names, in that it has no meaning in itself but is just the remainder of a prior operation. In Greek, *ouden* and *meden*, the usual words for "nothing," are both formed as negations of *hen* (one). Nothing, in Greek, means literally not one. *Ouden* (oud'hen) refers to "something that is not but could have been," while *meden* (med'hen) names "something that in principle cannot be."[45] Democritus's neologism, formed by dropping the prefix *me* or *ou*, is the subtraction of a negation. Den is the trace left by the evacuation of the last vestige of positivity still latent in the prefix "not." Stripped of its substantifying prefix, the particle points to what is neither one nor not one—something that is even less than nothing, "a decapitation of nothing."[46]

Den expresses the speculative truth of *Aufhebung*: it reveals a negativity more negative than any negation. The particle points not to a semantic plenitude or surplus of meaning but to a hypertrophy of emptiness—not a *Doppelsinn* but a *Doppelunsinn*—negativity redoubled. It is not that there are atoms floating in a void that then come into collision. Rather there is the void and there is also something that is even emptier than this void: a peculiar "subtraction after negation,"[47] a redoubled minus—a dash.

Such a reading of the ancient atomists clarifies why there cannot be any kind of stable linguistic atom that would be an ultimate signifying unit: there is no atom without the void, no atom (and no void) that is not the result of a prior splitting. The atoms are already split when they co-emerge with the void as their flipside. The atom is itself the pulverization of every atomic unit. And astoundingly Hegel learns from the atomists that something that is less than nothing can generate a world.

PART II

PUNCTUATIONS OF ABSOLUTE KNOWING

CHAPTER 4

HEGEL'S LAST WORDS

REBECCA COMAY

When all is said and done, to let go of a book is to go through a bout of mourning. Hegel's struggle to get the thing off gives separation anxiety a whole new spin. Craziness, hypochondria, missed deadlines, publisher's hassles, promises, more promises, bad postal service, no document backup, money problems, job insecurity—the usual academic nightmare—plus a dose of history: the Napoleonic horseman of the apocalypse, Jena under siege: Hegel's lawyer finally reassures him that, contractually speaking, acts of war do indeed count as extenuating circumstances. The manuscript somehow gets finished anyway, sent off nervously in installments, the postman braving enemy gunfire; arson, looting, chaos in the streets; Hegel frets, looks over the printer's shoulders, cringes, indulges in fantasies of instant republication in a new and improved edition, tacks on one of his trademark self-undermining prefaces, frets some more, procrastinates, suddenly has to find a new job, shamefully confesses dissatisfaction with his orphan text, shamelessly flogs the book anyway, preemptively defers judgment day (the usual way: caveat lector, don't leap to conclusions, my book needs slow reading, multiple rereadings, and, don't forget, it's just the "first part" of the system, it needs to be supplemented by the *Logic*, which in turn, and so on …), the thing still doesn't really sell, life goes on, new job, next book … The rest is history.

The focus of this chapter is much narrower. It involves the last two lines of the *Phenomenology* and the proleptic mourning work ("the undertakers are already at the door"[1]) performed as Hegel takes leave of the work that has consumed his energies since arriving at Jena to begin transcribing the "ideals of [his] youth"[2] into scientific (systematic) form. The thing has bloated. Whether or not the book conceptually exceeds the project announced in the introduction, Hegel has clearly ended up chewing more than he had bitten off when he set out to commit to paper the science of the experience of consciousness—science in its phenomenal aspect, as self-evident, and as (mere)

appearance. It's not my purpose here to engage in Frankenstein-style specu-
lations (did the book somehow start to *grow* somewhere around chapter 5?
chapter 6? an overdose of natural science? of cultural studies?) but just to note
the pressures on a work that chapter by chapter has been steadily slowing
down under the weight of its own accretions, until, abruptly shifting gears—
and as if to mime the synchronicity of its concluding vision (there were of
course also, as always, deadline issues)—it suddenly sprints forward to the
finish line. It's not just the traumatic abruptness of the last dash but also a
curious indeterminacy of the endpoint that intrigues me.

How (and when exactly) does the final leave-taking get registered? The context needs recapitulation. Absolute knowing, having "won the concept," has
just run through a breathless recapitulation of the entire sequence of its various misadventures—finally vindicated as learning experiences—in the
slightly esoteric shorthand that suggests at once a flashcard sequence learned
by rote and the cinematic flipbook of a deathbed vision. Having died a thousand deaths on the battlefield of experience, natural consciousness has mirac-
ulously survived, if only to tell the tale, according to a schema of allegorical
conversion similar to that elaborated in Dante's *Paradiso*: death, narrative resurrection—the metamorphosis of the pilgrimage of experience into its own
transcription. In a final flashback, absolute knowing suddenly rewinds and
fast-forwards, Krapp-like, through the highlights of its own history: some five
hundred pages of tortuously detailed exposition are compressed into nine
killingly elliptical paragraphs, which in their paratactic and occasionally arbitrary arrangement push to the limit the forward momentum of prose (as the
prorsus or *proversus*, i.e., linear procession). The shorthand gestures both to the
work's "verse-like" reversion to its own origins (its regression to draft, notes,
or outline) and to its decomposition into archival detritus: in the absolute
present of philosophy, sketch and ruin, project and memory, future and past,
converge. The repetition announcing the work's centripetal return-to-self
points to the irresistible force of fragmentation and decay. The self-abbrevia-
tion of the science is thus indistinguishable from its entropic disintegration
into disjoint phrases, titles, or labels, the commemorative labor from com-
pulsive mnemotechnic efficiency—or, as Hegel ridicules it in the preface, not
quite realizing that it might also be his own work he is describing, "a synoptic
table, like a skeleton with scraps of paper stuck all over it" (PH §51).

This miniaturization both describes and dramatizes the retroactive "annul-
ment [*tilgen*]" of time (PH §801): the overcoming of the fatal delay that had
produced consciousness's fundamental obliviousness to the significance of its
own experiences. (Hegel is here rigorously Aristotelian: time is the retarding
factor that prevents everything being given all at once and in advance.) The
almost illegibly formulaic compression of language in the concluding paragraphs of the *Phenomenology* announces the reversal of the temporal dilation

blocking the transparency of self-thinking thought. To close the book is to cancel the delay symptomatic of an unresolved gap between knowledge and its object. To "annul" time is, for Hegel, to "sublate" it,[3] to release it to its higher truth, that is, to convert it from being a mere "container"[4]—an alien "destiny and necessity" (PH §801)—to being the very substance or "filling" of spirit's project.

The shift from spirit's provisional appearance *in* time to its final vindication *as* time involves the recursive self-application of the concept. As the "existent concept," time needs to be "seized [*erfaßte*]" or "conceptualized [*begriffene*]" to become adequate to itself (PH §801), following an alimentary schema whose superficial proximity to Kant's own has been justly noted (most trenchantly by Werner Hamacher). Hegel hastens to point out the differences. In his Berlin lectures on the history of philosophy he will mock with biting sarcasm the "transcen-dental" aesthetic (Hamacher's uncharacteristically bad pun) interpretation of time and space as an oral-sadistic phantasm symptomatic of a disavowed breach between self and world:

> There are things-in-themselves out there, but lacking space and time; now consciousness comes along, which already possesses space and time within it as the possibility of experience, just as it already possesses mouth and teeth etc. as the conditions of eating. The things which are eaten possess neither mouth nor teeth, and just as consciousness imposes eating on things, so too it imposes space and time on them: just as it places things between mouth and teeth, so too it places them in space and time.[5]

Hegel is here ridiculing Kant for reducing subjectivity to the empty voracity that, failing to recognize itself in its object, unfailingly reinstates the gulf it seeks to eliminate as it appropriates the object through the jaws of the formal apperceptive apparatus. Such hunger reappears in the practical sphere as the "cold duty" that, forced to make do with itself as its sole enjoyment, is left gnawing on its own pieties—a "last, undigested lump in the stomach"—and thus displays all the conversion symptoms of the ascetic ideal: Hegel's terms are as always prophetically Nietzschean.[6] Hegel does not exactly renounce this oral phantasm but in a characteristic hypertranscendental move both prolongs and overcomes the Kantian schema by turning the critical bite back on itself such that the orifice between inner and outer, container and contents, is in turn involuted.

To overcome its merely "subjective" character as empty intuition, whether as the mathematical continuum of linear succession or as its historicist variations, time must turn its own bite back on itself, must submit to its own destructive logic. It must consume itself in the act of consumption.[7] As the "abstraction of consuming," time not only destroys the independence of its objects but must overcome its own external character as "container," "stream," or "river." It must absorb the seriality that it inflicts—the "not yet" symptomatic of an unresolved breach between knowledge and object—in the final synthesis that Hegel calls *begriffene Geschichte* (PH §808). In swallowing itself swallowing, time therefore marks itself as not only objective but absolute—a "conceptualized and conceptualizing intuiting" rather than a "merely intuited concept" (PH §801)—a self-seizure in which time "fills" and "fulfills" itself, but also renders itself impotent in its own engorgement: it checks its own violence.[8] Time withdraws itself as it draws itself inward (to evoke a Heideggerean register), a whirlpool arresting the stream of becoming (to recall Benjamin's formulation,[9] an "abstraction [*abstrahieren*]" that in drawing back from the self-presentation of spirit marks at once the latter's apogee and its blindspot.[10]

Self-consciousness in this way "enriches itself until ... it has sucked into itself the entire structure of what is essential to it"—a digestion (*verdauen*) (PH §808) whereby what is absorbed is already determined as spirit's own essence, and thus every bite effectively a self-bite—an involution of and on the inside. But since such suction has effaced the opposition between inside and outside, what appears from one angle as ingestion or contraction must be viewed with equal cogency as an excretion or expansion whereby spirit "releases" itself toward a zone of untrammeled sensuous immediacy—time and space as "free contingent happening"—which it posits as a determinate negativity to be recuperated as its own other (PH §807).[11] The "continuing existence" of the outside thus reinstates the subject in its heroic sublimity—a self-possession forged in the act of self-dispossession.

Thus the circle closes just where it breaks open: absolute knowing asserts its "supreme freedom and assurance" (PH §806) in its controlled regression to a natural prehistory that it embraces in a kind of *docta ignorantia* or feigned amnesia regulated by the analogical, Kantian-style, subjunctive of the "as if." "Spirit has to start afresh *as if* for it all that preceded were lost and *as if* it had learned nothing" from past experience.[12] The passage continues with a last-minute reversal: "But recollection, the inwardizing [*Er-innerung*] of that experience, has preserved it and is the inner being and in fact the higher form of the substance." The truth of absolute knowing as recollection is the fiction of an absolute forgetting.

Let's set aside the well-trodden objections, from Nietzsche through Bataille, that discern in the "supreme assurance" of the philosopher the bogus renunciations and fetishistic disavowals of the loser wins. ("Spirit has to start afresh *as if* all ... were lost. ... But memory ...."). Let's also set aside the interesting paradox lurking in this gesture of willed renunciation—a tension amplified in the *Logic*'s closing reference to the "drive" or "resolve" of the logical idea to "let itself go"[13]—with its Schellingian associations and its more contemporary resonances, for example, in Heidegger's notion of *Gelassenheit*, in the Proustian "search" for contingency, or indeed in the active forgetfulness of which Nietzsche writes. It's the Saturnine aspect of the operation that fascinates me. Sluggish, torpid, "sunk into the night of its own self-consciousness," absolute knowing digests what it encounters and secretes what it has assimilated as its own excrescence (PH §808). The subject simultaneously reaps and lays waste to the harvest of its history in a philosophical potlatch or Saturnalia—a moment of kenotic expenditure in which the speculative reversal from loss to gain is again reversed: "To know one's limit is to know how to sacrifice oneself" (PH §807).

What is at stake in Hegel's decision to end the tale under the sign of Saturn? The ambivalence of the figure is immediately striking. A figure of both prodigality and privation, at once infinite abundance and insatiable destruction, the "inscrutable Kronos" stands, in Hegel, for the power of unchecked natural consumption. Having castrated his father Ouranos, Kronos proceeds to devour his own progeny—monstrous violence curbed only by a feminine cunning that will parallel that of reason itself. Tricked by Rhea into vomiting up his own children, the Titan is banished to deepest Tartarus—"at the edges of the world, beyond the limits of self-consciousness"[14]—a primal repression of nature that for Hegel marks the violent inauguration of human history proper. Kronos will resurface as the Roman harvest god Saturn, figure of the golden age of abundance and unfettered freedom, whose rituals will involve the utopian role reversals whereby masters wait on slaves at the beggar's banquet. Plutarch is the first to make the phonetic link between Kronos and Chronos—cannibal father with "sharp-toothed time"—and the Titan's scythe will henceforth oscillate between castrating knife and agricultural implement, with images proliferating of a senile Father Time rapaciously gorging on his own offspring (think of Goya's famous painting of Saturn gnawing on his bloody infant).

Oscillating between morose melancholia and obscene enjoyment, between traumatic loss and libidinal excess, such a figure anticipates the perverse father (Lacan's père-vers) who makes his cameo appearance in Freud's Totem and Taboo. Slow, ponderous, weighed down by a gravitas that by the Renaissance signals the ascendancy of philosophical genius, at once the stony blockage of thought and its inspiration, Saturn will acquire during the Baroque period the trapping of voracious bibliomaniac cramming. Astrological tradition adds a treacherous quality of indecisiveness, theologically glossed as the hesitancy born of acedia, the deadly sin of indolence, as portrayed in the icy fifth circle of Dante's hell. Could such an undecidable figure—the very figure of indecision—serve as the final figure of the dialectic? Walter Benjamin thought so.

And what is at stake in Hegel's decision to sign off with a quotation from Schiller? What is the force of this interruption? Is philosophy, unable to complete its own thought, forced to raid the grave and abandon itself to stupid, mechanical citation? Or is there heroism in this self-mortification? Hegel's cannibalism of Schiller can be read in opposed ways—either the dereliction of philosophy or its ultimate vindication: the fate of speculative reason hangs in the balance.

Every epigraph has a fatal ambiguity. A foreign body lodged at the margins of the text, it simultaneously confirms and undermines the integrity of the work it demarcates. It marks the book's involution toward an outside that both is and is not its own to appropriate, and as such stages the aporia of narrative termination. The epigraph thus functions as a kind of double tombstone: it provides an epitaph both for the body of the text whose end it countersigns and for the corpus of borrowed speech it mangles. What does it mean to ghostwrite one's own ending so as to survive through one's own ancestor: who is burying whom? The mortuary logic of this transaction needs inspection.

According to Hegel's elliptical account of the transition to absolute knowing, spirit has risen phoenix-like from the ashes of figurative thought and language: the final achievement of rationality is to pronounce the funeral oration for religious-aesthetic *Vorstellung*. This is Hegel's version of Christian sacramental theology. Spirit performs the last rites over the corpse of poetry by translating finite body—language in its most recalcitrant, carnal particularity—into infinite spirit: the worldly object is relinquished in being introjected, abbreviated, "digested." Psychoanalytically, we can regard this as a work of mourning. This contrasts with the melancholic approach to loss: in this case, the living corpse is cannibalistically taken up within the fractured vault of the self, where it forms an indigestible pocket of internal extimacy and imposes a limit to symbolization.[15] In refusing the substitutive work of language, the melancholic not only maintains the lost object in hallucinatory persistence but congeals language itself into a corpselike thing: words and even the diacritical absence punctuating these become magical fetish objects, stripped of symbolic efficacy, no longer substitutes for the thing but perversely identified with it as they hover in the mouth as frozen, inassimilable remainders.

Is Hegel a mourner or a melancholic? In signing off with this scrap of Schiller, does he contradict or confirm his own infamous pronouncement of the supersession of the "poetry of *Vorstellung*" by the "prose of *Denken*"?[16] Is this the triumphant absorption of the aesthetic or a testimony to its persistence: display of a trophy or confession of defeat? These questions are not intended to revive the weary quarrel between philosophy and poetry, but to explore what might still be at stake in it. If Hegel's channeling of Schiller invites at least two incompatible explanations—it could point either to the transparent potency of thought or to a surd of irreducible opacity—this uncertainty has implications not only for the fate of art in the narrow sense, but for everything tied up with this: history, religion, politics, the whole theater of the body and its hungers. But these are not the only options.

Why quotation, why poetry, why Schiller, why this poem, why these lines, why this peculiar rendition? These questions have a cumulative force. Why, at the pinnacle of the subject's self-affirmation, does it suddenly resort to the stammering of the mechanical memory?[17] And why is it poetry it chooses to recite? The *Encyclopaedia* will also end with a quotation, but to a very different effect: in this later work it is a philosopher, Aristotle, who is recruited, under his own name, writing in the Greek language and in the Greek script and of a God whose vigilant self-sufficiency and uninterrupted productivity will collect and redeem the scattered moments of our own discontinuous existence as surely as day follows night. Not even the intrusion of a dead language and foreign script can cloud the transparency of self-thinking thought.[18]

Why this poet? A self-described "hermaphrodite"[19]—half-poet, half-philosopher—Schiller will be sliced up and repeatedly cannibalized by Hegel to the end of his life. Snippets of his verse keep resurfacing, usually unattributed, throughout Hegel's work: Hegel will quote him repeatedly in the Berlin period—in the later lectures on religion, in the *History of Philosophy*, and in a much-reviled passage in the *Philosophy of Right*, to which I'll return. He will continue to quote him despite or because of his own deepest misgivings about Schiller's entire project. Despite the poet's failure to "break through the Kantian barrier," to bridge the abyss between noumenal freedom and corporeal enjoyment[20]—in short, his failure to be the thinker of fulfilled modernity—Hegel will not stop serving up the poet's membra disjecta, mangled but recognizable, like half-chewed morsels.

The stakes are high: it is 1806, Napoleon is at the door, the carcass of the revolution is about to be shipped over to Germany—that "unreal land" where, it was thought, the tempest of French revolutionary freedom could be parried by the forces of spiritual advance (PH §595). Having already undergone its own religious revolution by way of the Protestant Reformation, Germany would have been already immunized against the fever of political revolution, leaving it free to seek out its real battles in the cultural arena.[21] Schiller had expressed the wager of a generation: we don't need *that* kind of revolution. Only through aesthetic revolution can we forestall the short circuit of politics into terror. Only through beauty do we inch our way toward freedom. When Schiller dies in 1805, just one year before the completion of the *Phenomenology*, he takes to the grave the promise of aborted revolutionary possibilities. I will come back to this.

Why this particular poem? Hegel is not the first to get his hands on it. First published in 1782, "Die Freundschaft" has already been pulverized, recycled, and parodically reinvested, by none other than Schiller himself, who started to borrow from it almost immediately upon publication. In a patchwork prose work of 1786, the *Philosophische Briefe*, a disenchanted protagonist, Julius (perhaps an avatar of the young Schiller), regurgitates scattered lines of the earlier poem as an embarrassing specimen of his own irretrievable youthful enthusiasm. "Die Freundschaft" was from the outset condemned to ironizing self-citation. [22]

Why this poem now? And why these lines, with their lightly veiled Eucharistic content and hints of Saturnalian enjoyment? As the scene of creation coalesces with the scene of resurrection, Hegel's book loops back to its own beginnings: absolute knowing revisits sense certainty's initiation into the "Eleusinian mysteries of consumption" just as it recalls the Bacchanalian revel of natural experience from the sober perspective of the last judgment. In the twilight of recollection, the fever of prephilosophical experience is retrieved as "transparent and simple repose." [23]

And why, finally, this particular rendition? Hegel's version of the couplet effaces the deep ambiguity pervading Schiller's lines. In cutting off the final distich from the immediately preceding verses, Hegel exactly reverses the force of Schiller's poem. The final stanza of the poem describes an isolated Creator—a "friendless world-master"—forced to seek company in his own mirror image. When the poem was first published, in 1782, Schiller had appeared to celebrate this fusional model of reconciliation, but by the mid-1780s, when he starts recycling his own verses, he has begun to suspect the narcissism of the scenario. [24] "Die Götter Griechenlands"—whose three versions would have been well known to Hegel (he dwells on this poem obsessively in the *Aesthetics*)—uses identical imagery to describe the unbearable alienation of the modern Christian world: a friendless God rules in splendid isolation on Saturn's toppled throne, encountering only his own image projected into the void.

Why close off the story of spirit's self-fashioning with this image of formless excess and evanescence—foam overflowing its own container and as ephemeral as the froth of the sea? Does Schiller's distich overflow the margins of Hegel's book as a kind of hallucinatory reminder of what has been foreclosed in the drive to symbolic reparation? Or is the chalice a kind of Holy Grail—a promise of succor both to the wounded subject, pilloried on the pathway of despair, and to the wounded text, tortured on the crux of its own illegibility? Or (these options are not mutually exclusive) perhaps the foam recalls the *aphros*—the semen dripping from the dismembered phallus of Ouranos, first victim of Kronos's violence—sea foam from which pleasure-giving Aphrodite is born. This precious substance was once thought to provide a euphoric counterweight to the melancholia afflicting dry, cold souls. [25]

To every question one could amass competing arguments to produce the double column of responses that captures the typical range of reactions to Hegel to date. As a renunciation of authorial sovereignty, the recourse to quotation could spell either the subject's regression to the stammering of the unhappy consciousness or its accession to the universal symbolic community. The appearance of poetry could indicate either a regression to the vagaries of *Vorstellung* or a sign of philosophy's most prodigious powers of absorption. The tribute to Schiller could indicate either a residue of unresolved Kantianism or the tombstone of a safely buried past. The invocation of friendship could testify either to the lure of narcissism or to the inextinguishable pungency of the revolutionary fraternal ideal. And the dollop of foam? This could mark either the self-putrescence of the system or the generative ferment of the Idea. It could mark either the spiritual disappearance of nature or a mere residue of natural disappearance—a fleeting apparition of meaningless contingency as it fizzles out without a trace.

To be sure, Hegel almost imperceptibly tips the balance by subtly rewriting Schiller's words. Torn out of context and from a less-than-perfect memory—neither strict citation nor free paraphrase, neither perfectly embalmed nor fully metabolized—the verse hovers in the limbo between receptivity and spontaneity, between repetition and interpretation. How exactly does Hegel remember Schiller at this junction? Here is the Schiller couplet, in context, as it concludes the final stanza from "Die Freundschaft" in the original version of 1782. Every word, every mark on the page, should be strictly noted.

> Freundlos war der grosse Weltenmeister
> Fühlte *Mangel*—darum schuf er Geister,
> Sel'ge Spiegel *seiner* Seligkeit!—
> Fand das höchste Wesen schon kein gleiches,
> Aus dem Kelch des ganzen Seelenreiches
> Schäumt *ihm*—die Unenlichkeit.

> [Friendless was the great world-master
> Felt a *lack*—and so created spirits,
> Blessed mirrors of his *own* blessedness
> But the highest being still could find no equal.
> From the chalice of the whole realm of souls
> Foams up to *him*—infinitude.]

Here is Hegel's revision, also in context, as the interminable final sentence of the *Phenomenology* suddenly lurches to a halt:

> The goal, absolute knowing, or Spirit that knows itself as Spirit, has for its path the recollection of the Spirits as they are in themselves and as they accomplish the organization of their realm. Their preservation, seen from the side of their free existence appearing in the form of contingency, is history; but regarded from the side of their comprehended organization, it is the science of knowing in the sphere of appearance: the two together,

comprehended history [*begriffne Geschichte*], form alike the inwardizing [*Erinnerung*] and the Calvary of absolute Spirit, the actuality, truth, and certainty of its throne, without which it would be lifeless and alone; only—

from the chalice of this realm of spirits
foams forth for it its own infinitude.

[aus dem Kelche dieses Geisterreiches
schäumt ihm seine Unendlichkeit.][26]

A series of elisions manages to scrub out what in Schiller's original seems to point to a surd of inassimilable alterity. The rephrasing of spirit's isolation—the rewriting of indicative description (Schiller: "friendless *was* the great world-master") as counterfactual conditional (Hegel: "without which it *would* be lifeless and alone")—siphons away from the verse the painful reference to divine lack, which is absorbed within the block of philosophical prose surrounding the poem, where "actuality, truth, and certainty" serenely assert their power. In the penultimate line, Hegel's substitution of "dieses Geisterreiches" for "des ganzen Seelenreiches" not only converts passive soul (the sleep of reason, anthropological immediacy) into the active reciprocity of finite and infinite spirit.[27] By rewriting Schiller's definite article as a demonstrative—*this* spiritual world (our world: there is no other)—Hegel also manages to recast the scene as a sacramental performative, which is in turn is endowed with the universality of the concept. Human rationality has acquired the redemptive potency of the Eucharistic *hoc est*.[28] Religion is no longer necessary for redemption, which is why it is irrelevant who picks up the cup: it is the human world that "foams forth" and offers itself to God's consumption. God is here imbibing his own creation, rather than the other way around.

Hegel's substitution of a possessive pronoun for Schiller's definite article, in the last line, grammatically binds infinity with its maker—an effect reinforced by the erasure of both the poet's italics (in German, the spacing visually highlighting God's isolated particularity) and his dash (the stroke graphically separating creature from creator): Hegel provides a typographical suture of the ontological fissure separating God from world. In Schiller, the transition from lack to satisfaction, from loneliness to friendship, is as precipitous as the dash that announces it. Hegel smooths over this transition. Both traumatic lack and its correlative on the battlefield of enjoyment—friendlessness, on the one hand, the foaming surplus of jouissance, on the other—are absorbed in the philosophical rewriting that erases context, grammar, and punctuation. Between Schiller's last word and Hegel's lies the almost imperceptible difference between the bad infinite of finitude or indeterminacy and its philosophical homonym. A gesture of erasure marks without remarking on this difference.

Has Hegel here bitten off more than he can chew? Might it be that the cost of swallowing poetry, of remembering Schiller's words speculatively, without "accent" or punctuation, is the reduction of language itself to an indigestible remainder? In his mature philosophy of language, Hegel will argue that the speculative purification of language requires a mortifying passage through the mechanical memory: language must disintegrate into a succession of meaningless signifiers in order to be semantically reinvested as the medium of Denken.[29] Rote memorization—habit-induced idiocy—permits the cathartic forgetfulness that marks the birth of thought. To use language philosophically we must empty it of all previous associations: evacuated of meaningful content, the mind becomes a tabula rasa for self-thinking thought. And yet vacuums can fill and mechanisms can paralyze. Hegel elsewhere compares a hypertrophic automatism to the dyspepsia of an organism unable to assimilate what it ingests. His examples are conventional but revealing: excessive reading, writing, the numbing rituals of organized religion.[30]

Hegel's readers, from Schelling through Deleuze, have never stopped seizing on the rapaciousness of a thought that, by finding sustenance in its own antithesis, has come to epitomize the imperialism of a system that manages to assimilate even its own excrement as food for thought. (Such self-consumption corresponds precisely to Nietzsche's definition of nihilism.[31]) "The Spirit is the belly turned mind and rage is the mark of every idealism."[32] While the visceral energy of the attacks suggests an addictive fascination on the part of Hegel's critics (why this obsession with Hegel's diet? why keep snapping at such stale bait?), the polemics tend to overlook just how peculiarly the alimentary metaphor functions for Hegel. If from beginning to end—from Bacchanalian tumult to foaming chalice, from the Eleusinian mysteries to the decapitated cabbages on the guillotine—if Hegel never stops ruminating on the figure of digestion, if he voraciously seizes on the image, obsessively keeps reworking it, this is as if to digest, soften, assimilate precisely what in the image resists metabolization.

The spirit and the letter are at odds. The tension between the figurative and the literal senses of consumption, between spiritual absorption and corporeal ingestion, highlights an essential ambiguity lurking in the very concept (of course a metaphor) of Er-innerung. The literal truth of "innering" turns out to be anything but what it figuratively posits. This ambivalence also introduces a crucial dissonance between Hegel's own figural practice and the metafigural theory that would contain it.

On the one hand: the metaphor of eating presents a model of interiorization underwritten by the liquefaction of the material sign—the "convivial communication"[33] uniting a community of readers nourished by the unimpeded flow of thought. Friedrich Kittler has argued that such an oral fantasy defines the "discourse network around 1800"—a fantasy connected to the pedagogical practices of the epoch, and culminating in Goethe's maternal phantasmagoria of reading as a sucking at the "breasts" or "wells of life."[34] The fantasy assumes the priority of the signified as the guarantor of translatability: Goethe's "pure perfect substance" that survives the translation of poetry into prose. For Hegel this will be expressed as the ultimate interconvertibility of the arts: in the *Aesthetics*, poetry notoriously enters as the "total art," which metabolizes all the other arts into its own medium while in turn submitting to its own paraphrase into conceptual language. Reduced to a s onorous membrane, saturated with spiritual content, the poetic medium deflates into a "mere external designation" that dissolves without residue into thought.[35]

On the other hand: if the metaphor speaks of translation, the literal invocation of the drives points to a somatic residue that can only impede the passage to the ideal. This is spelled out in Hegel's analysis of desire (*Begierde*). Failing to elaborate the object, the voracious subject keeps on demolishing it, only to relapse into the repetitive circle of mere life. Every act of assimilation thus exacerbates the exteriority it wants to cancel: it generates a mere "feeling" of unity[36] that unfailingly reinforces the vacancy at its core. Since such blockage defines the act of digestion, it is curious to encounter this as the figure for absolute knowing and its hermeneutic. Analyzing the eucharist, in the *Spirit of Christianity*, Hegel proposes an analogy between the trope of consumption and the trope of reading.[37] The interpretation of the written word, like the swallowing of the wine and bread, would seem at first glance to dissolve the mortified objectivity of the thing; it performs the "destruction of the soulless"—the negation of the negation—that crystallizes the event of resurrection. If the analogy breaks down as soon as it is introduced (Hegel emphasizes that, unlike the host, the text resists metabolization, it fails to vanish as a thing), it is immediately reinstated, in that the permanence of script and the evanescence of food prove to be symmetrical manifestations of the same failure to mediate. Both testify to an intransigent nonidentity. The disappearance of the host signals an irremediable split between faith and sensation—between "living forces and the corpse"[38]—while in its stony persistence the text presents a surd of unsurpassable materiality.

Eating and reading therefore culminate in their antitheses: the empty mouth, the fractured text—inedible, illegible alterity. Eating concludes in hunger—"something divine was promised and it melted away in the mouth"[39]—while reading confronts the opacity of the written text. The destructive enjoyment of the thing betrays a profound failure to mediate the material world, which returns in the form of obscene, death-bearing matter. Hegel alludes to the churchgoer's obsessional fantasies of contamination. "Many a man is afraid he will catch from the common chalice the venereal infection of the one who drank before him," a fear dramatized by the funereal clothing that stages the sacramental ritual as a rite of death; community is reduced to the contagious promiscuity and hypochondriacal suspicion that spell the disintegration of the social bond. Communion is revealed as an event of absolute expenditure—"purposeless destruction for the sake of destruction"[40]—a negativity that points both to the "infinite pain" of Christianity,[41] its "mournful hunger for the actual," and to its kernel of obscene enjoyment.

These two aspects are intimately connected in the young Hegel's analysis of Christianity. Christianity's failure to mediate its antitheses condemns the believer to an "endless, unquenchable, unappeased craving"[42] where the positivity of the object continues to affront the subject as the "stain" of contingent, unworked matter.[43] This stain appears as the rotting body of Christ— the "real human form" that accompanies the risen savior as an extraneous appendage weighing him down with the gravitational tug of fleshly matter.[44] An unbridgeable schism thus arises between an otherworldly God and the "ruins of this body."[45] In producing only a "monstrous combination" rather than an "actual unification"[46] of its antitheses, religion condemns humanity to "the truth and harshness of [its] Godlessness."[47] In the sacramental meal "enjoyment is overleaped."[48] It fails precisely to the extent that it succeeds all too well: jouissance is missed because it comes always already too soon. Thus the ultimate degradation of the host to excrement: to worship the holy wafer is, according to Hegel's gleeful *reductio*, already to worship the mouse shit to which this may be contingently reduced (the Catholic Church lodged a complaint about Hegel for saying this),[49] and announces the perversion of Christianity into "the most disgusting and revolting spectacle that was ever witnessed."[50]

In his Berlin lectures on the *Philosophy of Nature*, Hegel will dwell on the human mouth as the physiognomic signpost of the speculative union of contraries. The body itself performs the work of philosophical mediation; it offers a kind of carnal syllogism. As the switching station of ingestion and expression the mouth not only demonstrates the essential reciprocity between inside and outside[51] but provides a "concrete center" in which the "highest" and "lowest" functions of humanity, speaking and eating, find common abode.[52] The mouth is one of those speculative "knots"—a "point of unity" that by linking heterogeneous somatic functions allows the organism to transcend the entropic chaos of mere life. As Hegel's description proceeds, however, the adverbial connectives pile on with increasingly anxious insistence:

> Thus the mouth, for example, belongs to the particular system of sensibility for example, *insofar* [*insofern*] as it contains the tongue, which is the organ of taste, as a moment of the theoretical process. The mouth *furthermore* [*ferner*] has teeth, which are its extremities, their function being to seize upon

what is outside, and to grind it. The mouth is *besides* [*außerdem*] the organ of the voice and speech; *other related sensations* [*andere verwandte Empfindungen*] such as thirst are *also* [*auch*] located there; laughing, and *also* [*auch*] kissing are matters for the mouth *as well* [*gleichfalls*]. The mouth *therefore* unifies the expressions of many sensations.[53]

The syntax of this astonishing passage should be noted: Hegel moves from conjunction to adjunction to near asyndeton as he continues to heap up a series of increasingly vacuous connectives, right up to the dazzling non sequitur that concludes the list. Even as Hegel claims to be inferring spiritual unity from the scattered functions of the organism, the splintered grammar of his language undoes the integrity it is deductively asserting ("therefore ..."). Lest you think I'm being whimsical, just recall that it is Hegel who teaches us to notice such details and who underscores the significance of this kind of fissure between rhetoric and logic. The second chapter of the *Phenomenology* impersonates the dissociative stammer of consciousness in the throes of self-annihilation; marooned on its own contradictions, the perceiving subject is reduced to spitting out conjunctions like magical talismans designed to ward off the fragmentation at its core. The salt is white and it is *also* cubical and it is *also* salty. I see, and I *also* hear, and I *also* smell ...

The same anxiety also hovers in the *Aesthetics*, where Hegel dwells on the artistic challenge of representing a body part that hovers between bestial and spiritual attachments and therefore demands the most rigorous measures of containment. After identifying the face as the spiritual focal point of the body, the site of the human in the animal, Hegel emphasizes the visual disruption threatened by the mouth: not only is it a snoutlike reminder of animal hunger but it generates an inexhaustible repertoire of disconnected emotional display.[54] Hegel describes the various sculptural methods available for containing this visual disruption and converting the devouring mouth into a speaking mouth: the accentuation of the "Greek profile" (the spiritual alignment of nose with forehead diminishes the visual impact of the hungry orifice);[55] the construction of the "Greek chin" (the rounded evocation of satiety announces a freedom from material want);[56] and the various ways of hiding the teeth and expunging from the lips all traces of animal desire. In the middle of his catalog of Hellenic perfection, Hegel suddenly thinks of Schiller's mouth. Neither too thin nor too full, the poet's lips demonstrate an exquisite freedom from appetite and a perfect demonstration of aesthetic *Bildung*:

> [Sculpture] has to remove from the shape and the cut of the lips what is purely sensuous and indicative of natural needs. Therefore it so forms the mouth as to make it, in general, neither over-full nor tight ... sculpture makes the lower lip fuller than the upper one, as was the case with Schiller; in the formation of his mouth it was possible to read the significance and

richness of his mind and heart. This more ideal form of the lips, in contrast to the animal's snout, gives the impression of a certain absence of desire, whereas when the upper lip protrudes in an animal we are reminded at once of dashing for food and seizing on it.[57]

One could choke on such language, and perhaps Hegel did. An eyewitness at Hegel's lectures at Berlin describes his strange way of speaking and the peculiarly strangulated quality of his voice. The passage needs to be read at length:

> I shall never forget the first impression of his face. Livid and loose, all features drooped as if dead. … When I saw him lecturing, I was unable at first to find my way into the train of his thought. Exhausted, morose, he sat there as if collapsed into himself, his head bent down, and while speaking kept turning pages and searching in his long folio notebooks, forward and backward, high and low. His constant clearing of his throat and coughing interrupted any flow of speech. Every sentence stood alone and came out with effort, cut in pieces and jumbled. Every word, every syllable detached itself only reluctantly to receive a strangely thorough emphasis from the metallic-empty voice with its strange Swabian accent, as if each were the most important. Nevertheless, his whole appearance compelled such a profound respect, such a sense of worthiness, and was so attractive through the naiveté of the most overwhelming seriousness that, in spite of all my discomfort, and though I probably understood little of what was said, I found myself captivated forever. … He faltered even in the beginning, tried to go on, started once more, stopped again, spoke and pondered; the right word seemed to be missing forever, but then it scored most surely; it seemed common and yet inimitably fitting, unusual and yet the only one that was right. … Now one had grasped the clear meaning of a sentence and hoped most ardently to progress. In vain. Instead of moving forward, the thought kept revolving around the same point with similar points. But if one's wearied attention wandered and strayed a few minutes before it suddenly returned with a start to the lecture, it found itself punished by having been torn entirely out of the context. … The most wonderful stream of thought twisted and pressed and struggled, now isolating something, now very comprehensively; occasionally hesitant, then by jerks sweeping along, it flowed forward irresistibly. But even those who could follow with their entire mind and understanding, without looking right or left, felt the strangest strain and anxiety.[58]

Despite the auditor's efforts to reign in the anxieties provoked by Hegel's body language and by the bodily pressure of his language—the professor's sagging body is uplifted by his majesty of spirit, his sputtering voice is dignified by the seriousness of his message, his jerky argument is smoothed over by his intellectual composure—the description continues on relentlessly for pages. Hegel's student cannot exorcise the pressure of this strange voice that seems to prolong itself through its interruptions and to draw energy from its own defeat. In the cough, signification is suspended and language comes to the brink of silence.

If the dash is the written equivalent of the cough or stutter—a graphic hiatus—Hegel's final gamble is to erase this fissure within Schiller's text. He dashes out the dash. His elision would seem to efface not only the ontological gap between creator and created, and not only the fault line between philosophical prose and the poetry it would metabolize as conceptual fodder. It also erases the scar within language itself with which the body bears witness to its own hungers. The wounds of spirit heal, writes Hegel famously, and leave no scar (PH §669). In this sense there can be no last words in, of, or by Hegel—only the imperceptible gesture of effacement on which the transparency of his own language rests. But precisely as a gesture, the erasure returns language to the body at the moment of abjecting it. If Hegel effaces the traces of his own interventions with the stealth of a burglar, adjusting the dative of "Kelch" to fit the new metrical requirements, lest the ear hesitate or the tongue falter,[59] he cannot efface the violence of his own effacement. It will leave its mark in unexpected places.

In punctuation marks, writes Adorno, the check the writer draws on language is refused payment.[60] The puncture in the text is the ejected remainder of the process of symbolization: it marks not only the remnant left behind by spirit's self-interiorization but its presupposition. Noting a modern discomfort in the presence of such notations, Adorno remarks that reason has good reason to suppress these marks; it needs to efface the trace of its own bodily inscription. Quotation marks remind Adorno of hungry mouths: they betray an unquenchable thirst for the stuff we can neither quite remember nor quite forget within the recycled swill of history. Dashes, he continues, mark the hiatus of thought—"mute lines into the past" through which the unanswered demands of history continue to press their claim.

With a single stroke, Hegel erases Schiller's dash—and with it the dashed hopes of an entire generation. Marx's quip about Germany being the only country that is forced to suffer a restoration without having undergone its own revolution—the paradox of a counterrevolution in the absence of any revolution—articulates this aporia precisely.[61]

Hegel's elision thus cannot fail to evoke the crisis of signification embodied by the Terror—the "coldest and meanest of all deaths, with no more significance than chopping off a head of cabbage or swallowing a mouthful of water."[62] Lest this culinary metaphor seem haphazard (and the gulp of water—without a bubble of effervescence: emphatically not wine—evokes Hegel's description of a modernity so parched in abstraction, so thirsty for content, that it gladly settles for a sip of water),[63] we must recall that the Terror was persistently troped as cannibalistic: print after grisly print depicts the guillotine as a flesh-eating monster. In *Dantons Tod* Georg Büchner will compare the revolution to a Chronos devouring his own children.

In detaching itself from this scene of melancholy consumption, Hegel's final erasure unfailingly repeats the traumatic effacement it would cover over. The almost unreadable grammar of Hegel's final clause, the strange anacolouthon of its coda—a lonely monosyllabic *nur*, followed by a seemingly superfluous dash, carelessly dashed off as if by accident (erased, tellingly, in Miller's translation[64]), followed by a line break, followed by the mangled quotation—points to a residual fissure within the finished book.

Squeezed out of the poem, Schiller's dash has migrated to the borderlands of philosophy where it exerts a curiously ambiguous force. It could create a kind of *cordon sanitaire* between philosophy and poetry (the opposition standing in for a panoply of well-rehearsed epistemological-metaphysical distinctions); it could point to a philosophical takeover of poetry's resources. But it could also reorient the entire enterprise.[65] If so, Hegel's intervention does not so much pacify interruption as it reinscribes within philosophy a new opportunity for self-invention.

In this light, we should also reconsider the infamous hyphen in *Er-innerung* (PH §808). Even while graphically emphasizing the intensification of interiority, the mark registers a split within the self-remembering self. The hyphen negates the inwardness it simultaneously underscores. It subtracts what it underlines. The *Bindestrich*—in German, a "binding stroke"—unbinds what it ties together. The hyphen turns an ordinary word into a speculative word: it is punctuation, not semantics, that produces the effect of *Doppelsinn*; speculative overdeterminacy is a function of metonymic adjacency rather than metaphorical density—displacement rather than condensation. It is not meaning but punctuation that causes thought to stumble. At this point of fracture, philosophy is forced to pause at the memory of possibilities still unrealized. As late as 1831 Hegel will identify the Revolution as a "knot whose solution history has to work out in the future."[66]

Schiller does not stand for the "aesthetic" in a narrowly literary sense or even for the claims of a generalized aesthetic—the (new or old) materialist package of embodiment, sensibility, and affect that has become so ethically inflated in recent years. In fact, Hegel has spent much of the *Phenomenology* demonstrating what an equivocal category the aesthetic has come to be. If "art" has already come to an end—"beautiful fruit" in the museum[67]—this is not because its force is exhausted but only because its ideological charms have worn thin; beautiful illusion no longer provides consolation for the deficiencies of existence.

Aestheticism is not an isolated problem in the *Phenomenology of Spirit*: it is the persistent temptation that has plagued the entire "Spirit" chapter— from the beautiful harmony of Greek *Sittlichkeit* to the gorgeous fragmentation of the beautiful soul. (In his searing satire of the Romantic genius Hegel manages to demonstrate that even dissonance can be pacifying.[68]) The jury is still out whether Hegel's final solution to the antinomies of spirit—the magic wand of forgiveness—manages to discharge aestheticism or subtly reproduces it.[69] The final portion of the spirit chapter presents a sustained engagement with the many varieties of German aesthetic ideology circa 1800, and the political stakes are high. But there is one notable exception.

Surprisingly, there is no obvious engagement with Schiller in this climactic section of the "Spirit" chapter; the mantle of postrevolutionary philosophy somehow passes directly from Kant through Fichte to German Romanticism. Hegel does not give Schiller's experiment the dignity of a rebuttal: there is no word about the play drive, nothing about the aesthetic state, and Hegel says nothing about Schiller's attempt to extract from beauty an antidote or prophylactic to revolutionary terror. The omission is striking given the thoroughness with which Hegel catalogues all the available (German) philosophical options in the aftermath of the French Revolution; no standpoint, no matter how minor or marginal, has been left unexplored. Only after the performance is over does Hegel bring Schiller on stage: he introduces the poet at the very last minute if only in order to dismiss him. Schiller is called on to perform the final curtain call although he was assigned no lines in the last act.[70]

There are no pages more pressured than in the last chapter of the *Phenomenology*: it's as if the accelerated tempo is trying to compensate for the dilatory pace of the preceding several hundred pages (Hegel will retrospectively characterize the trajectory as a languid succession of "slow-moving" images). There's an almost Proustian temporal economy at work in the "Absolute Spirit" chapter. Proust takes ten pages to describe a second of awakening, thirty pages to describe a sip of tea, four hundred pages to transcribe a dinner party ... and alludes casually to "several years in the sanitarium" in a single sentence. Hegel takes ten pages to describe the fleeting encounter with a vanishing "now" point. That's much longer than it will take him to recapitulate the book's entire narrative in the final chapter.

Hegel's final dash functions as a kind of caesura in the Hölderlinian sense: it forces a brake on the momentum. It produces a kind of profane katechon: it delays the end. It introduces a "counter-rhythmic interruption" in which temporal relations are completely reconfigured.[71] In Hölderlin, the caesura stalls the forward rush of language—the rapid "exchange of representations" along the forced continuum of time. In the caesura, language itself momentarily comes into focus: intransitive speech prolonging itself in the apparent withdrawal of speaker, auditor, referent, subject matter, and context, a kind of communicability prior to communication—"pure language," in Benjamin's sense.[72]

Hölderlin's privileged example is Sophoclean tragedy, but the idea can be adapted. In his "Remarks on Sophocles," Hölderlin comments on the crucial positioning of the caesura: like a dam, the caesura needs to be installed at the critical spot where it can staunch the tidal wave of language—at just the right distance from the site of greatest dramatic intensity to be able to intervene effectively, just on time to protect one part of the work from the torrential pressure of the other. When the dramatic action is most concentrated at the beginning of the work, the caesura should be set up toward the end: the interruption marks off a protected zone in which the end is sheltered from the pressure of the beginning. When the greatest intensity is toward the end, the caesura needs to be set up near the beginning; the break protects the early phases of the drama from being swallowed up by the terminal acceleration. The barrier can also be seen to function as a fulcrum: it creates "balance" or "equipoise" (*Gleichgewicht*) between the two parts of the work despite their manifest differences in length, content, or style. It redistributes the weight or gravitas so as to protect one side from the overpowering pressure of the other. (I'm paraphrasing loosely just to underscore what's pertinent for my purposes; my hydraulic metaphor is not quite right, and Hölderlin's own use of a mechanical figure is idiosyncratic.) *Antigone*, with its piling up of action and intensity in the first scenes, exemplifies, for Hölderlin, the first model; *Oedipus*, with everything heaped up catastrophically at the end, the second. In the *Logic*, the caesura is introduced at the outset, virtually the instant the book finally starts going. It appears in the *Phenomenology* only at the very, very end. The break is inserted at the last possible moment—possibly even after the last moment—when the book is technically over and Hegel lays down his pen and hands over his text to his own precursor for completion.

We can read the dash as a minus sign: Hegel *subtracts* Schiller. With this gesture he also invites us to reread the entire *Phenomenology* as an immense procedure of subtraction: the story as a whole tells of the gradual divestment of every last shred of unelaborated positivity confronting, blocking, and frustrating (but also seducing, placating, and narcotizing) thought. This procedure will ultimately have to include among its objects not only the usual suspects—all those lumps of congealed motility and productivity (the various fetishes of nature, art, God, the human, the nation, the congregation, the collective singular of universal history, to name only the most obvious)—but consciousness itself, with its own incorrigible tendency to self-monumentalization. Hegel's final purge, at the end of the *Phenomenology*, takes self-consciousness to the brink of extinction: he will have redefined the very terms of subjectivity. In this sense, the *Phenomenology* itself amounts to nothing but a gigantic dash: the negation sign that stakes out the outer limit of the text is the abbreviation and condensation of the negativity that's been streaking through the book from the first page.

But—and this is where the *Phenomenology* reaches its internal limit—this procedure of subtraction will need in turn to be subtracted. Negation must be purged of its own tendency toward self-reification. Even negativity—"autonomous" or self-relating negativity—can congeal into yet another positivity and be fetishized as one more "fundamental operation." The dash is the trace left by the *Phenomenology's* operation of effacement; it will be the task of the *Logic* to efface this trace. The *Phenomenology* ends with the appearance of disappearance; the *Logic* will mark the disappearance of this very appearance. The *Logic* will enact a subtraction of subtraction—a kind of subtraction forward (by analogy with Kierkegaard's "repetition forward").

The dash functions as a peculiar placeholder in that it stands in not for any positive or even negative content (even nothingness is far too monumental). It reveals that even the void—emptiness itself—is a result: the blank space is generated by the inscription that presupposes it. The dash carves out (by marking) the emptiness that it simultaneously (also by marking) ruins. The dash is therefore the speculative sign par excellence: it incarnates the "magic power" of negativity. It marks the coincidence of destruction and construction. It is in this sense the perfect inscription of dialectical *Aufhebung*.

We can also read the dash as a kind of hyphen. It stakes out the interstitial zone in which occurs the interminable transition from the *Phenomenology* to the *Logic* and back again. To speak more precisely, the dash marks the transition from *Phänomeno-logie* to *-Logie* to *Logik* simpliciter. It marks the moment when the implicit genitive in *phenomenology* is dropped and the suffix finally comes to stand alone. In the end, strictly speaking, there can be neither a *Logik* nor a *Phänomenologie*, but only a *-Logik*. An invisible hyphen marks the disappearance of the two books into their secret fold.[73]

The hyphen flickers between the *Phenomenology* and the *Logic* like the grin of the Cheshire cat—pure anaphoric reference untethered from every referent, like a pronoun pried loose from every antecedent. It points to the ambiguous place of the *Phenomenology* in the system and conjures up all the interminable questions: is the *Phenomenology* the introduction or the first part, is it outside or inside the system, is it dispensable or indispensable, inessential or essential, is it a kind of Wittgensteinian ladder you're supposed to throw away once you get there (and if so, does the act of throwing away itself need continual restaging, which would require keeping the ladder on hand if only to be able to keep on demonstrating its superfluity); or is the whole point of the exercise to demonstrate precisely that *there is no there, there*—an insight that would make any ladder at once superfluous and insufficient? The answer is, of course, both none of the above and all the above, but it will take the entire *Logic* to demonstrate just why such questions are ill-formed, just as it will have required the entire *Phenomenology* to demonstrate why we can't stop ourselves from continually posing them. It is the terrible anticlimax of the *Phenomenology* to reveal that the ether we've been seeking is just the air we've been breathing from the very beginning; it will be the accomplishment of the *Logic* to demonstrate the breathtaking power of this deflating insight.

We can also read the dash as a partial object—a twin forever awaiting its own complement. The dash is a strange mark, late to arrive in European writing systems, almost unique among punctuation marks. Unlike the period, which arrives just once in every sentence, and unlike parentheses or quotation marks, which come only in pairs, the dash can either stand alone or in a couple. It can signal a unique turning point or a provisional deviation, a decisive derailment or a temporary detour. Preceded by a single dash, words can be set loose or ejected; they can wander off, they can fall away, they can be expelled, they can be brought back sharply like a dog on a leash. Followed by a single dash, words are left hanging; the reader is inevitably pushed back to the beginning, and compelled to start reading the sentence again. Placed between a pair of dashes, words are framed and contained, subordinated to the main drift of the sentence like an eddy within a current. It's never certain, when you first encounter a dash, whether the mark will be one or two, and this uncertainty forces an impossible double tempo in reading. You must simultaneously race ahead and hold back. The possibility of a repetition invites the eye to scan forward—you wait for the mark to duplicate itself—and forces you to hold your breath until the main topic resumes. The absence of repetition forces you to adapt to the sudden change of direction; there will be nothing more—

One or two: this uncertainty defines the dash, and this ambiguity chimes with the most intractable antinomy of Hegel's thought. Even the *point de capiton*—the "quilting point" that retroactively tethers the phrase and brings it to legibility—is never final: every point can and must be repeated, every speech act demands a sequel that may or may not arrive.

CHAPTER 5

HEGEL'S FIRST WORDS

FRANK RUDA

> Hegel ... does not begin with a principle or with a foundation. ... Thought is
> a decision—
> —Jean-Luc Nancy[1]

Hegel's *Science of Logic* is one of the strangest "objects" in the history of philosophy.[2] Its strangeness provoked Adorno to make the following observation:

> In the realm of great philosophy, Hegel is no doubt the only one with whom
> at times one literally does not know and cannot conclusively determine
> what is being talked about, and with whom there is no guarantee that such a
> judgment is even possible.[3]

The *Logic* "resists understanding"[4] more than any other of Hegel's texts but
also more than any other text in the history of philosophy. One reason for this
comes to the fore if one reads one of its infamous claims—allegedly the most
immodest of them all—from its introduction. There Hegel states that "the
content of pure science," the "veritable matter" of the science of pure thought
that the *Science of Logic* is about to present, is what he calls "objective thinking."[5] We are in the "realm of pure thought."[6] It is pure thought because after
the proceedings of the *Phenomenology of Spirit*, thought "has sublated all reference to an other and to mediation."[7] Thought is alone. It no longer (and at the
same time not yet) has any relation to an other.

But what does it mean to present pure thought—to present the realm of
thought in which thought thinks nothing but thought itself? It is "the exposition of God as he is in his eternal essence before the creation of nature and a
finite mind."[8] Reading the *Logic* and comprehending it is to read the mind of
God before he created the world.[9] This is not the expression of a megalomaniac madman.[10] Hegel has a strong argument for it. If the *Logic* delivers what
it promises, namely the "laws" of "thought *as such*,"[11] and if God has thought

before he created the world, he must also have used "the necessary forms and self-determinations of thought"[12] that any thought has to rely on. If this book aims at exposing God before the creation, this cannot but seem immodest. But it is necessary. As Hegel once noted:

> God before the creation of the world is alone. ... God is not the true God if he does not manifest himself outwardly. For God is God only in the act of creating the world.[13]

As soon as one achieves the "standpoint" of God before the creation of the world, it becomes clear that before the creation, God is not yet truly God. There is less megalomania than disappointment. To become who he is, he needs to create. His creation is self-creation: God before the creation can only be thought after he created (the thought that thinks what he thought before he created is postfestum). He is what can only be thought of as a retroactive, retrocreative effect of his own creation. Beginning is—even for God—a true speculative problem.

The act of creation must thus be linked to God's essence. Yet God is not identical to it. Here a peculiar parallax emerges: in the beginning there is an act of creation (making God into God for us), but there is also something not creative but static (God prior to creation). The unity of differences of creation, of movement and stasis, is the beginning. As soon as we start thinking God prior to his creation, we see that we must inscribe the act of creation into his essence, but we also have to recall that he precedes his creation. He will have become truly what he was before the creation after the creation. Against this background one might go as far as to claim that the problem of beginning (creation) is the problem of the Logic.

Hegel insists that the Logic begins without any presupposition: it "cannot presuppose any ... forms of reflection and laws of thinking"[14] After getting through the Phenomenology one made the move from an "unpurified and therefore unfree thinking"[15] to the point where "the freedom of spirit begins."[16] Purification takes place before the Logic, in the Phenomenology. In it we get the "education and discipline of thinking."[17] This means: "The Notion of logic has its genesis in the course of the exposition and cannot therefore be premised."[18]

We embark on an endeavor about which nothing can be said in advance and this implies that it is radically autonomous—a free logic of freedom. Heinz Eidam claims that "freedom is probably the only thing that solely presupposes itself,"[19] by presupposing that it can only be freedom when it is freed from any presuppositions (of what freedom is). If we only know what the Logic is after it has run its course, this implies that it is impossible to know where, when, and how it begins. But it is clear that its whole "division must be … immanent to the Notion itself."[20] Recall the table of contents: the *Logic* begins with two prefaces—written in 1812 and 1831—that are followed by an introduction to the notion of logic and its general division. Then the first book ("Book One: The Doctrine of Being") begins. Yet it does not begin immediately. Hegel inserts a further text, "With What Must the Science Begin?," includes a brief explanation of the "general division of being," and before finally starting, inserts another very brief section ("Section One") on "Determinateness (Quality)." Where does the *Logic* begin? With the prefaces, with the introduction, or with Book One?

One might argue with Hegel that "the superscriptions and divisions, too, which appear in this system are not themselves intended to have any other significance than that of a list of contents."[21] But what about the things they are dealing with? Already Feuerbach remarked that for Hegel "the *presentation of philosophy* is to be taken as the essence of philosophy itself."[22] But just glancing at Hegel's presentation, it is hard to trust one's eyes when all sense certainty is bracketed. What the *Logic* presents "cannot be stated beforehand"[23] and thus "a definition of [its] science … has its proof solely in the already mentioned necessity of its emergence."[24] If the *Logic* presents thought without an other (having purified itself from "ordinary, phenomenal consciousness" and its "errors"[25]), the problem of how to begin is an immanent problem of thought's exposition of pure thought. How to begin with thought when the thought of beginning—all presuppositions are suspended—must at the same time be the beginning of thought?

BEGINNING, NOT YET BEGINNING,—

To begin—before properly beginning with the beginning—by providing a brief account of what Hegel says about beginning: All the preliminaries only aim at "doing away with [all] preliminaries,"[26] demonstrating their futility. This is an initially necessary move: before we deal with the thing itself we must get rid of the things that are not the thing (of thought) and must begin with thinking beginning. How to do this? Did we now just begin when asking this question, even before beginning? Hegel answers negatively by stating that we can never begin with a definition: "The definition with which any science makes an absolute beginning cannot contain anything other than the precise and correct expression of what is *imagined* to be the *accepted* and *familiar* subject matter and aim of the science."[27] A definition would, per definition, ground a science (of *Logic*) on something external to that very science. Yet in the *Logic* we know that we do not know what the precise subject matter of the science is—it is only within this science that we can find it out. This is also why we cannot begin with any presupposed principle. *Beginning needs to be unprincipled.*

This is "the difficulty ... that thinkers have become aware of ... in recent times."[28] But against reifying "the *subjective* act ... as an essential moment,"[29] "the logical beginning ... can be taken ... either as a mediated result or as a beginning proper, as immediacy."[30] That is, at the beginning "there is Nothing [es Nichts *gibt*]."[31] There is nothing that can be taken as immediate or mediated. Because this nothing is the result of the cleansing efforts of the *Phenomenology*. Its achievement is "ridding oneself of all reflexive determinations and opinions whatever."[32] The beginning of the *Logic* is thereby an always already mediated beginning, and the result of this self-negating mediation is immediacy.[33] In this process all appearances are subtracted and signed over to disappearance to ultimately reach the purity of—absolute(ly pure)—knowing. What is left after negating mediation by means of mediation is (a) nothing. After the *Phenomenology* we cannot do anything but "take up, *what is before us* [aufzunehmen, *was vorhanden ist*]";[34] the only "thing" we can actually take up is this very nothing of mediation.

Immediacy is thus a product of the self-subtraction of mediation, but this product is nothing to start with. We have nothing in our hands but the purified purity of knowledge, of a knowledge so pure that it "ceases itself to be knowledge."[35] Even absolute knowing disappears, leaving nothing but an absence. We end up (and start) with a knowledge indistinguishable from nonknowledge, a knowledge that disappears as much as all phenomena disappeared with the *Phenomenology*. Creation and decreation coincide—"a circle in which the first is also the last and the last is also the first."[36] The subtraction of all presuppositions is a precondition for the *Logic*, but it is not *its* beginning.[37] The *Phenomenology* is its "presupposition,"[38] but if the precondition for the *Logic* is the disappearance of appearances, then the purity of pure knowing is bound to disappear itself. We end up with a disappearance of disappearance, an absence not even of something being absent. There is nothing left to disappear except disappearance itself. It is *necessary* to make a beginning and to take the disappearance of appearances (determinations, mediations, etc.) as a prerequisite. Yet it is strictly *impossible* to ground anything on the disappearance of disappearance. Houlgate emphasizes that a true "beginning must be the beginning of *thought*";[39] however, this beginning is not yet made with the disappearing outcome of the *Phenomenology*. For what can be deduced can also (retrospectively) be analyzed. And Hegel insists "that which constitutes the beginning, the beginning itself, is to be taken as something unanalyzable."[40] To truly begin—without relying on presuppositions—is to *begin with beginning*. This is to say: "The beginning must be an absolute ... it *may not presuppose* anything, must not be mediated by anything nor have a ground; rather it is to be itself the ground of the entire science."[41]

The only thing that can make a beginning is a beginning. This is the logical consequence to be drawn from the result of the *Phenomenology*—the disappearance of the process of disappearance culminating in pure know-ing[42]—from which nothing can be derived and from the properly knotted structure of the concept of beginning (as beginning of thought and thought of beginning). For the *Logic* as science of pure thought, whose concept we just attained and that is just about to disappear again, the beginning is both *logically necessary and logically impossible* (i.e., undeducible and unanalyzable). One has to begin, yet one cannot. *Immediately*, there is only one thing at hand: "All that is present [*vorhanden*][43] is simply the resolve [*Entschluss*], which can also be regarded as arbitrary, that we propose to consider thought as such."[44] If there is a knotting together of necessity and impossibility in the beginning, we need a nothing that can be considered "*vorhanden*," present, at hand; a noth-ing[45] that does equally contain mediation and immediacy. Hegel's name for it is resolve, *decision. In the beginning there is a decision, an immediate decision.* But what does it decide? It does not decide anything concretely; it is thus not only a fully immediate but also a fully *indeterminate decision.*

The decision only decides (that) it(self) (has consequences for thought); this is an indeterminate decision that immediately introduces a realm of con-sequences, but that remains fully indeterminate: an indeterminate immediacy. With such decision in scission (as it is split between the act of deciding and not deciding anything concrete), one is "*immediately* in the consequences."[46] The decision is itself a (de-)scission: it is characterized by an affirmative and by a negative moment.[47] Yet the decision is so immediate and so inde-terminate that one cannot presume any form of relation between the nega-tive and positive moments. It is split in two, without any relation between the Two of scission: "This insight is itself so simple that this beginning as such requires no preparation."[48] The only thing to begin with is beginning itself, the beginning of thought in decision, grounded in the absence of a begin-ning (i.e., not grounded at all). And the only thing we can (begin with is to) decide to think, if we decide to begin, is the being of this very absence. There is something strange and peculiarly nonderivable, nonanalyzable, *nondialectical about and in the beginning*; it can only be an immediate, indeterminate decision in scission. One must begin, one cannot begin, one has to begin, one will begin—*Not without a decision.*

—DECISION, PURE DECISION,—WITHOUT ANY FURTHER HESITATION

"Being Comma Pure Being Comma Dash": Hegel's first words. This seems mysterious.[49] After all the preliminaries, at the "beginning" of the first book, at the beginning of the "Doctrine of Being," these words appear. After nearly seven hundred pages in which he re- and deconstructed every-thing, an endeavor necessary to write any words at all, these are his first ones. First, Hegel reconstructed, presented, and exposed the whole process of the becoming of "absolute knowing": he presented how and why consciousness initially bound to unquestioned assumptions liberates itself from them to be able to relate to "pure thoughts, spirit thinking its own essential nature."[50] This movement traversed "every form of the *relation of consciousness to the object*"[51] and at the true beginning of the *Logic* we solely deal with the pure immanence of thought. Disappearance has disappeared, a decision took place.

The *Phenomenology* does not lead Hegel to write any words proper that could be part of a pure science of pure thought. The only words that he could have written were phenomenological, disappearing words, arguing that this project—under the banner of a pure science—is necessary and can and must be thought, presented, and developed. But he could not have written any lasting words to begin this science with. No words of beginning, no beginning signifiers even. He could have written only phenomenologically disappearing (speculative) words, no *pure* (speculative) words (and signs). After the reconstructive verification of the concept of science, Hegel includes all the preliminary texts before he actually begins writing anything at all. All we have before us are prerequisites, necessary preconditions—not one single word of the pure science has seen the light of day so far. Then after about seven hundred pages of preparation, it ultimately happens: Hegel finally pulls out his pen and begins the *Logic*, "Book One," "Chapter 1," with "Being Comma Pure Being Comma Dash." One should recall that even in the last edition of the *Logic* Hegel never changed this beginning a single bit, although he himself stated that it would be necessary to revise the whole project "seven and seventy times."[52] The beginning once written down was never altered; it was decided once and for all.

If any true beginning allows for some "free play"[53] of the arbitrariness of thought (which is an implication of the idea that in the beginning there is a decision), it also holds that "considered from its negative aspect, this business [of the *Logic*] consists in holding off the contingency of ordinary thinking and the arbitrary selection of particular grounds—or their opposites—as valid."[54] This means that even if "knowing what one is saying" or writing "is much rarer than we think,"[55] the beginning of the *Logic* presents us with such a rare case: Hegel did know what he was doing.

Why then "Being Comma Pure Being Comma Dash"? Why is there a constellation of "being" and a comma? Why then a constellation of being and pure being? Why does the whole syntagma end with a dash? Why a comma before the dash? To begin, one can again take up a remark by Adorno:

> Being, pure Being,—without any further determination, an anacoluthon that tries with Hebelian cunning to find a way out of the predicament that "indeterminate immediacy," even if clothed in the form of a predicative statement like "Being is the most general concept, without any further

determination," would thereby receive a definition through which the sentence would contradict itself.[56]

In German the anacoluthon is also called *Satzbruch*, a breaking up of the sentence. The Greek term *an-akolothous* combines the privative prefix *an* ("not, without") with the Greek word for "following, consequential." The anacoluthon thus stands for a breaking up of a sentence in which there is something that does not follow, a non sequitur. Literally, it translates as "without completion." Ernst Bloch—who astoundingly misses it in his commentary on the *Logic*[57]—argues that this rhetorical trope is always accompanied by an "interrupting tone of language"[58] that brings living speech into written syntax and makes them almost indistinguishable. In an interview, he further elaborates:

What is in itself clear can also be clear in its presentation. … This is different from what is fermented, self-parturient, still in vogue. … It corresponds in language to that which moves, is opaque, to a new entry, to the anacoluthon. Such a language of "noncompletion" [*des "Unvollendbar"*] is not at risk of feigning completion where there is none, whereas a smoothed language obscures that which is to be said by its own smoothness.[59]

Hegel is in the beginning clearly not concerned with smoothing over anything and indicates by the very form of this nonproposition a necessary noncompletion, nontotalization.[60] The beginning is incomplete, incompleting, incompleted, *Bruch im Satz und des Satzes*, breaking up of and in a sentence.[61] In the beginning there is a break, a (de-)scission, a cut, a rupture within the opening sentence.[62] This might be why Hegel notes: "That which constitutes the beginning"—that is the beginning itself—"is to be taken as something unanalyzable."[63] Henrich has shown[64] that immediately after the publication of the *Logic* this was forgotten by most early readers. One can map some of the early criticisms—usually articulated apropos of the whole chapter on being and nothing—onto the very first words of the *Logic*. This will allow to discriminate interpretations that in the spirit of Hegel must be avoided when investigating his first words.

Thinkers like Trendelenburg,[65] von Hartman,[66] and others criticized the *Logic* in the 1840s,[67] mainly articulating three types of arguments apropos of the beginning. First, they maintained that being and nothing are simply two aspects of indeterminate immediacy (it is being because it is posited; it is nothing because it is posited without determinations). Hegel is just playing a trick. Second, indeterminate immediacy (a predicate) functions as the genus of being and nothing. But Hegel inverts genus and predicate. Third, the difference between being and nothing indicates no difference in or of meaning; rather it is a difference of "mere *words* whose meaning is one and the same namely indeterminate immediacy."[68] This third criticism is not really a criticism of Hegel, since it restates that being and nothing are not substantially different precisely because they are both indeterminately immediate: *"The pure being and the pure nothing is, therefore, the same."*[69] However, the difference of words is still a difference, a "pure difference,"[70] a difference within immediate absence of determination;[71] a difference without determination (or relation), as "they are not undistinguished."[72]

These criticisms can be related to the first "sentence" of the *Logic*: "being" and "pure being" are then either taken to name two aspects of the same indeterminate immediacy and therefore the form of the first sentence does not really matter; or Hegel is simply playing on a difference of words that cannot be a meaningful difference as it is not a difference in meaning. "Being" and "pure being" would be two different ways of saying the same thing: being in its immediate, abstract, empty, and indeterminate form. All these criticisms get into trouble verifying that Hegel knew what he was doing when he wrote his first words. Although even most of Hegel's critics agree that for him everything depends on the form of the presentation, it is often ignored when reading the beginning of the *Logic*. But even if the critics are correct, why did he not simply write down what he wanted to say? Why did he not begin with a sentence in a propositional form? Did it not matter? Is this a sufficient explanation for why he never bothered to change this very beginning?

BEING, PURE BEING

"Being Comma Pure Being Comma Dash"—this syntagma does not name two opposite but related aspects of the same indeterminate immediacy. It is rather as if "being" gains some determinacy—the determination of being indeterminate, its own purity, being pure being—only through the act of being repeated. Being through its repetition becomes "pure being." It is not even accompanied by an article. It is just "being." Thought's insistence on being's emptiness and meaninglessness forces it to state this emptiness twice.[73] But why then should "being" and "pure being" not be merely two names for the same "thing"? As one learns from the *Phenomenology*, when it comes to "objects" in general and to the peculiar not-without-object of the *Logic*, things are not that simple. One cannot simply rephrase the first sentence of the *Logic*—which is not a sentence since it does not have the structure of an "S is P" proposition[74]—and state that "there is being and it is pure." But why repeat "being" as "pure being"—without any article—in this syntagma, which also does not include a verb?[75]

There is a choice to be made here. Again a scission, a decision is needed: either one claims that (1) there is being and it (2) unfolds its inner determination: it is pure and without further determination—it is determined as being indeterminate. Then the whole beginning of the *Logic* is a beginning of and with reflection. The logic of reflection[76] is then not only at the horizon (as logic of essence) but already fully present from the very start; or there is being and this term, its positing and the decision to begin with it, is (1) unanalyzable and only through the (2) repetition of this act of positing one gains the purity of what is posited, and maybe even more than this.

This choice has immediate consequences. According to one interpretive path, the repetition (of "being" as "pure being") seems to be nothing but the repetition of *one and the same being*. This implies that *being is that which is* and its *repetition* within the syntagma further qualifies *how and what* being is: being is pure and abstract, without determination (i.e., negatively determined). One would start from what is *given*—being—and *differentiate* it further, unfold and explicate its implication, reflect on its inner determinations, even if these turn out to be indeterminate ones that ultimately lead—via the immanent contradiction of being solely determined as being indeterminate—to the identification of being and nothing. But if this were the starting point of the *Logic*, there would be no beginning in Hegel's sense. We would analyze being and the only thing unanalyzable would be the very nonbeginning of being, its givenness. On this side of the decision, one ends up with the following consequences: (1) One contends a *logic of the One*, of the one and same being. (2) Internal to it is a *logic of differentiation of the given* being. Being is One and differentiates itself: a logic of differentiation under "the law of the one."[77] But why repeat being as pure being in a nonpropositional syntagma if we are already within the realm of reflexive differentiation of a self-identical being? Why is there a repetition (in the syntagma) at all? This position might answer: Repetition is what drives being to necessarily differentiate itself. It would thus also be the ground from which we can afterward analyze the concept of purity and end up with the determination of being without determination, etc.

Such a position offers in the last instance the following interpretation of the syntagma: There is a *givenness* of the *One* (being) and the *repetition* is the mode of *differentiation* of the One (pure being). By means of iteration we attain ever-richer determinations until we reach the end of the *Logic*. Although this is a rather common interpretation it is fundamentally *idealist*—in a bad way. For if this were the case, Hegel would not begin at the beginning of his *Logic*. He would at least not begin according to his own concept of beginning: the beginning would disappear, because it would either be dissolved into being a mere result of the *Phenomenology* or, worse, Hegel would revert to a "Myth of the Given-being,"[78] a myth of being-given. He would then have reflected on being's givenness and the very idea of the beginning would have been relinquished. The *Logic* in this sense would *begin without beginning*.

To not begin with beginning—and thus reduce the dialectic of being, the objective logic, to an explication of the result of the *Phenomenology*—amounts to an idealist interpretation. It leads down an unavoidable path of necessity, a path of the necessary unfolding of implied inferences of concepts that are already at hand; it leads to a complete suppression of contingency (i.e., of decision) and thereby to a disavowal of beginning itself. For an idealist interpretation, beginning might appear difficult at first, but it turns out to never have been difficult after all. Idealist interpretations, in speaking about the beginning of the *Logic*, do not speak about the *beginning* and thus do not speak about the *Logic* (but about the *Phenomenology*).[79] This is because "every beginning that would not be in decision would be a given beginning and thus already derived, produced elsewhere."[80] We would end up with an endless iteration, a self-movement of the One and same being, differentiating itself through reflection. With and at the beginning such interpretations have always already arrived at the end (of the *Phenomenology*) and explain the passage from being to pure being just as they would explain the passage from being to nothing, from being to determinate being, etc. This goes against Hegel's own claim that indeterminate immediacy does not already entail any reflexive identity.[81]

But if we have to decide how to read the (decision at the) beginning, what is on the other—let's call it the materialist[82]—side of the choice? Here we emphasize the beginning qua beginning. If the beginning is not simply articulating two aspects of the same genus, the materialist can take up the third misreading and assume that in the beginning we deal with a repetition of signifiers without meaning.[83] This repeats something like a pure name (without reference or content) and thereby seems to produce something more, the purity of being (recall: there is not only the repetition of "being, pure being" but also of "nothing, the pure nothing"). The materialist can take the actual beginning (its form and shape) seriously by investigating why one is not dealing with two names for one and the same thing ("being" and "nothing" as names for indeterminate immediacy) and why there is a repetition in each paragraph dealing with each individual name ("being, pure being" and "nothing, the pure nothing").

Each name (if "being" and "nothing" are names[84]) then can be taken to be "divided, but divided into itself ... and each word is combined, but with itself."[85] Each of the two names is divided, divided into itself: a constitutive repetition making the name ("being" and "nothing") into what it is,[86] generating its purity. The materialist can then ask: What does lie in the name(s)?[87] She ends (up) highlighting the beginning, even emphasizing the beginning of (the givenness of) being. But how to do this? Henrich observes that

> the method of Hegel at the beginning of the *Logic* is thus the opposite of a construction. In it there is completely and utterly only one intention dominant: To render a concatenation of thought evident which withdraws from any construction, even though it is of speculative nature. If the *Logic* would state it [the concatenation], without taking the difficulties of understanding into account, this could only happen in the simple uttering of the words Being and Nothing.[88]

A materialist reading assumes that the beginning is neither derivable nor constructible. It is a *speculative beginning* (since it is the beginning of speculative science) in which everything counts; every detail must be taken into account. So, what about the repetition of "being" in the first syntagma? An analysis presented by Alain Badiou can help here. He claims apropos of the beginning of the *Logic* that there

> is a double inscription of identity under the form of two marks for which the referent is absolutely undifferentiated [he is referring to "being" and "nothing" and not to "being, pure being"]—what finds itself thusly inscribed by Hegel is the weakest sort of difference, the difference of two identical marks (two marks for the void) and their marking out of two differential places, two marks that do not differ except for their place.[89]

This means for the passage from "being" to "pure being": B_1 ("being") relates to B_2 ("pure being") as two signifiers do in a signifying chain. It is the marking of a minimal difference, a difference of a term that does not inherently differ from itself but only differs because of the (named) place where it occurs. B_1 is absolutely identical to B_2 (both are clearly B), and they differ solely due to the additional mark of the place (indexed by 1 or 2). Why is "being" not the very name for this logic? Being as the space of differential placements, as the idealist reading could argue?[90] The minimal difference that one needs to maintain a materialist perspective concerns the claim that "being" is not the name for the "space of places,"[91] in which the essentially undifferentiated terms are placed and thereby differentiated. It is rather itself one of the terms placed in this space. Being is not simply the genus that makes it possible to differentiate species; it is the genus that appears among the species ("being, pure being"). There are thus again two options, another decision: being could be the "space of placements"[92] and then the question arises what is placed in this very space. An idealist answer would be: being itself. Being for an idealist would be that which places itself in the very "space of places" that it is. Being is the self-positing of its own difference within itself: *being as immanently autodifferentiating is idealist*.

But the materialist, taking up another detail, can ask a simple question: Why does Hegel write "Being Comma Pure Being"? The materialist answer: Being is the space of places in which something that is *not* being is placed. This something that is not being—not-being, maybe rather the *"being" of a "not"*[93]—is placed in it and this is why Hegel has to indicate it with the reference to purity in the repetition of being as "pure being." For that which is not-being—but also not-nothing—to come-to-being, it has to be placed in the space of places that is being. If there is a true beginning in the *Logic*, something new happening, two questions arise: (1) What is it that is not, or what is the "not," the not-nothing, not-being, that is placed? (2) If even being itself is placed, since it occurs in the space of places that it seems to delineate (and this is why it has to be placed twice), "where" is this space of places placed?

It is difficult to see what a materialist reading ends up with. One can outline two aspects ex negatively. First, one cannot be following a logic of one and the same being, as being is itself one of the terms of a difference ("being, pure being") and thus refers back to something else, to something that is the "not" of "not"-nothing,[94] "not"-being. Second, this means the concept of repetition here does not imply a logic of (auto)differentiation. There is indeed a differentiation pertaining to the places of terms, but this is not caused by one term differentiating itself within the space that it opens up. Rather a materialist can infer that "being" through its repetition as "pure being" bears the mark of its inscription, of its own positing, of its own logical commencement. In contrast to the idealist reading, *one begins with the beginning*. "Being" is one of two terms in a series of two terms. But it has not been demonstrated that it also grounds this series. It might be that "being"—as unanalyzable immediate consequence of the decision that begins the *Logic*—is itself placed in "something," occurs "somewhere." But where could being be said to occur? *Where* does it begin? Hegel's first words give us only a mute index to answer this question—"a silence in words."[95] The mute clue is the comma that separates "being" and "pure being."

COMMA

Adorno noted that punctuation marks have their own "physiognomic status"[96] that cannot be separated "from their syntactical function," so that they are "by no means exhausted by it."[97] A comma, for example, standing between two or more terms of the same quality incorporates what it enables. It embodies and enables a series, a logic of difference and differentiation. For Adorno punctuation marks in general operate like musical signs: the comma indicates a "weak phrasing,"[98] the semicolon a strong one.[99] But "in punctuation marks ... history has left its residue."[100] A comma thus silently points through its very physiognomy to something that does not lie on the same level but somehow "below," "beneath," "under," or with reference to history: "before" or "prior" to the series of differences. The very stroke of the comma points to this "dimension." The comma does two things at once: on the one hand it embodies the principle of differentiation and seriality. It is the mark of weak difference. But on the other it also points to and silently hints at that which somehow enables these differences, this series, lying "prior" to it. That is, what enables the series does not appear in it. It is "something" that is only silently indexed by the mark that enables the differentiation.

The comma is a mark of difference in a double sense: it embodies the weak difference of two terms that stand on the same stratum and—as if difference was related back onto itself[101]—it physiognomically indicates another type of difference, which is *in difference to the series of differences*. It marks what is other than weak difference (not being another weak difference), without being the other of being on the level of being—as Hegel is quite explicit, being is so indeterminate that it does not stand in any relation, not even in a negative one to anything (else). Being and nothing therefore are in a "relation" of *beziehungslose Verneinung*, "negation devoid of any relation ...—what could also be expressed if one so wished merely by 'not.'"[102] Being does not imply nothing and nothing does not imply being, but they have always already passed into each other. This means that "the transition in question is not yet a relation."[103] One neither begins with an already established relation (between being and pure being) nor with pure relationality (being as space of placements without any "outplace"[104]). Relation implies that there is already determination. But *in the beginning, there is no relation*.[105]

We thus start with an absence, the absence of relation: there is only a "not," a negation devoid of relation; a pure "not" that is the trace of cutting the (Borromean) knot (of how to begin) by deciding to begin. Through the comma, we come to think that "there is" an other that is not another, another type of difference "prior" to the weak differences, which can only be accessed through them. It is prior to weak difference but does not simply (say temporarily) precede it. This other difference is not-(a-weak-)difference; it is *in-difference*, *indifferent* to (at least weak) differences. And what stands in difference to weak differences differs from them so profoundly that it cannot appear on the same level (i.e., of being). We must think *not-being*, which is neither yet being nor yet nothing: not-being, not-nothing[106]—without any further negation thinkable.

Even though the comma marks the difference of two terms on the same level, the comma does not inscribe a conceptual articulation of another type of difference into the series; the way it points to it is less than conceptual. With it there is less than *the* concept of another difference. The comma is rather an embodiment of this other type of difference: in its very physiognomy it indexes it without conceptualizing it. It is like "*the outside* of language, but it is not outside it."[107] This second type of difference that is accessible only via the weak differences as that which lies prior to them (while enabling them) can be called "strong difference."[108] One attains its idea by applying the principle of difference, whose mark is the comma, to itself. But does this not imply there *is* some movement of reflection that manifests in the comma? To start answering this question one has to take into account that we not only have one sign in the opening syntagma but three (!): a comma, another comma, and a dash.

COMMA COMMA

Dolar states that after "Being Comma Pure Being Comma Dash" Hegel notes "Nothing Comma the Pure Nothing Semicolon" and so we get something "like form before form, the mere form of redoubling."[109] But this form before form, this mere form of redoubling, not only occurs in the repetitive transition from being to nothing but also in the very first nonproposition of the *Logic*. Not only being but also the comma is repeated, so what to make of this? If the comma can be read as embodying that which instantiates a series of weak differences and is at the same a silent mark of the strong difference enabling this series, the combination of "comma" and "comma" implies a redoubling of this very embodiment.

One can (heuristically) distinguish between the two operations of the two commas: on a first level—of weak differences—one not only attains an incorporation of the principle of the series of weak differences but also a kind of meta-syntagmatic effect: a potentialization of seriality, an iteration of iterativity. The second comma indexes—again silently—the fact that seriality can be serialized; iteration can be iterated, turning it into iterability proper. Thus the second comma indexes the very form of repetition before the repetition of (the/any) form, a repetition that only repeats itself. It embodies repeatability as such. The combination of "comma" and "comma" can therefore be read as formalizing the (potential) infinity of the series of weak differences. There cannot only be infinitely many weak differences, but there can be infinitely many infinite series of weak differences on the level (the presentation[110]) of being. This minimalist formalization of repeatability as such does not imply that any sort of relation is already established, rather this repetition that does not repeat anything precedes all relation (of negation, determined identity, etc.).[111] Thus it silently indicates that the repetition of repetition precedes everything (that can be articulated). It is the establishing ground for relation.

This insight is formalized by redoubling the comma: "comma comma" is the formula of repeatability. But it cannot be articulated in a propositional form. There is nothing mystically ineffable or irrational about it, rather this formalization is completely logical (we are still dealing with the *Logic*). Hegel knew how to formalize (and to think) the infinitization of infinite series of weak differences whose prerequisite is "that there is the Two," for only "metaphysics posits the One, and forever gets tangled up in deriving from it the Two."[112] Hegel starts with the Two—two "beings," two "commas," the *Phenomenology* and the *Logic*. The Two prevails in the beginning (of the *Logic*[113]) because it is only the Two that can mark repeatability (as repetition of the very form of repetition). This is what can be deciphered on the first level of reading the two commas.

But what about the dimension of not-being, not-nothing, and the strong difference that the first comma silently pointed at? The second comma repeats the first's physiognomic effect: the "not" indexed by the first comma (not-being, not-nothing, not-relation, etc.) is thus indexed again. It seems necessary to index the "not" twice, not to substantialize the "not" (as an abyssal, primordial Ur-negativity). The second comma thus operates in two ways. First, it repeats the indexing move of the first comma and indicates that there is not *one* place of the not-being, not-nothing (the place indicated by the first comma), but that it is rather everywhere. It is not only that which grounds the series of weak differences but also the infinitization of this very series. It therefore has to be "universally included"[114] in every series of weak differences although it never appears as an element of any series. It needs to be indexed twice to avoid the assumption that this very not-being, not-nothing could be thought of as being identical (or as *one* "not" underlying the series of weak differences).

Second, the two commas mark the formal structure of the parallax as such. It seems necessary to index the same "not" twice because what is indexed by the redoubling of the comma is only accessible in passing (through the series of commas), more precisely through repetition: through the repetition of repetition.[115] Only by repeating the embodiment of the series of weak differences is one able to access that which can only be accessed via repetition.[116] One needs the *consequential passing move* from one to the other. Otherwise there could still be a negative relation (something not appearing in the series of weak differences it grounds). Even the form (of repetition) before the form needs to be split in Two. This is because the "not" is not-one, not-multiple, not-being, not-nothing, etc.[117] It therefore can only be marked by multiplying the mark, by repeating the repetition. All of this seems radically speculative, yet it gets worse: there is also the dash.

COMMA DASH

Heinz Eidam states without further elaboration that

> if the Hegelian Logic is or is supposed to be a logic of freedom, then the decision, which it took at the beginning and forgot again in the very same moment, lies in the inaudible dash that is perceivable only as pause, as interruption in the flow of arguments.[118]

In the dash lies the decision. How to then conceive of the relation between the comma(s) and the dash in the syntagma? If the commas point to "something" that seems to lie "beneath" the series of iterating differences, the dash also embodies different things at once. First, it seems to physiognomically incorporate the very horizontality of weak differences. It is as if the dash incorporates the opening up of a space of determinations that all take place within the realm of weak difference. It embodies the (sub)stratum on which the whole move from "being" to "pure being," from "nothing" to "the pure nothing," to "becoming" and afterward to "determinate being," will take place. But second, "the dash is built to interrupt."[119] The dash at the end of the (first part of the) syntagma interrupts it, cuts it off. Thereby the *Gedanken-strich* introduces a pause, a break. It embodies this very break: it is a thought of pausing thought; a thought of interrupting thought; it is a *Strich durch den Gedanken*, a dash through thought that is at the same time *Gedanke des Strichs*, the thought of a barring of thought. Eidam argues:

> Being, pure being, without any further determination—[he strangely repositions the dash] is it Being thought, namely as the Being thought without any determinations at all that as such cannot be thought? Or is it the non-thought being that as "being-posited of non-thought" must be posited and thus however be thought to be able to think it at all as non-thought? One could have the idea that it must be both and both at the same time. But, pardon me, is one supposed to still think this?[120]

One can think it if one takes it seriously that one has to *think an interruption of thought within thought*. What does the dash interrupt if it is the physiognomic embodiment of interruption? It first interrupts and cuts into repeatability. The dash embodies something so singular, so unique, it breaks off any possibility of being inscribed in the form (before form) of being repeated. It is *unrepeatably singular*—the comma is repeated, the dash is not; it appears as interruption of the repetition of repetition. It embodies a pure "not."

It is not a sign of a determinate negation, rather a sign of subtraction, as a minus, not minusing anything concrete or determinate. It is the "not," the pure subtraction not subtracting (from) anything. It is a subtraction subtracting the *sub-* (the level of the repeatability of indeterminate being, the space of places) and leaving a mere *traction*. After the *Phenomenology* emptied out and subtracted all determinations and after deciding to begin, the *Logic* begins with a subtraction even of the *sub-* of the *sub-traction*. In the beginning there is only a *-traction* embodied by the dash. In it manifests the barring of (the) substance (of thought) itself, of the *sub-* of *sub-stance* (as much as of the *sub-* of *sub-traction*), leaving a mere *stance* that gains *traction*. The dash embodying the *decision* is the sign where the voided *sub-stance* is embodied in a singular *stance* in which all repetition of repetition is put on hold, paused, interrupted. The dash like the commas before thus has a specific "validity without significance,"[121] a speculative meaning.

The dash is the *embodied stance of a de-scission*[122] that marks the end of the syntagma by indicating its very beginning—that is, the decision. In this sense, the dash is the *speculative sign for Aufhebung*. It can be read as the invisible, unperceivable link between all the prefixes of the (coming) speculative vocabulary of the *Logic*,[123] enabling the very composition of the speculative words. It can become visible when there is a speculative turn in a sentence, an interruption of thought, pointing to a stance to be taken. This is what it embodies at the end[124] of the beginning of the *Logic's* first syntagma. Reading, thinking the dash is thinking what one cannot think; the barring of the substance of thought, the pure stance. It is as if one bars the thought one just had because the thought of a barring of thought is itself constitutive of thought (as that which cannot be thought). In it "the immanent counter-turn [*Gegenwendigkeit*] of the speculative sentence"[125] is embodied. The dash is the speculative sign, embodying the stance of a decision, indicating the advent, an event of thought.

Yet it also has to be read in sequence with the other (speculative) signs, with the commas: the physiognomic "direction" into which the index (of the not-being, not-nothing) changes when the dash is read in this sequence. It is as if the syntagma thereby designates a move against the running of the clock. This is Hegel's quarter turn.[126] It is as if the move from comma to dash is indicating another form of temporality: the temporality of retroactivity, as if the dash marks the *advent of retroactivity*. To apply this idea to the totality of the syntagma, "Being Comma Pure Being Comma Dash," then, could be read as follows: "being is what it will have been through the occurrence of pure being in the series of weak differences." This means that indeterminate immediacy is a product, but a retroactive product of the advent of retroactivity itself. This can be related to the redoubling of the commas (repeatability) in the following way: the beginning of the *Logic* demonstrates that retroactivity is itself a retroactive phenomenon. What will have been indeterminate immediacy will have been what it will have been when it will have become what it will have become.

That is, B_1 ("being") stands in a relation to B_2 ("pure being") that retroactively constitutes B_1 as being qualified by B_2: being is pure being that can only be accessed via the repetition of being as pure being (and the redoubled indexing marks of the commas, when read together with the dash). But in thinking this retroactive movement of constitution and negative determination of being—by adding B_2, the determination of indeterminacy— "something" else emerges. If we begin with "Being Comma Pure Being Comma Dash" and if the dash indicates the advent of the logic and temporality of retroactivity (related to the stance of the decision) applied to being itself, what does it mean when it is applied to the beginning itself? What lies retroactively before the retroactivity when retroactivity begins with being but does not end with it? This question is related to Henrich's comment that "the formalization of Hegel's logic finds its greatest, maybe unsurmountable difficulties in its beginning."[127] How to formalize that which can only be accessed via formalization, via the logic of weak difference as that which retroactively lies prior to it and even retroactively precedes the retroactivity at work within it? How to formalize that which—pertaining to the unanalyzability of the beginning—can only be formalized as unformalizable?

SEYN KOMMA REINES SEYN KOMMA GEDANKENSTRICH

In "Matrix" Jacques-Alain Miller develops an argument compatible with the beginning of Hegel's *Logic*. Hegel writes—before the beginning of the *Logic*—that in the beginning there is "*Sein und sonst nichts*," "being, and nothing else." [128] Miller begins the same way: "The All [*Le tout*]. Outside of which, therefore, nothing." [129] If one postulates a totality—say, all there is—one claims that there is nothing except this all: "There is only All there is and nothing else." But this proposition implies that one posits nothing as much as the All. Between the two of them there is only a negation devoid of all relation. For the All to conceptually remain what it is supposed to be and to avoid contradiction, it needs to repeat itself, attempting to integrate the nothing that occurred into it: one posits A_1 (the "All" in "there is the All, and nothing else") and one also posits N_1 (the first "nothing else" outside the All); one is then conceptually forced to generate A_2 (a second "All there is" that seeks realize the conceptual claim of the A_1). Thereby "N causes the reduplication of A." [130]

This engenders an infinitely progressing stratification; the same paradoxical structure is repeated on ever-higher strata: there are infinitely many Alls, which stand in a relation of order to one another. A_2 follows A_1, etc. The logic of this repetition can simply be formulated as the series of "All-Nothing-All." Nothing forces the All to repeat itself; it is the reason for the compulsion to repeat the All. Thus one can infer that it is always the same All and the same nothing that repeat although they are through the repetition placed on each and always higher strata. Each All (say, A_5 encompassing the nothing of A_4) bears the mark of this stratificatory process: 5 is the mark of the inclusion of N_4 into A_5. But with A_5 N_5 emerges, too. The All cannot ever encompass nothing but also not not include the nothing (in its concept) when posited—this is why there is all there is, and *nothing* else from the beginning. To begin with the being of one All is always to begin with Two, with the All, and with nothing.

This means the nothing confronts the All with being not-all, as it lacks nothing. The All is always lacking what is not-all (nothing); nothing always precedes the All. But didn't we start with positing the All? Yes. But the second All was engendered to include the first nothing that coemerged, and this process continues infinitely. This means that a strong difference (i.e., of nothing and the All) never appears on the same level. It only appears in the relation of one All (say, A_2) to another (A_1) but there is simply *no relation between the All and nothing*. So why does nothing precede the All? Miller claims that this stratificatory process of the different Alls engenders the question of *where* the first All is posited. He answers: because the nonrelation between the All and nothing grounds the stratification of the Alls, the first All must be posited in an unstratified "space," for otherwise the first space would simply be another All and therefore come with a specific nothing that it lacks. So if one asks where the All (or being) is posited as stratifying space of placements, for Miller it has to be "a place—where there is nothing."[131] But if any place is somehow determined by something it lacks, even this (ultimately initial) place where there is nothing needs to be determined by something it lacks. But what it lacks is lack itself. It is a place where even nothing is lacking—lack is lacking. It is a place where there is *less than nothing. This is the beginning.*

When Hegel claims that in the beginning there is "being and nothing else," doesn't he insist on the same point? If the task of the *Logic* is "to bring to consciousness the *logical* nature which animates spirit, drives it and is effective in it,"[132] couldn't one claim that which drives consciousness is precisely less than nothing? One might interpret the first version of Hegel's beginning "Seyn, reines Seyn,—"[133] such that even "Beyng" itself—with a "y" instead of an "i"—is indexing the peculiar not-being, not-nothing, not-something that is less than nothing. The "y's" seem to physiognomically index that *being is routed. Routed or placed somewhere where there is less than nothing,* since nothing coemerges with being. But one can in a materialist way think the "before"; one can (retroactively) think the advent of retroactivity. If the materialist hypothesis in reading the beginning of Hegel's *Logic* holds, this does have enormous consequences for how to read the rest of it. Because as Henrich rightly observes,[134] the beginning keeps repeating throughout the *Logic* as something necessarily impossible to sublate. A constant repetition of de-scission. The necessary impossibility of the beginning in this sense is never done away with; it insists on the higher logical strata until the end (as the immediate repeated as result). It then would be this nondialectical kernel of the whole dialectical development that can never be sublated; it can only be taken up as what is (always) "before" us.

If such a materialist reading can be upheld, this would not mean that Hegel starts with being as space of placements and that he also does not start with one and always the same being; yet he also does not start with a repetition of the one being or with a twofold placing of being (as being and pure being; or a being and nothing). Rather, it is only via the repetition of the being (as being and pure being), only via a repetition that introduces differences into that which is placed twice, that one could be able to think that the one being will always already have been Un-One. The first nonproposition of Hegel's *Logic* then indicates that being is neither inherently multiple nor One, but it is Not-One with a dash relating Not and One; it is not substance, it is stance. It is not-all and not-nothing. It is *less than nothing* that is also less than One: the beginning itself will (always) have been Un-One (taking up precisely the un- of un-mittelbar, "immediate"). It will have been Un-Eins as the *real* (being of the) beginning, the (real) *real* of and in the beginning of being and of nothing. From such a perspective one can claim that dialectics is somehow always an attempt to cope with Un-One, the Un-Eins at its roots, at its origin, its Ur-Sprung. In the end: *Dialectic is itself and will always have been Un-One, Un-Eins*—but this is just the beginning.

THE POINT IS TO LOSE IT

"Entschluss"
Kühn mag der Göttersohn der Vollendung Kampf sich vertrauen
Brich dann den Frieden mit dir, brich mit dem Werke der Welt.
Strebe, versuche du mehr, als das Heut und das Gestern, so wirst du
Besseres nichts als Zeit, aber auf's Beste sie sein!

"Resolve"
Boldly may the son of God trust in the achievement of the struggle.
Then break peace with yourself, break with the accomplishments of the
world.
Strive, try more than the today and the yesterday, and you will become
Nothing better than time, but time at its best!

—G. W. F. Hegel, from a poem written in 1801, read aloud by his students on
the tenth anniversary of his death[1]

Heinz Eidam claims that "if the Hegelian logic is a logic of freedom, then the
decision, which it took at the beginning and forgot again in the very same
moment, lies in the inaudible dash that is perceivable only as pause, as interruption in the flow of arguments."[2] The decision that kickstarts the *Logic* is
inscribed in its first sentence in the form of the dash. The dash is the speculative sign of an enigmatic "resolve" that originates somewhere prior to the
space of reasons and is necessarily overlooked within this space. "All we have
before us is simply the resolve [*Entschluss*], which can also be regarded as arbitrary, that we ... consider *thinking as such*."[3] This resolve is neither the result
nor the premise of an inference. It appears, rather, as a suspension of inferential reason—a withdrawal from the form of the syllogism or *Schluß: Entschluss*.
This resolve appears at the very beginning of the *Logic* and reappears at the
end in another form. Dieter Henrich remarks that "the end, the most determinate thought, is derived from the fact that a beginning was made. ... This is

an *absolute* fact."[4] This "absolute fact"—Hegel's answer to the Kantian "fact" of reason—confirms Hegel's philosophy as a philosophy of *Entschluss*, of resolve.

Yet there is not only one dash but two—one at the end of the *Phenomenology* and one at the beginning of the *Logic*. In the almost inaudible hesitation that inaugurates the *Logic* there is already an echo of a prior hesitation, and this ruins any illusion of the possibility of a pure beginning. Even the inaugural stutter of the *Logic* is a borrowed one. Every repetition is the echo of an earlier repetition. Between these two dashes opens up the interstitial space in which thinking learns what it means to move from one side of the Moebius strip to the other and back again. Within this transitional space philosophy rehearses the question of what it means to begin anew. The beginning move seems to vanish, but there is a compulsion to reinscribe this vanishing move in every step that follows, and this repetition throws us back to an even earlier rehearsal. Henrich is right to point out that the beginning, for Hegel, is "the source of a unsublatable ambiguity [*unaufhebbarer Zweideutigkeit*]."[5] We move on, yet we keep repeating, we seem to make progress, yet only in returning, we backslide, and yet we lurch forward. Ent-*schluss* and Er-*innerung*, repetition and advance, repetition in advance.

We suggested that the blocked movement of the speculative sentence offered a paradigm of the nonrelation between the *Logic* and its other side. The *Phenomenology* had demonstrated the historical significance of this blockage. It had raised the political stakes of a new beginning. How is thinking to proceed—*what is to be done?*—in a world where freedom is no longer the birthright of a sovereign subject and where there is no longer the consolation of aesthetic reconciliation? The achievement of the *Phenomenology* was to dismantle every voluntarist (Kantian or post-Kantian) possibility of subjective decision grounded in a given faculty. In order to resolve, one must first release the *Entschluss* from the grip of any subjectivist interpretation. The stakes are high in the wake of the Terror of the French Revolution. Yet the enterprise itself comes with the danger of effacing the promise of political transformation altogether. The spectral presence of Schiller at the close of the *Phenomenology* serves as a reminder of both the stakes and the danger.

We have emphasized the speculative commitment that enables us to stumble on something that we otherwise would not even have noticed. The resolve is also therefore an abandon or release, *Entlassen*, a renunciation of agency at the heart of action. In other words, and it will have been the fundamental achievement of the *Phenomenology* to clarify this, Hegel is a resolutely non-voluntarist—post-Kantian, post-Fichtean, post-Romantic—thinker. Despite or because of the recursiveness of resolve—the decision to philosophize is ultimately a commitment to commit to thinking—this is not the act of a sovereign decisionism, decision for the sake of decision, if only because the decision itself lacks grounding in any stable subject of decision. We confront here the paradoxical condition of freedom: the determination to be determined by something that we (necessarily) encounter only contingently.

Although the word *Entschluss* does not explicitly appear in Hegel's official lexicon of speculative words (*Aufhebung*, *Urteil*, etc.), the term displays all the versatility of such a word.[6] *Schluss* in German has several meanings: inference, conclusion, syllogism, closure, and even end. The Ent- prefix marks an immanent negation, so the combination, *Ent-schluss* involves a repetition of negativity, a negation of negation. *Entschluss* therefore can mean "Not-End," "Un-End," "Ent-Ende" in German or "Ent-End" in German-English, "End-End," a repetition of the end that ends the end, an "Ent-Ending" or "End-Ending," an unending ending and an ended unending. Ending the end is no longer ending. It is the immanent explosion or expulsion of the end, a finitization of finitude and thus an opening to the infinite: this is the kernel of Hegel's idealism.[7] But this opening is not the simple opposite of closure. *Entschluss* rather names *un-closure*. It introduces a split and doubling into the end or *Schluss*. The *Entschluss* un-ends what seems to have (irredeemably) ended, forcing us not only to begin anew but to think of beginning in a new way. Hegel, the philosopher of the end, is the philosopher of the *Un-ende*, of unending.

This is why the *Entschluss* repeats at the end of the *Logic* in the form of *Ent-lassen*.[8] The *Logic* begins by presenting God's resolve to create the world, and it ends when this creation is decidedly finished or *resolved*—not resolved in the sense that there has been a resolution or reconciliation of antagonisms, and not finished in the sense that there is nothing more to say or do. Thinking comes to an end when it is (contingently) decided that it must be broken off—when the Idea lets itself go.[9] There is no creation without a repetition of the *Entschluss* that simultaneously initiates and cuts short the un-ending movement of thinking. The process of un-ending must come to an end if only to avoid collapsing into the endlessness of the bad infinite (and thus the reinstatement of voluntarism in the form of the infinite task).

Nature itself is therefore also released. This is perhaps why Hegel never wrote the planned book about nature, why there can be no fully conceptualized nature, why in the aftermath of the *Logic*, nature (and spirit likewise) could only be pointed to—elliptically, didactically, even naturalistically and numerically, in encyclopedic shorthand. The "big" *Logic* is not followed by a "big" *Nature*, as intended, but only by a "little" *Logic* (followed by two more "little" textbooks). Logic can only repeat itself, summarize itself, profess itself, replicate itself in piecemeal miniature. Creation as a whole has been decreated, and this means that both nature and history have been rendered forever incomplete.

The *Entschluss* that launches the *Logic* was already rehearsed in the silent *Entschluss* that closed the *Phenomenology*. Absolute knowing had announced itself with a gesture of renunciation or release—a letting go "of the subject from the form of its Self [*Entlassen seiner aus der Form seines Selbsts*]."[10] The subject gives up the form of "its" very "self." More precisely: it relinquishes the formal property of a "Self." (The substantifying German majuscule, for once, must be carried over, however unidiomatically, into English translation.) Selfhood ceases to be the substantial possession of a self-identical self. The terms of subjectification are being completely reconstituted—but so too, accordingly, the terms of reality itself. This release from the self (or "Self") can be identified with a "supreme freedom and certainty":[11] freedom, because it liberates us from the assumption that freedom is or could ever be in our possession, and the certainty of an anxiety that never deceives—the certainty that there is nothing in me (or outside me) on which my freedom is grounded.[12] It is in this sense that the sacrificial movement of absolute knowing is directly linked to "knowing one's own limits."[13]

The *Entschluss* can also be read as "not-syllogism," "not-inference" or "un-syllogism," "un-judgment," and "un-conclusion." The resolve that drives thinking does not follow deductively; it is not the premise or the conclusion of a syllogistic inference. There can only be an *Entschluss* where inference fails and where thought is therefore impeded from continuing as before. Like the speculative sentence, the *Entschluss* is not a proposition (*Satz*), but rather a "leap" (*Satz*) of reason.

There is therefore an irredeemable contingency at the kernel of rational necessity. The *Entschluss* that inaugurates the *Logic* "can also be regarded as arbitrary."[14] The decision to start thinking can be—but does not have to be—regarded as contingent. The contingency of the *Entschluss* is itself contingent—which implies that the decision can also be regarded as necessary. It is necessary that the beginning can be regarded as either contingent or necessary (but by the same token, therefore, it need not be regarded as either). The *Entschluss* is neither a necessary prerequisite for the beginning (although it can be argued that it is necessary to make a beginning) nor simply a contingent decision that happens to be taken at the beginning. *Entschluss* collapses the distinction between contingency and necessity by demonstrating the necessary contingency of both. The beginning is thus marked by an original undecidability, and this is precisely what makes the beginning "conceptually incomprehensible" (*unbegreiflich*).[15] There is no *Entschluss* without undecidability, because only what is undecidable calls for a decision.

The immediate aftermath of Hegel's death forced a kind of decision as the legacy immediately split into left- and right-wing factions—the young Hegelians pitted against the old, the *Hegelinge* against the *Hegeliter*. The split itself was motivated by the essential ambiguity lurking in the concept of *Aufhebung*,[16] which could be interpreted in either a revolutionary or a conservative manner—demolition or preservation, transformation or conservation. The right-wing *Hegeliter* (as they were called) took the *Logic* as a lens for deciphering the underlying rational structure of the world;[17] the left-wing *Hegelinge* saw in the *Logic* an invitation to recreate the world in the light of reason. The split would inevitably come down to a debate over the relationship between theory and practice—between absolute knowing and its worldly unfolding, between philosophy and politics.[18]

From the outset, the *Entschluss* itself became a point of contention that started to divide Hegel's heritage. The Hegelian right embraced the actually existing state of affairs as the expression of rationality. Some of its members nonetheless continued to celebrate the *Entschluss*, but they typically located this resolve in the sphere of the *Philosophy of Right*, where it was the prerogative of the monarch to add his seal of legitimacy to the political order through a final act of sovereign "decision."[19] The Hegelian left, in contrast, emphasized the disparity between the semblance of rationality and its actuality. This was only sometimes explicitly articulated in relation to Hegelian resolve. Usually Hegel's "young" followers reproached him for having so little of it, or for having the wrong kind. A standard complaint of left-wing Hegelians was that the conceptual abstractness of the *Logic* prevented Hegel from thinking about concrete practice and led to an arrogant transformation of all reality into empty determinations of thought—"the catastrophe of metaphysics."[20] Engels, later, would argue that Hegel did not draw the proper consequences of his own dialectic; this needed to be liberated from the constraints of the *Logic* in order to transform reality into a rational state (and to avoid seeing reason where there was none).[21] Yet Kierkegaard turned the *Entschluss* into the constitutive feature of individual existence, criticizing Hegel for misrepresenting it as the arbitrariness of a subjective decision and for bringing it into the tamed form of logical closure: Hegel's logical apparatus reduced the *Entschluss* to a *Schluss*.[22] Arnold Ruge believed that the realization of thinking took the form of a practical resolve that was itself determined by the exigencies of its concrete historical context.[23]

Hegel claimed that philosophy emerges "when a gulf has arisen between inward strivings and external reality." His attempt to found "a kingdom of thought"[24] provoked the left-Hegelian objection that even a revolutionary theory that remains a mere theory is practically useless.[25] Hegel's *Entschluss* was therefore read by his early left-wing critics as tantamount to another religion. A symptom of this was seen at the end of the *Logic*, where the absolute idea "resolves" to release itself into nature—for many readers, this seemed like "a new edition of the old God."[26] Although Hegel had pointed in the right direction by emphasizing the groundlessness of the *Entschluss*, he ended up endorsing a position in which there remains nothing but pure agency without agents—a seemingly inauspicious basis for emancipatory politics.[27]

The left- and right-wing Hegelian factions were not uniform camps and the divide between the two camps cannot be easily mapped onto the division between the *Phenomenology* and the *Logic*. Indeed, the later generations of the post-Hegelian left (paradigmatically the later Marx, Bakunin, and later Lenin) often showed a surprising preference for the *Logic* (and usually at charged political moments),[28] while the right often preferred the various versions of the *Realphilosophie* articulated in Hegel's lectures.[29]

But the split in the Hegelian aftermath is indicative of a problem that pertains directly to the *Entschluss*: the problem of orientation. (In fact, the preoccupation with "left" and "right" may well be symptomatic of this preoccupation and hearkens back to the early Kant.[30]) Orientation is a problem directly connected to the resolve, because after the *Phenomenology* it has become completely unclear where we are. "With what must the science begin?"[31] "Womit muß der Anfang der Wissenschaft gemacht werden?" The first question of the *Science of Logic* is a confession of disorientation. This is not simply the usual diligence about scientific protocol. The question expresses a fundamental uncertainty about place. The subject lacks the initial "wherewithal" requisite for any scientific undertaking. Absolute knowing has brought us to this point of uncertainty: the condition for starting afresh is to clear away the basic coordinates of our symbolic universe.

We are at the limits of phenomenology: our exact historical-cultural location is inscrutable or untenable and we can no longer take for granted the habitual coordinates of space and time. We have relinquished every kind of givenness: there is no longer any objective principle to coordinate either thought or action. And we have arrived at a stopping place or "station" where every standard fails to stabilize and where we are therefore forced to question our unthinking commitment to upholding standards in the first place. Absolute Knowing releases the self-conscious subject from the compulsion to self-measurement that was its defining hallmark from the outset of the *Phenomenology*.[32]

Descartes had wagered that the only option for a traveler who is lost in the forest where all trees look alike is to arbitrarily choose a direction and stick to it as faithfully as possible. Only in facing the abyss of a freedom freed can we retrieve a new orientation and undertake a transformation of practice on the basis of a knowledge that we did not know we had—a knowledge so pure "it ceases itself to be knowledge."[33] Only through such a resolution opens up, *entschließt*, a path to truth.

Philosophers have hitherto only *interpreted* the world. For Hegel the point is to *lose* it—to delete it, suspend it, destroy it, dash it to pieces—to refuse the world as we know it and create a new one. The point is to punctuate history—to get the point, to get to the point, to bring things to the point of transformation.

It is in this sense that the dash is the perfect translation (and this is true in all languages, even in German) of Hegel's untranslatable master term: *Aufhebung*—

ABBREVIATIONS OF WORKS BY HEGEL

Aes (1–2): *Hegel's Aesthetics: Lectures on Fine Art*. 2 vols. Trans. T. M. Knox. Oxford: Oxford University Press, 1975.

Äs (1–3): *Vorlesungen über Ästhetik*. 3 vols. In *Werke*, vols. 13–15. Frankfurt am Main: Suhrkamp, 1986.

Encyclopaedia I: The Encyclopaedia Logic (with the *Zusätze*): *Part 1 of the Encyclopaedia of Philosophical Sciences with the Zusätze*. Trans. T. F. Geraets, W. A. Suchting, and H. S. Harris. Indianapolis: Hackett, 1991.

Encyclopaedia II: Philosophy of Nature. 3 vols. Trans. M. J. Petry. London: Allen and Unwin, 1970.

Encyclopaedia III: Philosophy of Mind. Part Three of the Encyclopaedia of the Philosophical Sciences (1830 edition). Trans. William Wallace and A. V. Miller. Oxford: Oxford University Press, 1971.

ENZ (1–3): *Enzyklopädie der philosophischen Wissenschaften im Grundrisse* [1830], 3. vols. In *Werke*, vols. 8–10, Frankfurt am Main: Suhrkamp, 1986.

ETW: "The Spirit of Christianity and Its Fate." In *On Christianity: Early Theological Writings*. Trans. T. M. Knox. New York: Harper, 1948.

GC: "Der Geist des Christentums und sein Schicksal." In *Frühe Schriften, in Werke*, vol. 1, 274–419. Frankfurt am Main: Suhrkamp, 1971.

HLL: Lectures on Logic: Berlin, 1831. Bloomington: Indiana University Press, 2008.

HPh (1–3): *Lectures on the History of Philosophy*. 3 vols. Trans. E. S. Haldane and F. H. Simson. Lincoln: University of Nebraska Press, 1995.

Letters: The Letters. Bloomington: Indiana University Press, 1984.

PH: Phenomenology of Spirit. Trans. A. V. Miller. Oxford: Oxford University Press, 1970.

PHÄ: *Phänomenologie des Geistes*. In *Gesammelte Werke*, vol. 9. Hamburg: Meiner, 1980.

PHH: *The Philosophy of History*. Trans. J. Sibree. Mineola, NY: Dover, 2004.

PhRi: *Outlines of the Philosophy of Right*. Trans. T. M. Knox, ed. Stephen Houlgate. Oxford: Oxford University Press, 2008.

RPh: *Grundlinien der Philosophie des Rechts oder Naturrecht und Staatswissenschaft im Grundrisse*. In *Werke*, vol. 7. Frankfurt am Main: Suhrkamp, 1989.

SL: *Hegel's Science of Logic*. Trans. George di Giovanni. Cambridge: Cambridge University Press, 2010.

SL1: *Hegel's Science of Logic*. Trans. A. V. Miller. London: Allen and Unwin, 1967.

VGP (1–3): *Vorlesungen über die Geschichte der Philosophie*. 3 vols. In *Werke*, vols. 18–20. Frankfurt am Main: Suhrkamp, 1986.

VPG: *Vorlesungen über die Philosophie der Geschichte*. In *Werke*, vol. 12. Frankfurt am Main: Suhrkamp, 1986.

Werke: *Werke in zwanzig Bänden*. Ed. Eva Moldenhauer and Karl Markus Michel. Frankfurt am Main: Suhrkamp, 1986.

WL (1–2): *Wissenschaft der Logik*. In *Werke*, vols. 5–6. Frankfurt am Main: Suhrkamp, [1812] 1986.

NOTES

PREFACE

1. "Aber Philosophie partiell—Priesterstand isoliert Heiligtum—Unbekümmert wie es der Welt gehen mag" (G. W. F. Hegel, *Vorlesungen über die Philosophie der Religion*, vol. 3, *Die vollendete Religion* [Hamburg: Meiner, 1995], 97). "Aber diese Versöhnung ist selbst nur eine partielle, ohne äußere Allgemeinheit; die Philosophie ist in dieser Beziehung ein abgesondertes Heiligtum, und ihre Diener bilden einen isolierten Priesterstand, der mit der Welt nicht zusammengehen darf und das Besitztum der Wahrheit hüten" (G. W. F. Hegel, "Vorlesungen über die Philosophie der Religion II," in *Werke*, vol. 17 [Frankfurt am Main: Suhrkamp, 1982], 347).

2. PhRi, 16; RPh, 27–28.

3. Jean Hyppolite, *Genesis and Structure of Hegel's "Phenomenology of Spirit"* (Evanston, IL: Northwestern University Press, 1974), 541.

4. SL, 29; WL 1, 44. Emphasis in original.

5. Slavoj Žižek remarks that the twentieth century was not only profoundly anti-Platonic, as Alain Badiou has demonstrated, but also profoundly anti-Hegelian, which is why Lenin called in 1920 for the formation of a "society of the materialist friends of Hegel." Cf. Slavoj Žižek, *Less Than Nothing: Hegel and the Shadow of Dialectical Materialism* (London: Verso, 2012), 40–41; V. I. Lenin, "On the Significance of Militant Materialism," in *Lenin's Collected Works*, vol. 33 (Moscow: Progress Publishers, 1972), 227–236.

6. "*We were all Feuerbachians* ..." (Frederick Engels, *Ludwig Feuerbach and the End of Classical German Philosophy*, in Karl Marx and Frederick Engels, *Collected Works*, vol. 26, *Engels, 1882–89* [London: International Publishers 1991], 364).

7. For a catalog of the best-known (and a few lesser-known) clichés about Hegel, see Jon Stewart, ed., *The Hegel Myths and Legends* (Evanston, IL: Northwestern University Press, 1996).

8. PH §78, 50; PHÄ, /2.

9. PH §807, 492; PHÄ, 590.

10. PH §343, 208; PHÄ, 260.

11. V. I. Lenin, *Conspectus of Hegel's Science of Logic*, in *Collected Works*, vol. 38 (Moscow: Progress Publishers, 1976), 130.

12. Cf. Hegel, "How the Ordinary Human Understanding Takes Philosophy (as Displayed in the Works of Mr. Krug)," in *Between Kant and Hegel: Texts in the Development of Post-Kantian Idealism*, ed. George Di Giovanni and H. S. Harris, 292–310 (Albany: SUNY Press, 1985).

13. PH §807, 492; PHÄ 590.

14. "It can [*Es kann*: note the contingency] delight a thinker [literally: it can allow for a delight to thinking—*Es kann dem Denken eine Freude gewähren*] to come across [literally: to stumble across, *stoßen auf*; the shock, *Stoß*, is Hegel's answer to the Fichtean *Anstoß*] such words and to find the union of opposites naively shown in the dictionary as one word with opposite meanings, although this result of speculative thinking is nonsensical to the understanding" (SL, 12; WL I, 20–21).

15. PH §87, 55; PHÄ, 77. For an elaboration of this point see Rebecca Comay, "Resistance and Repetition: Hegel and Freud," in *Research in Phenomenology* 45 (2015): 237–266, esp. 248–249.

16. SL, 47; WL I, 68.

17. Concerning Hegel and the devil, Ernest Hello, a nineteenth-century French Catholic critic of Hegel, charmingly objected: "Hegel condensed the mistake; he systematized it, proffered it, so to speak, entirely, and entirely in a word. His formula is on the frontispiece of Satan's school, which henceforth scorns imitators by defying them to do better. Satan recognized himself in the Hegelian formula, admired it as one of his own; for Pride, Satan and Hegel together shout: Being and Nothing are identical" (Ernest Hello, *L'homme* [Paris: Perrin, (1872) 1921], 137–138; quoted in Jean-Luc Nancy, *The Speculative Remark: One of Hegel's Bons Mots* [Palo Alto, CA: Stanford University Press, 2001], 21). About thirty years earlier Schlegel had formulated a similar criticism: "The system of negation [Hegel's] is even a step worse than atheism or the *idolization of the I or self* (Fichte), a deification of negating spirit, thus in fact philosophical satanism" (Friedrich Schlegel, *Philosophische Vorlesungen aus den Jahren 1804 bis 1806: Nebst Fragmenten vorzüglich philosophischen Inhalts*, vol. 2 [Berlin: E. Weber, 1837], 497).

18. PHH, 5; VPG, 16.

19. Theodor W. Adorno, *Minima Moralia: Reflections on a Damaged Life*, trans. E. F. N. Jephcott (London: Verso, 2005), 29.

20. This again comes with the danger of aestheticizing Hegel's method and reading him as a "poetic" thinker (a Rancièrian avant la lettre). Adorno risks such a position in his *Three Studies*: "One must read Hegel by describing along with him the curves of his intellectual movement, by playing his ideas with the speculative ear as though they were musical notes" (Theodor W. Adorno, *Hegel: Three Studies* [Cambridge, MA: MIT Press, 1993], 123). Günter Wohlfart endorses the claim that the truth of Hegel's philosophy lies in its aesthetic substratum (Günter Wohlfart, *Der spekulative Satz: Bemerkungen zum Begriff der Spekulation bei Hegel* [Berlin: de Gruyter, 1981]; Günter Wohlfart,

Der Punkt: Ästhetische Meditationen [Freiburg: Karl Alber, 1986]). This will be at stake in Hegel's treatment of Schiller, as we will see.

21. Cf. Hegel's famous letter of 1805 to Johann Heinrich Voss, the German translator of Homer: "Luther made the Bible speak German, and you have done the same for Homer—the greatest gift that can be made to a people. For a people remains barbarian and does not view what is excellent within the range of its acquaintance as its own true property so long as it does not come to know it in its own language. ... I may say of my endeavor that I wish to teach philosophy to speak German" (Hegel, *Letters*, 107).

22. PH §63, 39; PHÄ, 60.

23. Cf. Karl Rosenkranz, *Georg Wilhelm Friedrich Hegels Leben* (Darmstadt: WBG, 1991), 361.

24. Gérard Lebrun, *La patience du Concept: Essai sur le discours hégélien* (Paris: Gallimard, 1972), 112.

25. Alexandre Koyré, "Note sur la langue et la terminologie hégéliennes," in *Études d'histoire de la pensée philosophique* (Paris: Gallimard, 1971), 220.

26. "Naïveté is the breaking forth of the ingenuousness originally natural to humanity, in opposition to the art of disguising oneself that has become a second nature. We laugh at the simplicity that is as yet a stranger to dissimulation, but we rejoice all the while over the simplicity of nature that thwarts [*einen Querstrich spielt*] that art" (Immanuel Kant, *Critique of Judgment*, trans. James Creed Meredith [Oxford: Oxford University Press, 2007], §54, 163).

27. Cf. PH §554, 338; PHÄ, 410.

28. "Um so schlimmer für die Fakten. " On Hegel's notorious (untraceable) saying, see Adorno, *Hegel: Three Studies* (Cambridge, MA: MIT Press, 1993), 31.

29. Friedrich Nietzsche, *Genealogy of Morals*, trans. Walter Kaufmann (New York: Vintage, 1989), 119.

30. Adorno writes: "Es bleibt uns, könnte man beinahe sagen, gar nichts anders übrig als die Borniertheit des Partiellen, um überhaupt zum Ganzen zu kommen, denn das Ganze haben wir nicht" ("We could almost say that there is nothing left for us but parochialism and partiality, if we are to reach the whole at all") (Theodor W. Adorno, *Einführung in die Dialektik* [Berlin: Suhrkamp, [1958] 2015], 53).

CHAPTER 1

1. SL, 7; WL I, 13.

2. SL, 7; WL I, 13.

3. SL, 7–8; WL I, 13.

4. Kant for Hegel regressed to the position of Locke. Cf. G. W. F. Hegel, *Faith and Knowledge*, trans. Walter Cerf and H. S. Harris (Albany: SUNY Press, 1977), 68–69; G. W. F. Hegel, "Glaube und Wissen," in *Werke* (Frankfurt am Main: Suhrkamp, 1986), vol. 2, 304.

5. Immanuel Kant, "On the Miscarriage of All Philosophical Attempts in Theodicy," in Immanuel Kant, *Religion and Rational Theology* (Cambridge: Cambridge University Press, 2001), 31.

6. Adorno states: "We may say perhaps that the enormous impact of the *Critique of Pure Reason* has its source in the circumstance that it was in effect the first work to give expression to the element of bourgeois resignation [*Entsagung*], to that refusal to make any significant statement on the crucial questions, and instead to set up house in the finite world and explore it in every direction, as Goethe phrased it" (Theodor W. Adorno, *Kant's Critique of Pure Reason*, ed. Rolf Tiedemann, trans. Rodney Livingstone [Stanford, CA: Stanford University Press, (1959) 2001], 6).

7. SL, 25; WL1, 38.

8. Gerard Lebrun describes the "drama of the understanding" as abstracting from all sensible content without ever putting into question "the representations deriving from association with the sensible" (this is why understanding exhibits "the same naïveté" as sensation). Lebrun, *La patience du concept* (Paris: Gallimard, 1972), 78.

9. SL, 8; WL1, 14.

10. Herbert Marcuse, *Reason and Revolution: Hegel and the Rise of Social Theory* (London: Routledge, 1955), 130.

11. SL, 8; WL1, 14.

12. "*ohne allen Begriff, in's Wilde.*" (See G. W. F. Hegel, "Solgers nachgelassene Schriften und Briefwechsel," in *Werke*, vol. 11, 251.)

13. PH §524, 319; PHÄ, 389.

14. SL, 8; WL1, 40.

15. SL, 9; WL1, 40.

16. Immanuel Kant, *Critique of Pure Reason*, trans. and ed. Paul Guyer and Allen W. Wood (Cambridge: Cambridge University Press, 1998), Bxii, 108.

17. Theodor W. Adorno, *Negative Dialectics*, trans. E. B. Ashton (London: Routledge, 1974), 3.

18. V. I. Lenin, *What Is to Be Done? Burning Questions of Our Movement* (New York: International Publishers, 1978), 60. Lenin uses this expression to criticize the argument justifying the reduction of political action to economic struggles either as "the most widely applicable" or as "the means" of collective intervention. This quip has been popularized by Slavoj Žižek. See, for example, *Less Than Nothing: Hegel and the Shadow of Dialectical Materialism* (London: Verso, 2012), 69–79. See also Marx on the "good side" and "bad side" of feudalism: "Feudal production also had two antagonistic elements which are likewise designated by the name of the good side and the bad side of feudalism, irrespective of the fact that it is always the bad side that in the end triumphs over the good side. It is the bad side that produces the movement which makes history" (Karl Marx, "The Poverty of Philosophy: Answer to the 'Philosophy of Poverty' by M. Proudhon," in Karl Marx and Frederick Engels, *Collected Works*, vol. 6, *1845–1848* [New York: International Publishers, 1976], 174).

19. We can see a similar forced choice in the case of the class struggle: Marx emphasizes that from the standpoint of the proletariat there will never be anything but irreconcilable antagonism; the phantasm of reconciliation is a strictly one-sided (i.e., ideological) construction that can only express the partial interests of the ruling classes. The proletariat is the "universal" class not because its claims are impartial—or because its enterprise, as *homo laborans*, is of universal human value (as in early Marx)—but because its predicament illuminates the irreducible need to choose. Its situation calls for a praxis in excess of production.

20. Here we can see the deep affinity between dialectics and deconstruction. On the bond between undecidability and decision, see Jacques Derrida, *The Gift of Death* (Chicago: University of Chicago Press, 2008); Jacques Derrida, *Politics of Friendship* (London: Verso, 2006); Jacques Derrida, *Adieu to Emmanuel Levinas* (Stanford, CA: Stanford University Press, 1999). Slavoj Žižek has repeatedly emphasized that in the face of an impossible choice, the solution is sometimes not to directly tackle the choice itself but rather to effect a change that alters the very coordinates of the choice. See, for example, Slavoj Žižek, *The Fragile Absolute, or Why the Christian Legacy Is Worth Fighting For* (London: Verso, 2000), 149–150.

21. This turn to formalism also informed the structuralist transformation of Marxist theory in the 1970s in France. "Althusser's students wilfully adopted the 'bad side' of an adamantine formalism to struggle against the spiritualist currents that provided a welcome reception to phenomenology in France and, in their view, obscured what was most revolutionary in the 'theoretical practices' of Marxism and psychoanalysis" (Knox Peden, "Introduction to Volume Two: 'The Fate of the Concept,'" in *Concept and Form*, vol. 2, *Interviews and Essays on the "Cahiers pour l'Analyse,"* ed. Peter Hallward and Knox Peden [London: Verso, 2012], 4). A similar turn informs many contemporary German readings of Marx, as demonstrated in Michael Heinrich, *Die Wissenschaft vom Wert: Die Marxsche Kritik der politischen Ökonomie zwischen wissenschaftlicher Revolution und klassischer Tradition* (Münster: Westfälisches Dampfboot, 2011).

22. There is obviously an anti-Hegelian tradition (one of the best paradigms is Deleuze), which for similar reasons opts for an exaggerated form of empiricism that will internally implode any given form. See also Gurvitch's "hyper-empiricism," n. 105 below.

23. Immanuel Kant, *Lectures on Logic* (Cambridge: Cambridge University Press, 1992), 527.

24. Fredric Jameson, *The Hegel Variations: On the Phenomenology of Spirit* (London: Verso, 2010), 54.

25. Jürgen Habermas, *The Theory of Communicative Action*, vol. 1, *Reason and the Rationalization of Society*, trans. Thomas McCarthy (Boston: Beacon Press, 1984), 24.

26. Cf. Jacques Lacan, *The Other Side of Psychoanalysis: The Seminar of Jacques Lacan*, vol. 17, trans. Russell Grigg (New York: Norton, 2007).

27. Cf. Sigmund Freud, "New Introductory Lectures on Psycho-Analysis," in *The Standard Edition of the Complete Psychological Works of Sigmund Freud*, vol. 16, ed. James Strachey (New York: Norton, 1990), 71.

28. Saussure is usually taken to have introduced this idea into linguistics. There is no meaning outside its practical and inferential production (there is no "left" without saying "this is not right," and without "right" being not "green, pig, door, sky," etc.). Semantic content emerges precisely from the differential system determining the position of a signifier. The deconstruction of the antithesis of content and form is plausibly associated with a kind of pragmatism: the material that humans deal with is generated by their practice (of dealing). Cf. Robert B. Brandom, *A Spirit of Trust*, unpublished MS, chap. 5, http://www.pitt.edu/~brandom/spirit_of_trust_2014.html.

29. Alain Badiou emphasizes the constitutive exception that forms the vanishing ground of any practice establishing truths: "There are only bodies and languages, *except that* there are truths." We may say that for Hegel, likewise, "There is only language and action, *except that* there is freedom." Rather than resting on a transcendental foundation, language surges forth in the element of contingency. Freedom does not only define action within a given normative framework, it also strangely inhibits it. This is to say that freedom is not a "fact of reason"; it emerges contingently and requires its own practical verification. It is something that happens—to us. See Alain Badiou, *Logic of Worlds: Being and Event 2* (London: Continuum, 2006), 4.

30. On this see also Christoph Menke, *Force: A Fundamental Concept of Aesthetic Anthropology* (New York: Fordham University Press, 2013).

31. Werner Hamacher, "Afformative, Strike," in *Walter Benjamin's Philosophy: Destruction and Experience*, ed. Andrew Benjamin and Peter Osborne (London: Routledge, 1994), 155–182.

32. SL, 463; WL2, 189.

33. Cf. Immanuel Kant, "An Answer to the Question: What Is Enlightenment?," in *Practical Philosophy*, ed. Mary J. Gregor (Cambridge: Cambridge University Press, 1999), 19–20. See also Žižek, *Less Than Nothing*, 980ff.

34. A frequent reaction to Gödel's theorem(s) is that the theorem itself falls under the verdict it articulates—which seems to prove that a choice needs to be made (both for or against consistency and for or against completeness) (Kurt Gödel, "On Completeness and Consistency," in *Collected Works*, vol. 1, *Publications 1929–1936*, ed. Solomon Feferman et al. [Oxford: Oxford University Press, 1986], 235–238).

35. Michel Foucault, "The Order of Discourse," in *Untying the Text: A Post-Structuralist Reader*, ed. Robert Young (Boston: Routledge, 1981), 69. One might also refer to this as materialism without matter. See Frank Ruda, *For Badiou: Idealism without Idealism* (Evanston, IL: Northwestern University Press, 2015), 9.

36. Quentin Meillassoux, *After Finitude: An Essay on the Necessity of Contingency* (London: Bloomsbury, 2010).

37. In this way "'matter' disappears in a network of purely formal/ideal relations." Slavoj Žižek, *Absolute Recoil: Towards a New Foundation of Dialectical Materialism* (London: Verso, 2015), 5.

38. PhRi, 15; RPh, 26.

39. PH §808, 493; PHÄ, 591.

40. G. W. F. Hegel, *The Difference between Fichte's and Schelling's System of Philosophy* (Albany: SUNY Press, 1977), 88; G. W. F. Hegel, "Differenz des Fichteschen und Schellingschen Systems der Philosophie" (1801), in *Werke* (Frankfurt am Main: Suhrkamp, 1986), vol. 2, 19.

41. PH §72, 45; PHÄ, 67. Emphasis added.

42. Hegel from his early years onward always praised this investigation as the core of the Kantian legacy: "In the principle of the deduction of the categories Kant's philosophy is authentic idealism" (Hegel, *The Difference*, 79). In the *Science of Logic*, Hegel describes Kant's "original synthesis of apperception" as "one of the most profound principles for speculative development" (SL, 520; WL2, 260–261).

43. Adorno: "Thus you can see here that what stands opposed to the concept of the given, namely the organization of mind to which something is given, is something that Kant himself regards as a kind of given" (Adorno, *Kant's Critique of Pure Reason*, 17).

44. This is in Hegel's seventh thesis: "Philosophia critica caret ideis et imperfecta est Scepticismi forma" (G. W. F. Hegel, "Habilitationstheses," in *Miscellaneous Writings of G. W. F. Hegel*, ed. Jon Stewart [Evanston, IL: Northwestern University Press, 2002], 170–171; G. W. F. Hegel, "Habilitationsthesen," in *Werke*, vol. 2, 533); emphasis added. For the context of this criticism, see Arsen Gulyga, *Georg Wilhelm Friedrich Hegel* (Leipzig: Reclam, 1974), 62ff.

45. PH §78, 50; PHÄ, 72.

46. Cf. Lebrun on Hegel's "hyperdogmatism" (Lebrun, *La patience*, 91).

47. Lacan has clearly seen this dilemma in "Kant avec Sade" (Jacques Lacan, *Écrits*, trans. Bruce Fink [New York: Norton, 2002], 645–670).

48. Hegel brings out the implications of this incomplete formalism in his criticism of Kant's practical philosophy: the categorical imperative is presented as a purely formal principle that allows me to discriminate moral from merely legal or prudential actions. Yet, even if I choose a particular maxim that does not contradict this formal rule, this too may nonetheless lead to contradictory consequences. Hegel's example of such a maxim is: Always help the poor! This does not contradict the form of the imperative, yet if this maxim becomes a universal law, poverty will be abolished and the maxim itself will become meaningless. This shows that there is content inscribed into what appears to be just a formal principle (cf. G. W. F. Hegel, *Natural Law: The Scientific Ways of Treating Natural Law, Its Place in Moral Philosophy, and Its Relation to the Positive Sciences of Law*, trans. T. M. Knox [Philadelphia: University of Pennsylvania Press, 1975], 80).

49. Sigmund Freud, "Fetishism," in *The Standard Edition of the Complete Psychological Works of Sigmund Freud*, vol. 21, ed. James Strachey, 147–158 (London: Hogarth Press, [1927] 1975). See also Rebecca Comay, *Mourning Sickness: Hegel and the French Revolution* (Stanford, CA: Stanford University Press, 2011), 81–117.

50. SL, 472; WL2, 195.

51. Adorno, *Hegel: Three Studies*, 11.

52. PH §165, 103; PHÄ, 153.

53. SL, 524, WL2, 267. Translation modified.

54. "It may be said that in general cognition begins with ignorance, for one does not learn to know something with which one is already acquainted. Conversely, it also begins with the known, for it is a tautological proposition that that with which cognition begins, what it therefore actually knows, is for that reason a known; what is as yet not known, and is expected to be known only later, is still an unknown. In this respect it must be said that cognition, once it has begun, always proceeds from the known to the unknown" (SL, 700; WL2, 502).

55. SL, 466; WL2, 187.

56. SL, 466; WL2, 187.

57. SL, 467; WL 2, 189.

58. "*a displaying of what it is*," "*ein Zeigen dessen, was es ist.*" SL, 466; WL2, 187.

59. Cf. Heinrich von Kleist, "On the Gradual Production of Thoughts Whilst Speaking," in *Kleist: Selected Writings*, ed. and trans. David Constantine (Indianapolis: Hackett, 2004), 405–410. Heinrich von Kleist, *Über die allmähligeVerfertigung der Gedanken beim Reden* (Frankfurt am Main: Dielmann, 1999). Cf. Hegel's statement that philosophy is only capable of becoming science if it unfolds on a "self-constructing path" (SL, 10; WL1, 17).

60. SL, 471; WL2, 194.

61. This is the opposite of what Adorno (citing Lukács as its author) called "flattening through depth [*Verflachung durch Tiefe*]." We are emphasizing a deepening through superficiality. See Theodor W. Adorno, "Zur gegenwärtigen Stellung der empirischen Sozialforschung in Deutschland," in *Gesammelte Schriften*, vol. 8, *Soziologische Schriften I*, ed. Rolf Tiedemann (Frankfurt am Main: Suhrkamp, 1997), 484.

62. PH §10, 6; PHÄ, 18.

63. SL 471; WL2, 194. There are affinities with Alain Badiou's "generic procedure" (cf. Alain Badiou, *Being and Event* [London: Continuum, 2007], 327–391). Cf. Hegel's formulation in the *Phenomenology*: "Truth is its own self-movement [*Die Wahrheit ist die Bewegung ihrer an ihr selbst*]" (PH §48, 28; PHÄ, 47).

64. "Interpretation [*Auslegung*] is, in short, the word for the aporia of interpretation" (Werner Hamacher, "The Promise of Interpretation: Remarks on the Hermeneutic Imperative in Kant and Nietzsche," in *Premises: Essays on Philosophy and Literature from Kant to Celan*, trans. Peter Fenves [Cambridge, MA: Harvard University Press, 1996], 133).

65. Quoted by Benjamin in Walter Benjamin, *Understanding Brecht* (London: Verso, 2003), 110.

66. This is of course Hegel's caricature of the Egyptian mysteries, which suggests that there is an "Egyptian" moment at the heights of absolute knowing.

67. PH §807, 492; PHÄ, 590.

68. Psychoanalysis describes such paradoxical resolve as the "choice of neurosis." What does it mean to "choose" to be governed by an unconscious that erodes the power to choose and that reveals itself only in the effects it forces?

69. The phrase is Napoleon's, made famous by Lenin in "Our Revolution" (1923) and elsewhere to capture the necessary flexibility of revolutionary military strategy. See *Lenin's Collected Works*, 2nd English ed., vol. 33 (Moscow: Progress Publishers, 1965), 476–480.

70. On "acting before hearing," see Emmanuel Levinas, *New Talmudic Readings* (Pittsburgh: Duquesne University Press, 2007), 30ff.

71. SL, 468; WL2, 194. Emphasis in the original.

72. Johann Friedrich Blumenbach, "Über den Bildungstrieb (Nisus formativus) und seinen Einfluß auf die Generation und Reproduktion,"*Göttingisches Magazin der Wissenschaften und Literatur* 1, no. 5 (1780): 247–266, ed. Georg Christoph Lichtenberg and Georg Forster.

73. Johann Wolfgang von Goethe, *The Metamorphosis of Plants* (Cambridge, MA: MIT Press, 2009). This book aimed at exposing "the true Proteus who can hide or reveal himself in all vegetal forms."

74. SL, 677; WL2, 471.

75. Already the early Hegel spoke of the overcoming of natural life (with its egoistic strivings) in the practice of love (cf. G. W. F. Hegel, "Love," in ETW, 302–303).

76. Spirit is only what it makes of itself and "what it knows of itself" (*Encyclopaedia III*, §385, Zusätze, 21; ENZ3, 33).

77. John Bellamy Foster has made a similar argument for a materialist concept of nature that dispenses with the metaphysical assumption that nature is well ordered and homeostatic. See John Bellamy Foster, *Marx's Ecology: Materialism and Nature* (London: Monthly Review Press, 2000). Emphasizing the artificiality of the life of spirit, Hegel is reported as having stated: "Man dies out of habit because he has fully inhabited life [*sich ganz eingewohnt im Leben*], when he has so inhabited himself, he dies" (G. W. F. Hegel, *Vorlesungen über Rechtsphilosophie 1818–1831*, vol. 4, ed. Karl-Heinz Ilting [Stuttgart: frommann-holzboog, 1974], 407). "Nature's malfunction [*die Ohnmacht der Natur*]" is an expression of nature's "contingency, caprice and lack of order … [its] inability … to hold fast to the realization of the concept" (*Encyclopaedia II*, §250, 215–215; ENZ2, 34–36).

78. PH §452, 270; PHÄ, 332.

79. "Logical life as idea" is different "from natural life as treated in the philosophy of nature, and from life in so far as it is bound to spirit." SL, 677; WL2, 470–471.

80. PH §51, 30, PHÄ, 21.

81. PH §51, 31, PHÄ, 22.

82. PH §28, 16; PHÄ, 48. Hegel's incessant attack on the mortifying work of formalism includes, inter alia, a condemnation of "dead propositions" (PH §45, 26; PHÄ, 44), "lifeless schema" (PH §50, 29), "skeleton" (PH §51, 31), "dead necessity" (PH §378, 227; PHÄ, 279), "dead words and letters" (PH §554, 338; PHÄ, 410), "the deadness of abstraction" (PH§689, 420; PHÄ, 507), "dead forms" (SL, 27; WL1, 41), "dead bones of logic" (SL, 32; WL1, 48), "dead, motionless determinations" (SL, 180; WL1, 247), "dead mechanical aggregates" (SL, 455; WL2, 172), and "dead forms of thought" (SL, 676; WL2, 469).

83. Cf. ETW, 254; GC, 371. "To conceive of pure life means trying to abstract from every deed, from everything which man was or will be." Hegel writes in this context that "pure life is *being*."

84. See Mladen Dolar, "The Comic Mimesis," *Critical Inquiry* 43 (Winter 2017): 570–589, 584.

85. SL, 749; WL2, 568.

86. PH §90, 58; PHÄ, 82. In the *Phenomenology* Hegel states that "to judge a thing that has substance and solid worth is quite easy, to apprehend [*fassen*] it is much harder, and to unite [*vereinigen*] both, to produce its presentation [*seine Darstellung hervorzubringen*], is the hardest thing of all" (translation altered) (PH §3, 3; PHÄ, 13).

87. Cf. PH §85, 54; PHÄ, 77.

88. Jacques Lacan, *The Seminar of Jacques Lacan*, Book X, *Anxiety*, ed. Jacques-Alain Miller, trans. A. R. Price (Cambridge: Polity Press, 2014), 100.

89. Martin Heidegger, "What Is Metaphysics?," in *Pathmarks*, ed. William McNeill (Cambridge: Cambridge University Press, 1998), 88; see also Martin Heidegger, *Being and Time* (New York: Harper & Row, 2008), §§30, 40.

90. PH §194, 117; PHÄ, 153.

91. SL, 30 (translation modified); WL, 45.

92. In the *Phenomenology*, Hegel uses *Angst* and *Furcht* ("anxiety" and "fear") interchangeably. See PH §74, 74; PHÄ, 70 (*Furcht vor der Wahrheit*: fear of truth) and PH §80, 52; PHÄ, 74 (*Angst vor der Wahrheit*: fear of truth).

93. Hegel, *Encyclopaedia* 1, 4–5; ENZ1, 14.

94. "Es ist klar, daß keine Darstellungen für wissenschaftlich gelten können, welche nicht den Gang dieser Methode gehen und ihrem einfachen Rhythmus gemäß sind, denn es ist der Gang der Sache selbst" ("No expositions can be accepted as scientifically valid that do not follow the course of this method and are not in tune with its simple rhythm, for it is the course of the matter itself") (SL, 33; WL1, 50; translation modified).

95. Compare readings that stress the open-endedness of Hegel's system. For a critique of this approach, see Gérard Lebrun, *L'envers de la dialectique: Hegel à la lumière de Nietzsche* (Paris: Seuil, 2004), 218ff, and Žižek, *Less Than Nothing*, 199ff.

96. "Art, considered in its highest vocation, is and remains for us a thing of the past [*ein Vergangenes*]" (Aes1, 11; Äs1, 25). Hegel's lecture transcripts show that Hegel himself never pronounced these legendary words, but the phrase nonetheless remains indissolubly attached to his name and deserves careful parsing. See Annemarie Gethmann-Siefert, *Einführung in Hegels Ästhetik* (Stuttgart: UTB, 2005).

97. SL, 65; WL1, 91.

98. "Wenn der Weltbau krachend einstürzt, treffen die Trümmer noch einen Helden" ("If the world were to fall to pieces, the ruins would still sustain the undaunted") (Flaccus, *Carminum liber tertium*, ode III, verses 7–8). The tension between the German and English translations could not be starker.

99. PH §808, 493; PHÄ, 591.

100. Hegel invites this association with his (untranslated) citation of Aristotle at the end of the last book of the Encyclopaedia: "ἡ δὲ νόησις ἡ καθ᾽ αὑτὴν τοῦ καθ᾽ αὑτὸ ἀρίστου, καὶ ἡ μάλιστα τοῦ μάλιστα. αὑτὸν δὲ νοεῖ ὁ νοῦς κατὰ μετάληψιν τοῦ νοητοῦ· νοητὸς γὰρ γίνεται θιάνων καὶ νοῶν, ὥστε ταὐτὸν νοῦς καὶ νοητόν. τὸ γὰρ δεκτικὸν τοῦ νοητοῦ καὶ τῆς οὐσίας νοῦς, ἐνεργεῖ δὲ ἔχων, ὥστ᾽ ἐκεῖνο μᾶ ον τούτου ὃ δοκεῖ ὁ νοῦς θεῖον ἔχειν, καὶ ἡ θεωρία τὸ ἥδιστον καὶ ἄριστον. εἰ οὖν οὕτως εὖ ἔχει, ὡς ἡμεῖς ποτέ, ὁ θεὸς ἀεί, θαυμαστόν· εἰ δὲ μᾶ ον, ἔτι θαυμασιώτερον. ἔχει δὲ ὧδε. καὶ ζωὴ δέ γε ὑπάρχει· ἡ γὰρ νοῦ ἐνέργεια ζωή, ἐκεῖνο δὲ ἡ ἐνέργεια· ἐνέργεια δὲ ἡ καθ᾽ αὑτὴν ἐκείνου ζωὴ ἀρίστη καὶ ἀΐδιος. φαμὲν δὲ τὸν θεὸν εἶναι ζῷον ἀΐδιον ἄριστον, ὥστε ζωὴ καὶ αἰὼν συνεχὴς ἀΐδιος ὑπάρχει τῷ θεῷ· τοῦτο γὰρ ὁ θεός. ..." Encyclopaedia III, 315; ENZ3 §577, 395 (quoted from Aristotle, Metaphysics 1072b, 18–30).

101. Sigmund Freud, "Introductory Lectures on Psycho-Analysis," in The Standard Edition of the Complete Psychological Works of Sigmund Freud, ed. J. Strachey (New York: Norton, 1966), 29–48.

102. PH §20, 11; PHÄ, 24.

103. In line with this Lacan once remarked about psychoanalysis: "Pas science du tout"—"not at all science," but also "not a science of the all" (Jacques Lacan, Le moment de conclure: Séminaire XXV, http://staferla.free.fr/S25/S25.pdf).

104. This shows that "the dialectical sentence is always at the same time true and false" (Adorno, Einführung in die Dialektik, 71).

105. Although he did not develop this in a consistent manner, Georges Gurvitch spoke of the need for a "dialectical hyperempiricism." Cf. Georges Gurvitch, "Hyper-Empirisme dialectique," Cahiers Internationale de Sociologie 15 (1953): 3–33. We want to argue that in Hegel such hyperempiricism is indistinguishable from a speculative hyper-formalism. Cf. our comment on Deleuze above, n. 22.

106. In his 1914 Conspectus of Hegel's Book "The Science of Logic," Lenin assigns top grades to the end of the Logic ("excellent!," "très bien"). His last annotation, commenting on the very end of the Logic, comes with this startling praise: "Оченьхорошо (и образно)!" ("very good [and graphic]!"). Hegel's endeavor culminates in the convergence of the most abstract with the most concrete. "The concept as thought in general, as universal, as against the particularity of the things ... is their immeasurable abbreviation [die unermeßliche Abbreviatur]" (SL, 19; WL1, 29).

CHAPTER 2

1. Beckett uses this phrase in The Unnameable to refer to Mercier and Camier—just two of the many impossible couples (Hamm and Clov, Didi and Gogo, Pozzo and Lucky) that populate his work. See Samuel Beckett, Three Novels: Molloy, Malone Dies, The Unnamable (New York: Grove Press, 2009), 291. See Mladen Dolar, "Two Shades of Grey" (unpublished typescript).

2. Near bankruptcy, landlady pregnant with his child, war about to break out, and so on.

3. In 1811, when the first volume of the *Logic* was published, Hegel was the head of a *Gymnasium* (high school) in Nuremberg and had just married. He was unhappy because he was increasingly reluctant to be a servant of the university discourse and was forced to give up his initial idea that the *Logic* could serve as a teaching manual. He was also engaged in personal rivalry with his academic enemy Fries, who had just published his own *Logic*. In 1811–1812, Hegel's first child died.

4. Georg Lukács, *The Young Hegel: Studies in the Relation between Dialectics and Economics* (London: Merlin Press, 1975), 449.

5. Dilthey is quoted as having said this at the opening of one of his lectures (he took this judgment as a reason to return to the very early Hegel, even before the *Phenomenology*) (quoted in Hermann Glockner, *Beiträge zum Verständnis und zur Kritik Hegels sowie zur Umgestaltung seiner Geisteswelt* [Bonn: Bouvier, 1965], 485).

6. Hegel, *Letters*, 288 (to Sinclair). "Spanish boots" were torture devices used during the Middle Ages to extort confessions from criminals and apostates by putting immense pressure on the shinbone, often to the point of producing bone fractures. Hegel is torturing spirit (or inciting it to torture itself) to confess its role in world history. Remnants of this machinery produce the forced interpretations that Hegel's philosophy continues to invite. "The labour of the negative" (PH §19, 10; PHÄ, 24) turns philosophy into self-inflicted torture. Only by being forced to constantly confront its own limits does thought become thought. For Kant, pain is the index of a moral act (at least a negative index of the absence of pathological motives). For Hegel, thought begins with pain, yet there is no moral or meaning to be derived from this suffering other than this: thinking hurts.

7. As if anticipating this, Hegel writes in a letter to Niethammer: "The world spirit, this essential [power], proceeds irresistibly like a closely drawn armored phalanx advancing with imperceptible movement, much as the sun through thick and thin. Innumerable light troops flank it on all sides, throwing themselves into the balance for or against its progress, though most of them are entirely ignorant of what is at stake and merely take head blows as from an invisible hand. Yet no lingering lies or make-believe strokes in the air can achieve anything against it. They can perhaps reach the shoelaces of this colossus, and smear on a bit of boot wax or mud, but they cannot untie the laces. Much less can they remove these shoes of gods—which according to Voss's *Mythological Letters*, among other sources, have elastic soles or are even themselves seven-league boots—once the colossus pulls them on. Surely the safest thing to do both externally and internally is to keep one's gaze fixed on the advancing giant" (Hegel, *Letters*, 325).

8. "Ein Buch abstrusesten Inhalts ..." (letter to Niethammer [198] on February 5, 1812; cf. Hegel, *Letters*, 261). Hegel continues the letter, complaining about having to rush through the writing: "But the injustice of the times! ['Injuria temporum!'] I am no academic [*Akademikus*]. I would have needed another year to put it in proper form, but I need money to live." Note that *abstruse* in Latin (*abstrusus*) means literally "hidden" and "concealed," "pushed away" (from *trudere*, "to thrust, push"). Hegel's

self-description captures the hidden thrust and the thrust to hiddenness that drives the expansive self-revelatory movement of the Idea.

9. "In pressing forward to its true existence, consciousness will arrive at a point at which it gets rid of its semblance of being burdened with something alien, with what is only for it, and some sort of 'other', at a point where appearance becomes identical with essence, so that its exposition will coincide at just this point with the authentic Science of Spirit" (PH §89, 56–57; PHÄ, 81). Never one to underestimate the world-historical importance of his own endeavor, Hegel planned to reach this point "by Easter" of 1807 (see Hegel, *Letters*, 74 [to Schelling]); he similarly planned to publish the second edition of the *Logic* by Easter of 1832 (he died six months earlier) (Hegel, *Letters*, 670 [to von Cotta]). Walter Jaeschke notes that Hegel is constantly timing the publication of his work to coincide with resurrection day (Walter Jaeschke, *Hegel-Handbuch: Leben—Werk—Schule* [Stuttgart: Metzler, 2010], 319). In a similar vein, Franz Rosenzweig remarks that all the important moves in Hegel's life took place in the autumn: the moves to Tübingen, to Bamberg, to Heidelberg, to Berlin, and even his last move (death) (Franz Rosenzweig, *Hegel und der Staat* [Berlin: Suhrkamp, 2010], 11).

10. The *Logic* was criticized by Hegel's Nuremberg colleague, the mathematician Johann Wilhelm Andreas Pfaff, for presenting a movement so self-contained that it leaves no remainder: "There is no longer anything else left" (Hegel, *Letters*, 264–265).

11. SL, 753; WL2, 573.

12. Jacques Lacan, *The Seminar of Jacques Lacan*, Book XI, *The Four Fundamental Concepts of Psychoanalysis*, ed. Jacques-Alain Miller, trans. Alan Sheridan (New York: Norton, 1981).

13. This would seem to vindicate Hegel's early view that philosophy addresses that which "seems to have no meaning"—the "idea in its highest simplicity" that exists "in abstraction from everything else [Sie wird keine Bedeutung zu haben scheinen … die Idee in ihrer höchsten Einfachheit vorgetragen. … Diese Abstraction von allen anderen] " (G. W. F. Hegel, "Die Idee des absoluten Wesens …," in *Gesammelte Werke*, vol. 5 [Hamburg: Meiner, 1988], 264).

14. Hegel was only halfheartedly contemplating a second edition of the *Phenomenology* during this period (Wolfgang Bonsiepen and Reinhard Heede, "Anhang," in G. W. F. Hegel, *Gesammelte Werke*, vol. 9, *Phänomenologie des Geistes* [Hamburg: Meiner, 1980], 477).

15. On November 7, 1831, Hegel finished reworking the "doctrine of being" and submitted it to the printer, promising his typesetter to have the remaining revisions of the *Logic* finished within a few weeks. Hegel died one week later, leaving no evidence of having done further revisions on the remaining text.

16. SL, 21; WL1, 33.

17. When asked by Peter just exactly how many times it was necessary to forgive a sinner—seven, for example? (here Peter is already being magnanimous, since conventional etiquette only requires three times)—Jesus replies that one must be prepared to forgive as many as "seven times seventy" times over (Matthew 18:21–22). This is of course if you follow (with Luther) the Septuagint: ἑβδομηκοντάκις (seven times seventy). If Jesus had been quoted in Hebrew, he would no doubt have said שַׁ. מִיעָבְשׁ הָעַב—seven plus seventy (which precisely reverses the formula for revenge in

the Hebrew Bible: if Cain is avenged sevenfold, then Lamech is to be avenged seventy-sevenfold [Genesis 4:24]). This is in fact how the New International Version renders this verse in English: "Jesus answered, 'I tell you, not seven times, but seventy-seven times.'"

18. Wilhelm Raimund Beyer, "Wie die Hegelsche Freundesvereinsausgabe entstand: Aus neu aufgefundenen Briefen der Witwe Hegels," *Deutsche Zeitschrift für Philosophie* 15, no. 5 (1967): 564.

19. The *Encyclopaedia* is described in the first preface as being only a *Grundriss*, a ground plan or outline of the system, and therefore strictly not part of the system itself. The published version was released with an explicit deficiency: It saw "the light of day sooner than [Hegel] was otherwise minded to do" and furthermore "the brevity and compression that an outline makes necessary" requires supplementary "elucidation through oral commentary" (Hegel, *Encyclopaedia* 1, 4; ENZ 1, 14). Whether the explanatory additions inserted in the later editions of the *Encyclopaedia* enable a re-oralization remains debatable. The *Philosophy of Right* is a peculiar hybrid composition, insofar as it is an expansion of the "Objective Spirit" section of the third volume of the *Encyclopaedia*—thus a simultaneous abridgement and enlargement.

20. The title page of the first edition of the *Encyclopaedia* specifies that it is to be used together with his lectures—"zum Gebrauch seiner Vorlesungen." Hegel also calls it a "Leitfaden," a guiding thread, to his lectures (G. W. F. Hegel, *Encyclopaedia* 1, 1; ENZ 1, 11).

21. Given Hegel's legendary Swabian accent and his mesmerizingly idiosyncratic lecturing style ("discourse of the master" in every sense), the bureaucratic style of his textbooks is all the more striking. For a description of Hegel at the podium, see Günther Nicolin, ed., *Hegel in Berichten seiner Zeitgenossen* (Hamburg: Meiner, 1970), 177, 123, 188, 134; see also Walter Kaufmann, *Hegel: A Reinterpretation* (Garden City, NY: Doubleday, 1965), 357–360.

22. Friedrich Nietzsche, *Anti-Education: On the Future of Our Educational Institutions*, ed. Paul Reitter and Chad Wellmon (New York: New York Review of Books, 2016), 65.

23. Jaeschke argues that Hegel's work, in contrast to that of Fichte, Kant, and Schelling, was little known to the broader public in his own lifetime. Its impact unfolded only after his death—after Hegel's twilight had turned to the deepest night—a phase perceived by his pupils as the period in which spirit would finally realize itself. There are material factors: many of Hegel's early writings, including his Jena sketches, were not published, while his published works attracted little attention. By 1829 the *Phenomenology*, printed in 750 copies, was far from being sold out and had created little public interest (it would not be reprinted until 1832). The same fate befell the *Science of Logic*. So Hegel's influence originally sprang from his posthumously published university lectures. The debate is ongoing regarding what kind of system Hegel had in mind when he started to formulate the project at Jena, and how to situate both the *Phenomenology* and *Logic* in relation to the later (Heidelberg and Berlin) university-related works. In some respects the relationship between the books and the lectures is comparable to the relationship between the *Phenomenology* and the

Logic. Some see the lectures as a vulgarization of Hegel's thought, with all the distortions introduced by the unreliable student transcripts (Hegel never actually officially pronounced that beauty is the "sensuous appearance of the idea," for example; cf. Annemarie Gethmann-Siefert, Einführung in Hegels Ästhetik [Stuttgart: UTB, 2005]). Some readers see the Phenomenology as systematically self-undermining and thus inferior to the later system. Some privilege the earlier work as the core of Hegel's thinking, seeing the lectures as mere didactic devices. Some see his system as properly embodied in his lectures (as captured by their transcripts) while the encyclopedic formulation falls short of the oral exposition.

24. Cf. Rosenkranz, Hegels Leben, 202, 214.

25. On some modulations in Hegel's conception of his system, cf. Jean Grondin, Introduction to Metaphysics: From Parmenides to Levinas (New York: Columbia University Press, 2012), 184ff.

26. G. W. F. Hegel, "Logica et Metaphysica," in Gesammelte Werke, vol. 5 (Hamburg: Meiner, 1998), 272.

27. G. W. F. Hegel, "Diese Vorlesungen …" (fragment), in Gesammelte Werke, vol. 5, 259.

28. It is thus poignant that the last text Hegel wrote was the preface to the second edition of the Logic. For this and more context, see Mladen Dolar, "Being and MacGuffin," Crisis and Critique: "Hegel('s) Today" 4, no. 1 (2017): 82–101.

29. G. W. F. Hegel, Selbstanzeige, in PHÄ, 593.

30. See Hegel's announcement for his lectures on logic and metaphysics in 1802 (G. W. F. Hegel, "Vorlesungsmanuskripte: 1816–1831," in Gesammelte Werke, vol. 17 [Hamburg: Meiner, 1987], 5–33).

31. On this see Martin Heidegger, Hegel's Phenomenology of Spirit (Bloomington: Indiana University Press, 1994), 3ff.

32. In 1803–1804, Hegel announced his university lectures on the following classical topics (in which one can see the classificatory structure inherited from traditional academic philosophy): "philosophiae speculativae systema completectens a) Logicam et Metaphysicam, sive Idealismum transcendentalem b) philosophia naturae et c) mentis." On the divisions, see Ernst Vollrath, "Die Gliederung der Metaphysik in eine Metaphysica generalis und eine Metaphysica specialis," Zeitschrift für philosophische Forschung 16 (1962): 258–281. For a list of Hegel's courses at Jena, see G. W. F. Hegel, Briefe von und an Hegel: Dokumente und Materialien zur Bibliographie, ed. Friedhelm Nicolin and Johannes Hoffmeister (Hamburg: Meiner, 1977), 80ff; also see Hegel, Jenaer Systementwürfe, vol. 1, ed. Klaus Düsing and Klaus Kimmerle (Hamburg: Meiner, 1986), iii–xxxv. One should recall that the doctrine of God (theology) was traditionally assigned to the third branch of the three metaphysicae specializ inherited from Aristotle (i.e., (1) cosmologia, (2) psychologia, and (3) theologia naturalis). By the time Hegel launches his mature system, the place of theology seems to have been dispersed between the "general" and the "special" parts of systematic metaphysics. On the one hand, Hegel takes logic, as metaphysica generalis (ontology or "first philosophy," i.e., "scientia entis in genere, seu quantenus ens est"), to be an account of God's thought before the creation. On the other hand, God appears fully adumbrated in the figure of spirit—that is, within the

context of *philosophia mentis* (the philosophy of spirit). So theology is split between the *generalis* and the *specialis*: God himself becomes a floating signifier, shuttling between the universal and the particular parts of the system, without being assigned a designated volume of his own, while the *Logic* splits into a general (ontological) and a specific (theological) aspect.

33. Cf. Jaeschke, *Hegel-Handbuch*, 320.

34. The status of the "little" *Phenomenology* remains vigorously debated. Hyppolite describes the *Encyclopaedia Phenomenology* as presenting "a dialectic of awakening" in which spirit awakens from its natural or merely "anthropological" torpor and nature awakens to its own spiritualization. In other words, by tracking the birth of consciousness rather than taking it as a given, the "little" *Phenomenology* is actually bigger— it covers a larger territory—than its larger homonym (Hyppolite, *Genesis and Structure*, 60). Strikingly, Hegel identifies phenomenology with the subject matter of Kantian philosophy (he is presumably referring to the first *Critique*): "The Kantian philosophy is a phenomenology" (Hegel, *Encyclopaedia III*, §415, 156; ENZ3, 202).

35. The second edition of the *Encyclopaedia Logic* begins differently than the *Science of Logic*, on a seemingly historical note, by rehearsing the "three positions of thought with respect to objectivity" (namely empiricism, Kant, and Jacobi); in taking this historical point of departure, if not in the actual details, the encyclopedic *Logic* seems to be encroaching on the territory of the *Phenomenology*. In the *Encyclopaedia*, Hegel seems to have once and for all separated the *Science of Experience* and the *Phenomenology*; one is introducing the *Logic*, the other the awakening of spirit in the *Realphilosophie*.

36. Hegel, *Encyclopaedia* 1, 45, §19; ENZ1, 67.

37. When asked to prepare a school course on logic while he is working on the *Science of Logic*, Hegel rejects the offer, stating that "a new science cannot be presented in a textbook for the Gymnasium [Eine neue Wissenschaft kann nicht in einem Lehrbuche für Gymnasien vorgetragen werden]" (Hegel, *Letters*, 175). Why is the science new? Previously there had been no science that portrayed the creation of the world and universe from the perspective of the creator.

38. Immanuel Kant, *Critique of Pure Reason*, trans. and ed. Paul Guyer and Allen W. Wood (Cambridge: Cambridge University Press, 1998), A838/B866, 694.

39. The confusion deepened when in 1873 the shorter *Logic* was translated simply as *The Logic of Hegel* (*The Logic of Hegel*, trans. William Wallace [Oxford: Clarendon Press, 1873]) and then in 1894 as *Prolegomena to the Study of Hegel's Philosophy and Especially His Logic* (*Prolegomena to the Study of Hegel's Philosophy and Especially His Logic*, trans. William Wallace [Oxford: Clarendon Press, 1894]). The identical naming of the two *Logics* (Hegel had confused matters at the outset by calling both the "big" and the "little" Logic the *Science of Logic*) either led to the two works being conflated or to the later book being assigned the task of introducing the earlier one–a task previously supposed to be fulfilled by the *Phenomenology*.

40. We owe this insightful observation and other helpful archival assistance to Annette Sell from the Hegel-Archiv in Bochum, Germany.

41. Ernst Bloch remarked: "There are paragraphs, divisions of paragraphs, quotable material, all trimmed for the needs of teaching, although it did however not get easier. The condensation of the material in the *Encyclopaedia of the Philosophical Sciences* makes many things entirely incomprehensible" (Ernst Bloch, *Leipziger Vorlesungen zur Geschichte der Philosophie: Neuzeitliche Philosophie II: Deutscher Idealismus, die Philosophie des 18. Jahrhunderts*, vol. 4 [Frankfurt am Main: Suhrkamp, 1985], 265–266).

42. It is interesting that the standard English translation of the *Phenomenology* (but not the *Logic*) is presented in numbered paragraphs that do not exist in the German. The format not only perhaps reflects the empiricist heritage of Anglo-American philosophy but possibly also captures a secret "encyclopedic" tendency latent in the *Phenomenology* itself. This tendency is often expressed in the different assumptions about what the project is ultimately supposed to achieve—an ambiguity linked to the untranslatability of *absolutes Wissen*: either absolute *knowing* or absolute *knowledge*, either an activity of thinking or a body of achieved results, a distinction that goes back to the Kantian opposition between *Philosophie* (philosophy) and *Philosophieren* (philosophizing).

43. A symptom of this absence of relation is that the very category of relation has been eviscerated in the *Encyclopaedia Logic*: whereas the *Science of Logic* unfolds this category by recourse to the concept of the absolute and its modalities, the *Encyclopaedia* begins with so-called substantial relations, moves to causal relations, and finally ends with "interdependency." The *Encyclopaedia* thus appears to take substantial relations for granted and to lack any strong concept of relation—that is, any way of relating what is absolute (that is, truly independent).

44. The externality pervading the *Encyclopaedia* has affinities with the form of the negative judgment in Kant—a simple absence of relation or mediation that can always be converted into a positive judgment. In contrast, we are suggesting that the abyss between the *Phenomenology* and the *Logic* resembles an infinite judgment in the Kantian sense. Whereas the transitions within the *Encyclopaedia* display a simple lack of relation ("there is no relation" between the categories), the transition from the *Phenomenology* to the *Logic* is marked by an active nonrelation ("*there is* no relation" between one book and the other). For this idea of active nonrelation, see Slavoj Žižek, "A Modest Plea for a Hegelian Reading of Christianity," in Slavoj Žižek and John Milbank, *The Monstrosity of Christ: Paradox or Dialectic?* (Cambridge, MA: MIT Press, 2009), 33–34.

45. Cf. SL, 31; WL1, 46. The *Encyclopaedia* is the only published work of which Hegel prepared three editions during his lifetime as he kept adding further and further clarifications. Unlike with the re-editions of his actual books, he even tried to outsource these revisions to his former students, only finishing the job himself after they failed to meet his expectations. The *Encyclopaedia* was designed to be repeated in lectures and destined to be republished in more and more editions—a potentially endless repetition of a text whose vitality depended on its being incessantly reawakened. One could note many further differences between the two versions of the *Logic*, but we are here focusing only on the ones with immediate systematic consequences, leaving aside the fact that the distinction between objective and subjective logic is undone in the later *Logic*. An instructive discussion can be found in Jaeschke, *Hegel-Handbuch*, 327ff.

46. This is perhaps related to a peculiar modification of the logical category of life as we move from the *Science of Logic* to the *Encyclopaedia*. Whereas the *Science of Logic* discusses the living individual, the life process, and the species, the *Encyclopaedia Logic* barely touches on the concept of the species, which is only properly elaborated in the *Philosophy of Nature* (the second volume of the *Encyclopaedia*). The discussion of life is so condensed in the *Encyclopaedia Logic* that it is almost completely pushed out of the sphere of logic and reemerges in the sphere of nature—that is, in the realm of contingency.

47. Cf. SL 753; WL2, 573.

48. The "Reason" chapter, which had run to over one hundred pages in 1806, is condensed in the *Encyclopaedia* into a couple of paragraphs.

49. Art, religion, and philosophy, which had occupied the last part of the *Phenomenology of Spirit*, are even further separated from the encyclopedic *Phenomenology* and are given a distinct section of their own in the concluding chapter on absolute spirit.

50. In the third volume of the *Science of Logic*, published in 1816, Hegel seems to be softening his original claims for the systematic importance of the *Phenomenology of Spirit*: phenomenology finds its "higher truth" in philosophical psychology, "synonymous with the *doctrine of spirit*" (SL, 694; WL2, 494). This seems to diminish the stature of the earlier text and to weaken the claims made on its behalf in the *Phenomenology* and even in the earlier volume of the *Logic*, published just four years earlier. Pinkard points to the curricular pressures that Hegel was facing in starting his duties as a Gymnasium teacher in Nuremberg in the wake of the Napoleonic invasion. The directives of Niethammer's "General Normative" for Gymnasium pedagogy (as well as the time pressures caused by the late opening of the 1808–1809 academic year) forced Hegel to prepare a course covering "Introduction to Philosophy alongside Logical Drills" at the last minute. (The material corresponding to the second half of the *Phenomenology* fell more or less under the rubric of the second course assigned to Hegel, which was on "Religion, Right, and Duties.") To move quickly from propaedeutics to logic within the time frame of a single course, Hegel was "forced to cut short his dictation based on the *Phenomenology*, rapidly concluding with a section called 'Universal Self-Consciousness' and a one-paragraph dictation that in his marginal notes he titled 'Reason'" (Terry Pinkard, *Hegel: A Biography* [Cambridge: Cambridge University Press, 2000], 334). Pinkard notes that by the following academic year, Hegel had decided to continue with this plan except that instead of moving directly from "Phenomenology" to "Logic" he moved first to "Psychology" (identified in his dictation, as it will be a few years later in the third book of the *Logic*, as the "authentic doctrine of spirit"; ibid., 336)—a sequence he would continue to follow during his entire period in Nuremberg, and in all three versions of the *Encyclopaedia*.

51. Cf. Hegel, *Encyclopaedia* 1, §10, 33–34; ENZ1, 53–54.

52. PH §70, 43; PHÄ, 65.

53. PH §5, 3; PHÄ, 14.

54. "I have just noticed that the enclosed slip, which I had wanted to enclose yesterday and whose words I indicated are to appear on the back of the title sheet, has remained behind" (Hegel, November 13, 1831; *Letters*, 557).

55. Cicero, *Tusculan Disputations* (Cambridge, MA: Harvard University Press, 1927), Book II, chap. 1.

56. The fate and the precise contents of this slip of paper are impossible to reconstruct; it seems not to have been sent or not to have survived. One editor of the *Encyclopaedia* in any case decided to add a motto (from Sophocles) that Hegel had never asked for.

57. Hegel, *Encyclopaedia* 1, 18; ENZ 1, 33.

58. "The isolated situation which you seem to wish, with Cicero, to assign philosophy … it is far livelier … not merely to attack rationalism in general, in the abstract, but also to attack the rationalism of specific professors. Personality then becomes an issue only if contingencies are mixed in that have nothing to do with their teaching" (Hegel, *Letters*, 545).

59. Hegel repeats the sentiment in the second preface to the *Logic*: it is doubtful "whether the noisy clamor of the day and the deafening chatter of a conceit that takes pride in confining itself to just these interests, might still leave room for partaking in the dispassionate calm of a knowledge dedicated to thought alone" (SL, 22; WL 1, 34).

60. Philippe Lacoue-Labarthe and Jean-Luc Nancy, *The Literary Absolute: The Theory of Literature in German Romanticism* (Albany: SUNY Press, 1988).

61. G. W. F. Hegel, "Notiz zur Überarbeitung des Werks von 1807," in *Gesammelte Werke*, vol. 9, *Phänomenologie des Geistes*, ed. Wolfgang Bonsiepen and Reinhard Heede (Hamburg: Meiner, 1980), 448. Shortly after finishing the text, Hegel remarked that he wanted "to here and there clean the ship from ballast and to set it afloat" (November 16, 1807 [to Niethammer]; Hegel, *Letters*, 119).

62. "Notiz zur Überarbeitung des Werks von 1807."

63. Ibid.

64. It is the "*logical* nature that animates the spirit, that moves and works within it [*in ihm treibt und wirkt*]" (SL, 17; WL 1, 27).

65. Cf. PH §29, 17; PHÄ, 33. The *Phenomenology* presents the "embodied shape [of spirit's historical unfolding] reduced to abbreviated, simple determinations of thought."

66. SL, 37; WL 1, 55.

67. Cf., for example, Hermann Glockner, "Georg Wilhelm Friedrich Hegel: Entwicklung und Schicksal der Hegelschen Philosophie," in G. W. F. Hegel, *Sämtliche Werke*, vol. 22, ed. Hermann Glockner (Stuttgart–Bad Cannstatt: frommann-holzboog, 1964).

68. "The Hegelian dialectics was often—but superficially—assimilated to a *mobilism*. And it is undoubtedly true that the critique of the fixity of determinations can give rise to the conviction of an infinite dialectical process: the limited being has to disappear again and always, and its destruction extends to the very limit of our sight. … However, at this level, we are still dealing with a simple happening [*Geschehen*] to which one cannot confer the inner unity of a history [*Geschichte*]" (Lebrun, *L'envers de la dialectique*, 11).

69. Although he meant it unironically and sympathetically, Pöggeler raises the question whether the *Phenomenology* can be read as "a hermeneutic of the occidental world" similar to Tocqueville's (Otto Pöggeler, "Die Komposition der Phänomenologie des Geistes," in *Materialien zu Hegels "Phänomenologie des Geistes*," ed. Hans Friedrich Fulda and Dieter Henrich [Frankfurt am Main: Suhrkamp, 1973], 372).

70. PH §26, 14; PHÄ, 29.

71. Ludwig Wittgenstein, *Tractatus Logico-Philosophicus* (London: Routledge, 2001), 6.54, 89.

72. Cf. Hyppolite, *Genesis and Structure*, 56.

73. Rudolf Haym, *Hegel und seine* Zeit (Hildesheim: Olms, 1962), 234.

74. Otto Pöggeler, "Die Komposition," 329.

75. While working on the *Grundrisse* in 1857-58, Marx planned to develop his *Critique of Political Economy* (the title of his project in its entirety) in six volumes: capital, property, wage labor, state, foreign trade, and world market. See Karl Marx, *A Contribution to the Critique of Political Economy* (Moscow: Progress Publishers, 1977), 1. In the published editions of Marx's work the distinction between what Marx refers to as book and volume becomes obscure (he planned to publish volume 1 of *Capital* as book 1; books 2 and 3 were supposed to appear in a single volume, but as edited by Engels they each appeared as separate books and volumes). See Michael Heinrich, "Capital after MEGA: Discontinuities, Interruptions, and New Beginnings," *Crisis and Critique* 3, no. 3 (2016): 93–138.

76. "Unity" has always already gone forth "into twosomeness [*Zweiheit*]" (PH §138, 84). Cf. Mladen Dolar, "One Divides into Two," http://www.e-flux.com/journal/one-divides-into-two/.

77. Alongside the frequently noted break between the fourth and fifth chapters, and between the fifth and sixth chapters, there is also the puzzling break between the sixth and seventh chapters of the *Phenomenology*. Hyppolite characterized the transition to the "Religion" chapter as a leap from a phenomenology to a "noumenology," suggesting that the limits of phenomenology (that is, the limits of experience) are encountered in forgiveness.

78. Theodor Haering, "Die Entstehungsgeschichte der Phänomenologie des Geistes," in *Verhandlungen des dritten Hegelkongresses* (Tübingen: J. C. B. Mohr, 1934), 126. Along similar lines, Robert Solomon stated that it is "a slapdash manuscript. … Hegel did not know what he was trying to do" (R.C. Solomon, *In the Spirit of Hegel* [Oxford: Oxford University Press, 1983], 156).

79. For a helpful reconstruction, see Eckart Förster, *The Twenty-Five Years of Philosophy* (Cambridge, MA: Harvard University Press, 2012), 350ff.

80. Hegel, *Encyclopaedia* 1, 64 (translation modified); ENZ 1, 92.

81. Karl Hegel, quoted in Förster, *The Twenty-Five Years*, 350. Also see Bonsiepen and Heede, "Anhang," 492.

82. Otto Pöggeler, "Die Komposition," 334.

83. "Die Phänomenologie demnach wird zum Palimpsest: über und zwischen dem ersten Text entdecken wir einen zweiten" (Haym, *Hegel und seine Zeit*, 250).

84. Günther Nicolin,ed., *Hegel in Berichten seiner Zeitgenossen* (Hamburg: Meiner, 1970), 87.

85. PHH, 73; VPG, 104.

86. See Friedhelm Nicolin, "Zum Titelproblem der 'Phänomenologie des Geistes,'" *Hegel-Studien* 4 (1967): 113–123. Heidegger will see this double naming as the expression of Hegel's circle of circles, where the end repeats the beginning in a different form: "The proposition 'The experience of consciousness is thoroughgoing skepticism' and the proposition 'Phenomenology is the Golgotha of absolute spirit' join the completion of the work to its beginning. … Because phenomenology is experience, the beingness of beings, it is therefore the gathering of the appearing-to-itself upon the appearance out of the seeming of the absolute" (Martin Heidegger, "Hegel's Concept of Experience," in *Off the Beaten Track*, ed. and trans. Julian Young and Kenneth Haynes [Cambridge: Cambridge University Press, 2002], 152).

87. Cf. Hegel, *Selbstanzeige*, 593.

88. PH §89, 56–57; PHÄ, 80–81.

89. Pöggeler, "Die Komposition," 351.

90. Hegel, *Letters*, 114.

91. Cited in Richard Kroner, "Hegel heute," *Hegel-Studien* 1 (1961): 135.

92. Hegel, *Letters*, 95. The review Hegel complains about was written by his enemy Fries (whom Hegel first attacked in the first edition of the *Logic* and would attack more strenuously in the preface to the *Philosophy of Right*).

93. SL, 32; WL1, 48. "The discipline apparently most distant to life" (Hans Friedrich Fulda, "Zur Logik der Phänomenologie von 1807," 391).

94. See Douglas Ainslie, "Translator's Introduction" to Benedetto Croce, *What Is Living and What Is Dead of the Philosophy of Hegel* (New York: Russell & Russell, 1969), xi. Beatrice Longuenesse identifies the transition to the subjective logic as the point where Hegel assumes the "Standpoint of God" (a strange complaint, given that Hegel himself had expressly identified this divine standpoint as the essential starting point of the book (SL, 29). See Beatrice Longuenesse, *Hegel's Critique of Metaphysics* (Cambridge: Cambridge University Press, 2007), 165–191. A similar critique can be found in Vittorio Hösle, *Hegels System: Der Idealismus der Subjektivität und das Problem der Intersubjektivität* (Hamburg: Meiner, 1998).

95. "How can there be seemingly 'extralogical' moments in this logic?" (Annette Sell, *Der lebendige Begriff: Leben und Logik bei G.W. F. Hegel* [Freiburg: Karl Alber, 2013], 13).

96. E.g., SL 40–41; WL1, 59 and Hph 3, 438–441; VGP3, 337–338.

97. Kant, *Critique of Pure Reason*, A81–82; B106–107, 213.w

98. Jean Hyppolite, *Logic and Existence* (New York: SUNY Press, 1997), 58.

99. SL, 29; WL1, 44.

100. Consciousness "works through … the whole of experience" (Hyppolite, *Genesis and Structure*, 10).

101. Cf. Jacques Lacan, *Encore: The Seminar of Jacques Lacan, Book XX, On Feminine Sexuality: The Limits of Love and Knowledge, 1972–1973*, ed. Jacques-Alain Miller, trans. Bruce Fink (New York: Norton, 1988).

102. G. W. F. Hegel, "Fragment of a System," in ETW, 312; translation modified. G. W. F. Hegel, "Systemfragment von 1800," in *Werke*, vol. 1 (Frankfurt am Main: Suhrkamp, 1986), 422.

103. See Benedetto Croce, *What Is Living and What Is Dead of the Philosophy of Hegel* (New York: Russell & Russell, 1969), 193. Pöggeler describes the relation between the two books as taking the form of a "Zwiesel," a tree that has two trunks but one root (Pöggeler, "Die Komposition," 359).

104. "It develops to the full in two directions—the 'Science of the Phenomenology of Spirit' and the 'Science of Logic'" (Heidegger, "Hegel's Concept of Experience," 142–143).

105. "One might say that the greatness of Hegel's philosophy lies essentially in that these two quasi-trunks of dialectical thinking [*diese beiden Stämme gewissermaßen des dialektischen Denkens*], on one side the logical-speculative and on the other the trunk of experience, which I elaborated for you a moment ago with regard to the rift [*Zerissenheit*] and to alienation, that these two trunks are brought together, that their inner unity is presented within dialectics" (Adorno, *Einführung in die Dialektik*, 108–109).

106. Already the young Hegel had indicated the necessity for a twofold take on "being": "Being must be taken from a double point of view [by reflection], since reflection supposes that that to which it gives a reflected form is at the same time not reflected; i.e., it takes Being (i) to be the single thing in which there is no partition or opposition, and (ii) at the same time to be the single thing which is potentially separable and infinitely divisible into parts" (ETW, 257, translation modified; GC, 345). There is a crucial logical difference between the double and the Two: the double is two times One, whereas it is unclear how many precisely the Two is (it introduces a difference that makes the count as such problematic). See Lorenzo Chiesa, *The Not-Two: Logic and God in Lacan* (Cambridge, MA: MIT Press, 2016).

107. Alain Badiou remarks: "Dialectics states that there is the Two, and intends to infer the One from it as a moving division. Metaphysics posits the One, and forever gets tangled up in deriving from it the Two. There are others … who posit the Multiple, which is never more than a semblance since positing the Multiple amounts to presupposing the One as substance and excluding the Two from it" (Alain Badiou, *Theory of the Subject* [London: Continuum, 2009], 22).

108. PH §572, 348; PHÄ, 423.

109. Lukács rightly emphasized the nonpsychological force of these affects: "There are no moods in Hegel's philosophy" (Georg Lukács, *The Young Hegel*, 456). Very late in his life, contemplating the new edition of the *Logic*, Hegel expressed doubt "whether the noisy clamor of the day … might still leave room for partaking in the dispassionate calm of a knowledge dedicated to thought alone" (SL, 22; WL 1, 34).

110. This raises the question of what the term following this prefix signifies on its own. In the case of *Ver-stand* (understanding), the prefix indicates a displacement of everything standing and stable; Hegel describes the infinite power of the understanding to dissect and fluidify. But what is -*nunft* on its own? In Middle High German this term (from *nehmen*) designated the grasping of an opportunity—to take the liberty to do something, but also to steal.

111. Hegel notes "that the schism that arises in one of the parties and seems to be a misfortune, demonstrates rather that party's good fortune [daß also die in einer Partei entstehende Zwietracht, welche ein Unglück scheint, vielmehr ihr Glück beweist]" (PH §575, 351; PHÄ, 425). Happiness sometimes lies in dis-pair.

112. Lacan, *Anxiety*, 69ff. We encounter here what Günter Wohlfart calls "*Einzweideutigkeit*": an unambiguous ambiguity (Wohlfart, *Der Punkt*, 20).

113. Kant, *Critique of Pure Reason*, B29, A15.

114. Cf. Theodor W. Adorno, *Kant's Critique of Pure Reason*, trans. Rodney Livingstone (Stanford, CA: Stanford University Press, [1959] 2001). This is already the position of Carl Christian Erhard Schmid, one of the earliest committed Kantians (who brought Kant's thought to Novalis and others).

115. PH §178, 111 (translation modified); PHÄ, 145.

116. Letter of May 1, 1807, in Hegel, *Letters*, 80; *Briefe*, 161. Surprisingly, this is the definition Hegel gives of modern comedy. There is a "coming and going [Herüber und Hinüber] [that] makes possible ... infinitely many meaningful bewildering windings" (*Aes*, 1234, translation modified); *Äs3*, 570–571.

117. Hegel remarks that one of the reasons the middle section of the *Logic*, supposedly mediating between the beginning and the end, between being and concept, "is the most difficult ... part of the *Logic*," is because it "both assumes the distinctions as independent and at the same time posits their relationality as well" (Hegel, *Encyclopaedia 1*, §114, 179; ENZ1, 235–236).

118. SL, 113; WL1, 156.

119. SL, 30; WL1, 45. One can see this affliction at work not only in Kant's theoretical and practical philosophy, but also in his attempt, in the *Third Critique*, to connect these two spheres.

120. SL, 30; WL1, 45. Translation modified.

121. Cf. Lacan, *Le Seminaire, livre X, L'Angoisse* (Paris: Seuil, 2004), 15.

122. Martin Heidegger, "Aristoteles-Hegel-Seminar," in *Gesamtausgabe 4, no. 86: Seminare: Hegel-Schelling* (Tübingen: Klostermann, 2011), 39.

123. Hegel, *Letters*, 150. In the same letter he compares the combination to the bad taste of drinking sherry in the same mouthful as drinking tea (ibid.). (This can be contrasted to the empty taste of "poetic" pseudophilosophy, which Hegel compares to drinking chicory instead of coffee, and described as "neither fish nor fowl" [PH §68, 42; PHÄ 64]).

124. Hegel, *Letters*, 12.

125. Similarly, every sentence can be parsed in two ways: both as an ordinary proposition and as a speculative sentence. This is why Hegel insists on the need to read the *Phenomenology* at least twice (the same requirement holds for the *Science of Logic*). This double reading applies potentially not only to every sentences but to every element of the text: paragraph, word, punctuation. See Hegel's notice for the *Phenomenology* in the *Bamberger Zeitung*, discussed below.

126. Letter to Niethammer, November 1807; Hegel, *Letters*, 149.

127. SL, 83–84; WL 1, 116.

128. SL, 337; W 1, 273.

129. SL, 193; WL 1, 113.

130. See Comay, "Repetition and Resistance," *Research in Phenomenology* 45 (2015): 237–266.

131. SL, 112; WL. In German Hegel speaks of the "Rückfall in die vorherige, vergebens aufgehobene Bestimmung" (WL 1, 154).

132. Dieter Henrich rightly claims that the end of the *Logic* "is supposed to ground the insight into the necessity of a beginning of unsublatable immediacy" (Dieter Henrich, *Hegel im Kontext* [Frankfurt am Main: Suhrkamp, 1975], 93).

133. PH §73, 47; PHÄ, 69.

134. "All that we have to do to ensure that the beginning will remain immanent to the science of this knowledge is to consider, or rather, setting aside every reflection, simply to take up, *what is there before us*" (SL, 47; WL, 68).

135. PH §807, 492; PHÄ, 590.

136. PH §808, 492; PHÄ, 591.

137. Cf. Alain Badiou, *Le Séminaire—L'infini: Aristote, Spinoza, Hegel, 1984–1985* (Paris: Fayard, 2016), 300.

138. Cf. PH §165, 103; PHÄ 135–136.

139. "Antinomies really constitute all too poor a dialectic. Nothing beyond tortuous antitheses. I have, I believe, elucidated them in my Logic" (Hegel, *Letters*, 281).

140. PH §89, 56–57; PHÄ, 81. (The point comes through only in translation; the ellipsis is elliptically abbreviated in the original …)

141. Cf. Markus Semm, *Der springende Punkt in Hegels System* (Munich: Boer, 1994).

142. "If the world were to fall to pieces, the ruins would still sustain the undaunted" (SL, 65; WL 1, 91). For a discussion see Mladen Dolar, "Si fractus illabatur orbis, impavidum ferient ruinae," https://www.youtube.com/watch?v=liDeHZh4qJg&t=3271s.

143. SL, 29; WL 1, 44.

CHAPTER 3

1. The Miller translations of both the *Logic* and the *Phenomenology* omit the mark. See PH §808, 493, and SL 1, 82. Surprisingly the more recent and much improved edition

of the *Logic*, translated by di Giovanni, does not elide the dash, but it does omit the immediately preceding comma (SL, 59). The newest translation of the *Phenomenology* by Pinkard, forthcoming with Cambridge University Press, is in this respect (as in so many other respects) the most accurate (cf. https://www.marxists.org/reference/archive/hegel/works/ph/pinkard-translation-of-phenomenology.pdf). For further discussion of the destiny of this punctuation mark in various translations see below, 138, n.64.

2. Walter Benjamin, "The Task of the Translator," in *Selected Writings*, vol. 1, 1913–1926, ed. Marcus Bullock and Michael W. Jennings (Cambridge, MA: Harvard University Press, 1996).

3. PH §808, 493; PHÄ, 493. Translation modified. We have removed the personifying majuscules and replaced the deifying pronouns him and He with the impersonal and neuter pronouns it and its (referring to the antecedent spirit/Geist). We have also restored the dash immediately preceding the verse, which Miller has incorrected deleted.

4. SL, 59 (translation modified); WL I, 82.

5. Markus Semm, remarking that this sentence is not a proper sentence, for this reason takes "Pure being and pure nothing are the same" to be the actual first sentence of the *Logic* (Semm, *Der springende Punkt in Hegels System*, 80).

6. SL, 12; WL I, 20.

7. SL, 81–82; WL I, 114.

8. SL, 12; WL I, 20.

9. Sigmund Freud, "The Antithetical Meaning of Primal Words," in *The Standard Edition of the Complete Psychological Works of Sigmund Freud*, vol. 11, ed. James Strachey (London: Hogarth Press, [1910] 1957), 155–161.

10. Freud will similarly suggest that one only finds something accidentally when one was in some sense already looking for it, if only unconsciously (Sigmund Freud, "The Psychopathology of Everyday Life," in *The Standard Edition of the Complete Psychological Works of Sigmund Freud*, vol. 6, ed. James Strachey (London: Hogarth Press, [1901] 1960), 215ff).

11. PHH, 11 (translation modified); VPG, 23.

12. This is why there is no philosophical lexicon that a student should rely on when reading Hegel. Not every appearance of the word *aufheben* is philosophically noteworthy: often it simply refers to getting rid of something. *Erinnerung* is sometimes an ordinary memory. There are no terms of art in Hegel. Sometimes a cigar is just a cigar. Not every punctuation mark is of speculative interest. This is what makes the interpretive project so challenging.

13. Cf. Hegel's statement at Heidelberg: "The wise spirit, by expressing a universal, has expressed something that contains the concrete in itself. Its sentence is approved, tested, and purified through long experience. Another spirit can articulate the same sentence, yet here it simply entails something universal separated from the concrete"

(G. W. F. Hegel, *Vorlesungen über Logik und Metaphysik: Heidelberg 1817* [Hamburg: Meiner, 1992], 9).

14. PH §63, 39; PHÄ, 60.

15. Werner Hamacher, *Pleroma—Reading in Hegel* (Stanford, CA: Stanford University Press, 1998), 6.

16. See Robert Bernasconi, "'We Philosophers': *Barbaros medeis eisito*," in *Endings: Questions of Memory in Hegel and Heidegger*, ed. Rebecca Comay and John McCumber (Evanston, IL: Northwestern University Press, 1999), 77–96.

17. PH §58, 35; PHÄ, 56.

18. Hegel remarks that "picture-thinking [*Vorstellung*]" finds the speculative sentence "just as irksome as formalistic thinking" (PH §58, 35; PHÄ, 56). In fact, formalism is another version of picture thinking: the latter assumes a stable framework (S is P) within which it can find a passing content; the former disregards all content and turns its form of presentation (S is P) into another content.

19. PH §63, 39; PHÄ, 60.

20. "The study of philosophy is as much hindered by the conceit that will not argue as it is by the argumentative approach" (PH §67, 41; PHÄ, 62).

21. PH §60, 37; PHÄ, 62.

22. PH §62, 38; PHÄ, 59.

23. Hegel himself occasionally uses the language of the syncope: "The counterthrust in the rhythm of tact and melody comes out the clearest in what are called syncopations" (*Aes*, 918; *Äs3*, 170).

24. PH § 60, 37; PHÄ, 58 (translation modified). Hegel gives a formal account of this in the *Logic*: "'A is' is a beginning that envisages something different before it to which the 'A is' would proceed, but the 'A is' never gets to it. 'A is—A': the difference is only a disappearing and the movement goes back into itself" (SL, 360; translation modified; WL2, 44). Hamacher comments: "This expectation is in Hegel's modified writing of the proposition of identity as A is—A marked by a dash, a pause, a waiting sign. This demonstrates: A is, going out to this indeterminate other, already at it as its predicate and thus different from A. In this other it has gained a determination that does not belong to it as it was initially. But the proposition that is suspended in the dash and in the otherness it indexes even moves beyond this determination. The expected or thought difference disappears and gives way to a second A in which the proposition finds its beginning confirmed" (Werner Hamacher, "Das Nicht im Satz [der Identität]," unpublished typescript).

25. The experience of a counterthrust is not limited to philosophy, even though philosophy alone is able to account for this everyday experience. In a letter to Niethammer, Hegel describes how two forces directed toward one goal can hinder each other from attaining either goal (he had wanted to write earlier to tell Niethammer about his newborn baby, but had to take care of the children, which he could not do properly because he wanted to write the letter). Hegel then writes: "Such a bizarrerie of the relationship [*eine solche Bizarrerie des Verhältnisses*] can only be explained by philosophy

alone; incidentally even our experience familiarizes us with such counterthrust and offers us many examples of it" (Hegel, letter to Niethammer, July 19, 1812, in *Briefe*, vol. 1, 413).

26. G. W. F. Hegel, "[Über] Friedrich Heinrich Jacobis Werke. Dritter Band," in *Werke*, vol. 4 (Frankfurt am Main: Suhrkamp, 1982), 437.

27. PH §58, 36; PHÄ, 56. Hegel distinguishes this rhythm from the idle oscillation of *Räsonnieren*—"the subjective seesaw of arguments that sway back and forth [*subjektives Schaukelsystem von hin-und herübergehendem Räsonnement*], where basic import is lacking" (Hegel, *Encyclopaedia* 1, §81, 128; ENZ1, 172).

28. SL, 697; WL2, 498.

29. PH §48, 28; PHÄ, 47.

30. Ibid. Translation modified.

31. PH §13, 8. Translation modified; PHÄ, 20.

32. Slavoj Žižek, "Philosophy, the 'Unknown Knowns,' and the Public Use of Reason," *Topoi* 25, no. 1–2 (2006): 137–142.

33. Hegel, *Encyclopaedia* 3, §459 Anm., 215–218; ENZ3, 271–276; and see Jacques Derrida, "The Pit and the Pyramid: Introduction to Hegel's Semiology," in *Margins of Philosophy*, trans. Alan Bass (Chicago: University of Chicago Press, 1982), 69–108, and Jacques Derrida, *Of Grammatology*, trans. Gayatri Chakravorty Spivak (Baltimore: Johns Hopkins University Press, 1976), 24–26. Note that Hegel's negative comments on writing are generally confined to oral remarks—what he purportedly said in class rather than what he wrote.

34. Derrida, "The Pit and the Pyramid," 71.

35. Derrida, *Of Grammatology*, 26.

36. Hegel, *Encyclopaedia* 1, §98, 155; ENZ1, 206.

37. It is Epicurus and Aristotle who will assign weight and a body to the atoms, whereas Democritus claims that they have no weight whatsoever.

38. Wismann demonstrated that the characteristic traits Democritus assigned to the atoms—*rhysmos* (figure), *diathige* (succession), and *tropé* (position)—correspond to the fundamental features of writing as an incessant combinatory recoil: *rhysmos* designates the practice of writing, *diathigè* the specific configuration of letters, and *trope* names the "return," the looping back to where the movement started that is necessary to generate any signification (Wismann, *Les avatars du vide: Démocrite et les fondements du atomisme* [Paris: Hermann Editeurs, 2010], 28ff). Atoms themselves are nothing but "points swinging in the void" (ibid., 32).

39. Lucretius, *On the Nature of Things and the Universe* (Oxford: Oxford University Press, 1997), Book I, 825–830, 26.

40. Ibid., Book II, 142.

41. "Idealism in the higher sense, not [merely] subjective" (HPh1, 303–304; VGP1, 359). And: "The atom and the void are just simple terms. But we cannot here see

or find more than the formal fact [*dies Formelle*] that quite general and simple principles, the antithesis between the one and continuity, are represented." (HPh1, 306; VGP1, 362). Hegel's praise is all the more notable in that (like Kant before him) he is critical of the theory of the *clinamen* as a purely chance event: "The repulsion which shows itself in the concept of the One was assumed to be its fundamental force; it is not attraction, however, but chance, i.e., what is without thought, that is supposed to bring them together" (Hegel, *Encyclopaedia* 1, §98, 155; ENZ1, 206).

42. Cf. Wismann, *Les avatars du vide*, 32–33.

43. "The atom can be seen materially, but it is unsensual, purely intellectual" (HPh1, 303; VGP1, 358).

44. Dolar, "The Atom and the Void—from Democritus to Lacan," *Filozofski Vestnik* 44, no. 2 (2013): 22.

45. Žižek, *Less Than Nothing*, 59.

46. Dolar, "The Atom and the Void," 23. Dolar points out that *den* was translated as *othing* into English, as *ichts* into German, and as *ien* into French. Both Dolar and Žižek point to a comparable passage in Lacan: "Nothing, perhaps? No—perhaps nothing, but not nothing" (Jacques Lacan, *The Seminar of Jacques Lacan*, Book XI, *The Four Fundamental Concepts of Psychoanalysis*, ed. Jacques-Alain Miller, trans. Alan Sheridan [New York: Norton, 1981], 62).

47. Alain Badiou and Barbara Cassin, *Il n'y a pas de rapport sexuel* (Paris: fayard, 2010), 83.

CHAPTER 4

1. PH §71, 45; PHÄ 67.

2. Hegel, letter to Schelling, November 2, 1800 (*Briefe* 1, 56).

3. "Time is the Concept that *is there* [*da ist*] and which presents itself to consciousness as empty intuition; for this reason, Spirit necessarily appears in Time, and it appears in Time just as long as it has not *grasped* its pure Concept, that is, has not annulled [*tilgt*] Time" (PH §801, 487; PHÄ 584). The verb *tilgen* (with its hint of abstract negativity) is replaced in the next sentence with the more accommodating term *aufheben*: "[Time] is the *outer*, intuited pure Self which is *not grasped* by the Self, the merely intuited Concept; when this latter grasps itself it supersedes [*aufhebt*] its Time-form, conceptualizes its intuiting, and is a conceptualizing and conceptualized intuiting" (translation modified).

4. *Encyclopaedia* II, §258, *Zusätze*, 231; ENZ2, 50.

5. HPh3, 434; VGP3, 340–341.

6. HPh3, 461; VGP3, 369.

7. "The Kronos which engenders all and destroys that to which it gives birth" (*Encyclopaedia* II §258, Anm 230; ENZ2 49.)

8. "Time does not resemble a container in which everything is as it were borne away and swallowed up in the flow of a stream. Time is merely this abstraction of destroying. Things are in time because they are finite; they do not pass away because they

are in time, but are themselves that which is temporal. Temporality is their objective determination. It is therefore the process of actual things that constitutes time, and if it can be said that time is omnipotent, it must be added that it is completely impotent. The present makes a tremendous demand, yet as the individual present it is nothing, for even as I pronounce it, its all-excluding pretentiousness dwindles, dissolves, and falls into dust" (*Encyclopaedia II* §258, *Zusätze*, 231; ENZ2, 50).

9. Walter Benjamin, *The Origin of German Tragic Drama* (London: Verso, 1977), 44.

10. Cf. Werner Hamacher, *Pleroma—Reading in Hegel* (Stanford, CA: Stanford University Press, 1998), 225–226.

11. The ejection of nature involves a double genitive: spirit's self-excretion into nature as well as nature's own self-excretion. Life (nature in its highest form) is defined as a process of self-disgorgement—the "primal act of scission [Ur-teil] and expulsion of the sun and everything else" (*Encyclopaedia II* §357, *Zusätze*). The organism turns against its own externality: it "separates itself from itself ... expels its struggle, the bile which it has excreted, from itself" (*Encyclopaedia II* §365, *Zusätze*).

12. PH §808, 492; PHÄ, 590 (emphasis added).

13. SL, 843; WL2, 573.

14. G. W. F. Hegel, *Lectures on the Philosophy of Religion: The Lectures of 1827*, trans. P. Hodgson (Berkeley: University of California Press, 1988), 334n.

15. Sigmund Freud, "Mourning and Melancholia," in *The Standard Edition of the Complete Psychological Works of Sigmund Freud*, vol. 18, ed. James Strachey (London: Hogarth Press, 1960). Cf. Nicolas Abraham and Maria Torok, *The Shell and the Kernel*, vol. 1, trans. Nicholas T. Rand (Chicago: University of Chicago Press, 1994).

16. *Aes1*, 89; *Äs*, 123.

17. ENZ3 §§461–464.

18. ENZ3 §577.

19. Cf. Schiller's letter to Fichte of August 3–4, 1795, quoted in Friedrich Kittler, *Discourse Networks 1800/1900* (Stanford, CA: Stanford University Press, 1990), 156.

20. Hegel's ambivalence is palpable: "It has to be admitted that the artistic sense of a profound and philosophic mind has demanded, and expressed, totality and reconciliation ... as against that abstract endlessness or ratiocination, that duty for duty's sake, that formless intellectualism, which apprehends nature and actuality, sense and feeling, as just a barrier, just contradicting it and hostile. It is *Schiller* who must be given credit for breaking through the Kantian subjectivity and abstraction ... by intellectually grasping the unity and reconciliation as the truth and by actualizing them in artistic production. ... Even so, one feels that at one period of his life he busied himself with thought more than was advantageous for the naive beauty of his works of art" (*Aes1*, 61; *Äs1*, 89).

21. See Comay, *Mourning Sickness*.

22. Note the citational subtitle of the first edition of "Die Freundschaft (aus den Briefen Julius an Raphael; einem noch ungedruckten Roman)," in Friedrich Schiller,

Schillers Werke, Nationalausgabe, vol. 1, ed. J. Petersen and F. Beißner (Weimar: Hermann Böhlaus Nachfolger, 1962), 111ff. Schiller's subsequent rewriting of the poem, in the *Philosophische Briefe* (1786), introduces substitutions (*Wesenreiches* for *Seelenreiches*) and typographical elisions (the erasure of the original dashes and two of the three original italics) that anticipate Hegel's revision. The final stanza in Schiller's 1786 version reads as follows: "Freundlos war der große Weltenmeister, / fühlte Mangel, darum schuf er Geister, / sel'ge Spiegel *seiner* Seligkeit. / Fand das höchste Wesen schon kein Gleiches / aus dem Kelch des ganzen Wesenreiches / schäumt ihm die Unendlichkeit" (Friedrich Schiller, *Schillers Werke, Nationalausgabe*, vol. 20: *Philosophische Schriften*, ed. Benno von Wiese and Helmut Koopman [Weimar: Hermann Böhlaus Nachfolger, 1963], 125). While there is no evidence that Hegel had this version at his disposal when composing the *Phenomenology*, Schiller's own earlier revision is perhaps unsurprising, given that the poem has already been subordinated to the (fictional) framework of a "philosophical" epistolary correspondence; it has already been conceptually digested.

23. Cf. PH §47, 27; PHÄ, 46.

24. David Pugh argues that disillusion sets in as early as 1783. For a pronounced expression of the crisis, see the letter of October 5, 1785, cited in David Pugh, *Dialectic of Love: Platonism in Schiller's Aesthetics* (Montreal: McGill–Queen's University Press, 1997), 183.

25. Cf. Aristotle, *Problems*, 935b31–32. See the study by Raymond Klibansky, Erwin Panofsky, and Fritz Saxl, *Saturn and Melancholy: Studies in the History of Natural Philosophy, Religion, and Art* (New York: Basic Books, 1964), with Benjamin's comments in *The Origin of German Tragic Drama*.

26. Translation modified. See above, 131, n. 3.

27. On the transition from anthropology to phenomenology see *Encyclopaedia III* §412.

28. My reading departs from Katrin Pahl's illuminating discussion of this passage. See Katrin Pahl, *Tropes of Transport: Hegel on Emotion* (Evanston, IL: Northwestern University Press, 2012). Drawing on an earlier discussion by John McCumber, Pahl offers a different reading of Hegel's emendations of the last two lines of Schiller's verse. She argues that Hegel's introduction of the possessive pronoun and the demonstrative serve to mitigate rather than reinforce spirit's claim to absoluteness (she also unequivocally sees the epigraph as a philosophical concession to the "poetic"). My reading stresses rather the universalizing thrust of the demonstrative (as established in the first chapter of the *Phenomenology*) and the suturing effect of the possessive. From a grammatical perspective, mastery is strengthened in being individuated (in accordance with the singularizing logic of *die wahre Unendlichkeit*). My argument is that it is rather at a syncategorematic (even a typographical) level rather than a semantic or level that we are led to witness the unraveling of speculative mastery.

29. *Encyclopaedia III* §§461–464. Cf. Jacques Derrida, "The Pit and the Pyramid: Introduction to Hegel's Semiology," in *Margins of Philosophy*, trans. Alan Bass, 69–108 (Chicago: University of Chicago Press), 1982.

30. *Encyclopaedia I* §195. In his rectoral address at Nuremberg Gymnasium, Hegel underlines the relationship between linguistic mastery and digestion: "For it is the mechanical that is foreign to the mind, and it is this which awakens the mind's desire to digest the indigestible food forced upon it, to make intelligible what is at first without life and meaning, and to assimilate it" (G. W. F. Hegel, "Rede zum Schuljahrabschluß am 29. September 1809," in *Werke*, vol. 4, 319).

31. Cf. Friedrich Nietzsche, *The Will to Power*, ed. Walter Kaufmann, trans. Walter Kaufmann and R. J. Hollingdale (New York: Random House, 1967), §1066. "The new world-conception—The world exists; it is not something that becomes, not something that passes away. Or rather: it becomes, it passes away, but it has never begun to become and never ceased from passing away—it maintains itself in both—it lives on itself: its excrements are its food."

32. Theodor W. Adorno, *Negative Dialectics*, trans. E. B. Ashton (London: Routledge, 1974), 23.

33. Schlegel, quoted in Kittler, *Discourse Networks 1800/1900*, 70.

34. Johann Wolfgang von Goethe, *Faust* (Munich: Beck, 1984), 22.

35. *Aes*, 627, 964, 968; *ÄsII* 262, *ÄsIII*, 229, *ÄsIII*, 235.

36. PH §171, 108; PHÄ, 141.

37. I am indebted here to Werner Hamacher's brilliant exploration of Hegel's hermeneutics in *Pleroma*; see esp. 101–110.

38. ETW, 252; GC, 368.

39. ETW, 253; GC, 369.

40. ETW, 316; "Systemfragment von 1800," in *Werke*, vol. 1, 425. Hamacher sees in this relationless relation a key transition to speculative identity. The moment of unproductive consumption—the meal that does not nourish—marks the delay inherent in the movement of absolutization. See *Pleroma*, 181.

41. Hegel, "Aphorismen aus Hegels Wastebook," in *Werke*, vol. 2, 563.

42. ETW, 300; GC, 417.

43. ETW, 292; GC, 409; cf. ETW, 295; GC, 412.

44. ETW, 293; GC, 409. Cf. ETW, 297; GC, 414 and ETW, 292; GC, 408.

45. ETW, 318; GC 426.

46. ETW, 293, 296; GC 410, 412.

47. G. W. F. Hegel, *Faith and Knowledge*, trans. Walter Cerf and H. S. Harris (Albany: SUNY Press, 1977), 191. Hegel, *Glauben und Wissen*, in *Werke*, vol. 2, 432.

48. *Hegel Aphorismen aus Hegels Wastebook*, in *Werke*, vol. 2, 563.

49. HPh3, 55; VGP3, 538. See Hegel's letter to von Altenstein, April 3, 1826, responding to a priest's complaint, in *Werke*, vol. 11, 68–71.

50. PHH 382; VPG 460.

51. "The mouth ... has the dual function of initiating the immediate conversion of food into organic structures in the animal organism and *also*, in contrast to this inwardizing of the outer, of completing the objectification of subjectivity occurring in the voice" (emphasis added) (*Encyclopaedia III* §401, Zusätze, 88; ENZ3, 117).

52. "In many animals, the excretory and genital organs, which constitute the highest and lowest features of animal organization, are intimately connected; just as speech and kissing, on the one hand, and eating, drinking, and spitting, on the other, all focus on the mouth" (*Encyclopaedia II* §365, Zusätze, vol. 3, 164; ENZ2, 492).

53. *Encyclopaedia II* §355, vol. 2, 128; ENZ2, 456; translation slightly modified, emphasis added.

54. "It can vividly present the finest shades of derision, contempt, and envy, the whole gamut of grief and joy, by means of the faintest movements ... similarly, in repose it indicates charm, seriousness, sensitiveness, shyness, surrender, etc." (*Aes*, 736; *Äs1*, 394).

55. *Aes*, 729–730; *Äs1*, 385–386.

56. *Aes*, 736; *Äs1*, 394.

57. *Aes*, 736; *Äs1*, 394.

58. Hotho (1835), cited in Walter Kaufmann, *Hegel: A Reinterpretation* (Garden City, NY: Doubleday, 1965).

59. By changing Schiller's "aus dem Kelch" to "aus dem Kelche"—substituting a slightly archaic form of the dative—Hegel preserves the iambic pentameter. Thanks to John Zilcolsky for clarifying this.

60. Theodor W. Adorno, "Punctuation Marks," in *Notes to Literature*, vol. 1, trans. S. W. Nicholson (New York: Columbia University Press, 1991), 96.

61. Marx, "A Contribution to the Critique of Hegel's 'Philosophy of Right': Introduction," in Karl Marx, *Critique of Hegel's Philosophy of Right* (Cambridge: Cambridge University Press, 1970), 129–142.

62. PH §590, 360; PHÄ, 437.

63. PH §8, 5; PHÄ, 17. Cf. James Schmidt, "Cabbage Heads and Gulps of Water," *Political Theory* 26, no. 1 (Feb. 1998): 4–32.

64. A slightly random survey of some of the available translations shows the dash to be also missing (or sometimes misplaced) in the translations of the *Phenomenology* into Spanish, Danish, Slovene, Arabic, and Chinese, as well as in Baillie's earlier English translation. The punctuation is preserved in the French, Russian, Dutch, Turkish, Serbocroatian, and Greek translations, and is restored in Pinkard's forthcoming English translation. (Thanks to Simon Gros, Ferit Güven, Jens Hanssen, Gal Kirn, Artemy Magun, Gregor Moder, Carsten Pallesen, Mariano Siskind, Timothy Stock, Bart Zantvoort, and Xudong Zhang for all chiming in on such short notice.)

65. The dash also induces a retroactive uncertainty about the sentence it punctuates. It creates grammatical confusion: what part of speech is the word that immediately precedes it? Is *only* a conjunction or an adverb? Is Hegel saying: Spirit would be lifeless

and alone. [*pause*] *Only* (i.e., but, however): "From the chalice of the realm of spirits. ..."? Or is he saying: Spirit would be lifeless and alone—[*It is*] *only* from the chalice of the realm of spirts that ..."?

66. PHH 452; VGP 535.

67. PH §753, 455; PHÄ, 547.

68. The argument was prepared in Hegel's discussion of Diderot's *Rameau's Nephew* earlier in the same chapter.

69. See Comay, *Mourning Sickness*, chap. 5.

70. It is notably the young Schiller who is brought in to close off the *Phenomenology*—not the author of the *Ästhetische Briefe* (a text that will be crucially important in Hegel's *Aesthetics*), nor the playwright who had appeared at a decisive earlier moment in the "Reason" chapter of the *Phenomenology*.

71. Friedrich Hölderlin, "Remarks on Antigone," in *Essays and Letters on Theory*, ed. and trans. Thomas Pfau (Albany: SUNY Press, 1988).

72. Walter Benjamin, "The Task of the Translator," in *Selected Writings*, vol. 1, 1919–1923, ed. Marcus Bullock and Michael Jennings (Cambridge, MA: Harvard University Press, 1996), 253–263.

73. Cf. Samuel Weber's wonderful *Benjamin's -abilities* (Cambridge, MA: Harvard University Press, 2009). Weber highlights (by hyphenating) the insistent suffixes -*bar*, -*barkeit* (*Mitteilbarkeit*, *übersetzbar*, *Reproduzierbarkeit*, etc.) running through Benjamin's writings. Hegel helps us understand the diacritical labor that gives these suffixes their semantic power.

CHAPTER 5

1. Jean-Luc Nancy, *Hegel: The Restlessness of the Negative* (Minneapolis: University of Minnesota Press, 2002), 9.

2. This reading is indebted to and inspired by my dear friend Mladen Dolar in uncountable ways. Its idea originated in Ljubljana, during a late-night conversation with him.

3. Adorno, *Hegel*, 90. Adorno argues that the opacity of Hegel's text is not a flaw but part of the things themselves. Some have connected the intricacy of the *Logic* even to the hermetic tradition (cf. Glenn A. Magee, *Hegel and the Hermetic Tradition* [Ithaca, NY: Cornell University Press, 2001]).

4. Adorno, *Hegel*, 90.

5. SL 1, 50; WL 1, 40.

6. SL 1, 50; WL 1, 40.

7. SL 1, 69; WL 1, 68.

8. SL 1, 50; WL 1, 44.

9. A "diabolical heresy." Cf. Hassan Givsan, "Hegels Logik—die Frage des Anfangs: Kritik und Affirmation," in *Anfänge bei Hegel*, ed. Wolfdietrich Schmied-Kowarzik and

Heinz Eidam (Kassel: Kassel University Press, 2009), 70. Pinkard calls the aspiration of the *Logic* "strong stuff" (Pinkard, *Hegel*, 342). There is something literally diabolic about the *Logic*, something in it that gives a *primacy to the dia-bolon*, to a hurling ("bal-lein") across ("dia") of all things *over the sym-bolon*.

10. C. G. Jung claimed: "The peculiar high-flown language of Hegel … is reminiscent of the megalomaniac language of schizophrenics. … So bombastic a terminology is a symptom of weakness, ineptitude, and lack of substance." The language Hegel uses indicates a lack of substance, even: a lack in substance. C. G. Jung, "On the Nature of the Psyche," in *Collected Works*, vol. 8 (Princeton, NJ: Princeton University Press, 1969), 170.

11. SL1, 63; WL1, 60.

12. SL1, 50; WL1, 44.

13. HLL, 113.

14. SL1, 43; WL1, 35.

15. SL1, 38; WL1, 28.

16. SL1, 37; WL1, 27.

17. SL1, 42; WL1, 33. The only presupposition that we need for the *Logic* is the *Phenomenology*, which ensures that there are no presuppositions left. It is a "presupposition for a presuppositionless science" (William Maker, *Philosophy without Foundation: Rethinking Hegel* (Albany: SUNY Press, 1994), 85). The *Logic* does not begin with a liberated "I think." Instead it begins with an "if there is thought—it thinks" (in a way yet to be determined): the only thing we know—and we did not know this before the *Phenomenology*—is that we do not know this. This knowledge is indistinguishable from lack of knowledge. Habermas claims problematically that "from the very beginning Hegel presumes as given a knowledge of the Absolute" (Jürgen Habermas, *Knowledge and Human Interest* [London: Heinemann, 1981], 10).

18. SL1, 43; WL1, 36.

19. Heinz Eidam, "Der Anfang der Logik," in *Anfänge bei Hegel*, ed. Wolfdietrich Schmid-Kowarzik and Heinz Eidam (Kassel: Kassel University Press, 2009), 51–63.

20. SL1, 59; WL1, 55.

21. SL1, 55; WL1, 51.

22. Ludwig Feuerbach, "Toward a Critique of Hegel's Philosophy," in *The Fiery Brook: Selected Writings of Ludwig Feuerbach* (London: Verso, 2013), 61.

23. SL1, 43; WL1, 35.

24. SL1, 49; WL1, 42.

25. SL1, 45; WL1, 38.

26. Dolar, "Being and MacGuffin," 87.

27. SL1, 49; WL1, 42.

28. SL1, 67; WL1, 65.

29. SL1, 67; WL1, 65.

30. SL1, 68; WL1, 66.

31. SL1, 68; WL1, 66.

32. SL1, 69; WL1, 68.

33. It is "the immediacy as a product, as a result of a process" (Eidam, "Der Anfang der Logik," 59). Immediacy is *created absence*.

34. SL1, 69; WL1, 68.

35. SL1, 69; WL1, 68.

36. SL1, 71; WL1, 70.

37. This is a position first articulated by Bertrando Spaventa (see Bertrando Spaventa, *Scritti filosofici*, vol. 1 [Naples: Pierro, 1900], 215ff).

38. SL1, 68; WL1, 67.

39. Stephen Houlgate, *The Opening of Hegel's Logic: From Being to Infinity* (West Lafayette, IN: Purdue University Press, 2006), 49.

40. SL1, 75; WL1, 75.

41. SL1, 70; WL1, 68.

42. Eidam is correct when he emphasizes: "Its [the *Logic's*] ... initial spark is the insight into the logic of disappearance" (Eidam, "Der Anfang der Logik," 54).

43. What needs to be taken up is the resolve; we need to take it upon us. Hegel speaks of taking up (*aufnehmen*), which is one of the lexical meanings of sublation (*aufheben*). He thus indicates that sublation does not work as a transition from the *Phenomenology* to the *Logic*, as the beginning of the *Logic*.

44. SL1, 70; WL1, 68.

45. "As yet there is nothing [*Nichts*] and there is to become something" (SL1, 73; WL1, 71).

46. Alain Badiou, *Séminaire: L'image du temps présent II, 2002–2003*, session from May 14, 2003, http://www.entretemps.asso.fr/Badiou/02-03.3.htm.

47. Being and nothing are the affirmative and negative moment of this indeterminate immediacy decision in scission (cf. Henrich, *Hegel im Kontext*, 79).

48. SL1, 78; WL1, 79. This elimination of preliminaries mirrors the whole process of the *Phenomenology*. It is a *repetition in miniature*, a peculiar compulsion to repeat what has already been achieved, yet as this achievement is nothing, this nothing has to be repeated over and over again.

49. It has been claimed that "nothing is a deeper mystery in the *Science of Logic* than absolute origin"; however, maybe even more mysterious is the actual form it takes (cf. Thomas J. J. Altizer, *The Genesis of God: A Theological Genealogy* [Louisville, KY: Westminster John Knox Press, 1993], 15).

50. SL1, 28; WL1, 17.

51. SL I, 48; WL I, 42.

52. SL I, 42; WL I, 33.

53. SL I, 73; WL I, 72.

54. SL I, 37; WL I, 55.

55. G. W. F. Hegel, "Solgers nachgelassene Schriften und Briefwechsel," in *Werke*, vol. 11 (Frankfurt am Main: Suhrkamp, 1985), 249.

56. Adorno, *Hegel*, 120.

57. Cf. Ernst Bloch, *Subjekt-Objekt: Erläuterungen zu Hegel* (Frankfurt am Main: Suhrkamp, 1971), 155–168.

58. Ernst Bloch, "Gesprochene und geschriebene Syntax: Das Anakoluth," in *Literarische Aufsätze* (Frankfurt am Main: Suhrkamp, 1985), 565.

59. Michael Landmann, "Gespräch mit Ernst Bloch (Tübingen, 22. December 1967)," in *Bloch-Almanach* 4 (1984): 20–21.

60. Already with this first nonpropositional sentence Hegel achieved what he described as the "task" of the *Logic*: "To focus attention [zum Bewusstsein zu bringen] on this logical nature which animates spirit, drives in it, and is effective in it, this is the task" (SL I, 37; WL I, 27).

61. In his third remark on the beginning, Hegel claims that "because *being* is posited only as immediate, therefore *nothing* breaks forth from it only immediately [bricht das Nichts an ihm nur unmittelbar hervor; my emphasis]" (SL I, 99; WL I, 104).

62. Tugendhat criticizes the beginning of the *Logic* for "violating at every turn the insight of Frege that the primary logical—and … also the primary ontological—unit … is the sentence" (Ernst Tugendhat, "Das Sein und das Nichts," in *Durchblicke: Martin Heidegger zum 80. Geburtstag*, 132–171 [Frankfurt am Main: Klostermann, 1970]). Tugendhat is right: Hegel is not a Fregean, yet this is not a limitation.

63. SL I, 75; WL I, 75.

64. Cf. Henrich, *Hegel im Kontext*, 73–94.

65. Friedrich Adolf von Trendelenburg, *Logische Untersuchen* (Leipzig: Hirzel, 1840), 37ff.

66. Eduard von Hartmann, *Die dialektische Methode* (Berlin: Carl Duncker Verlag, 1868), 78.

67. Cf. Henrich, *Hegel im Kontext*, 77–79.

68. Ibid., 78.

69. SL I, 82. Translation modified; WL I, 83. The English translation does not follow the capitalization of the German text.

70. Dolar, "Being and MacGuffin," 95.

71. The minimal difference of emphasis can be situated between the *being of the absence of determination* (i.e., being) and the *absence of the being of determination* (i.e., nothing). Recall

the famous joke from Lubitsch's *Ninotchka*: a guy comes to a cafeteria and orders coffee without cream and the waiter replies: "Sorry, but we've run out of cream. Can I bring you coffee without milk?" (cf. Žižek, *Less Than Nothing*, 765). The difference between the two identical coffees (without cream / without milk) is a *difference within the without*, within the absence, a pure difference. Nonetheless it *is* a difference, since "can absence be the same?" (Dolar, "Being and MacGuffin," 95).

72. SL1, 83; WL1, 83.

73. Mladen Dolar rightly notes that "its absolute emptiness and meaninglessness ... is far more difficult to come to terms with than any deep hidden sense" (Dolar, "Being and MacGuffin," 86).

74. In his early wastebook Hegel noted: "It is not good for philosophy to have a proposition and be able to say: this *is* or *is nothing*" (G. W. F. Hegel, *Aphorismen aus Hegels Wastebook*, in *Werke*, vol. 2 [Frankfurt am Main: Suhrkamp, (1803–1806) 1986], 559).

75. Andrew Haas rightly remarked that this sentence "lacks a verb—for Hegel cannot even say that being *is*" (Andrew Haas, *Hegel and the Problem of Multiplicity* [Evanston, IL: Northwestern University Press, 2000], xxiii).

76. On this see Henrich, *Hegel im Kontext*, 95–156.

77. Badiou, *Theory of the Subject*, 55.

78. Wilfrid Sellars, *Empiricism and Philosophy of Mind* (Cambridge, MA: Harvard University Press, 1997).

79. This is like psychoanalytic "screen-memory, a fantasy formation" that obfuscates that one resolved the question of how to begin by claiming one always already had begun. This is what Žižek describes as "postmetaphysical" anti-Hegelian thought (cf. Žižek, *Less Than Nothing*, 239).

80. Nancy, *The Restlessness of the Negative*, 9.

81. Henrich emphasizes that "this interpretation can ... not be carried out without changing the meaning and systematic position of the *Logic* from the ground up. If the *Logic* wants to develop the determination of thought for itself and one from the other, the reflection upon their being thought cannot be regarded as its motive" (Heinrich, *Hegel im Kontext*, 82). Eidam seconds this: "Being, pure being thus must—au fond—not be a reflexive expression" (Eidam, "Der Anfang der Logik", 56). And Dolar argues: "Being is not determined in relation to essence, for this is already a reflexive move, ... Hegel's vulgate: everything is reflexive, split, redoubled, yet Hegel here insists again and again that being is reflectionless, non-split" (Mladen Dolar, "Reading Notes on Hegel's *Logic*," unpublished typescript).

82. A "materialist" reading repeats the initial gesture of the *Logic*: it simply takes up what is before us.

83. Fink elaborates apropos of Lacan that "being, in Lacan's work, is associated with the letter—the letter ... being the material, nonsignifying face of the signifier, the part that has effects without signifying" (Bruce Fink, *The Lacanian Subject: Between Language and Jouissance* [Princeton, NJ: Princeton University Press, 1995], 119).

84. Eidam's comments: "One cannot say that at the beginning there is or there exists Being and that this Being in its indeterminacy is the same as Nothing. Then one would have two things—or representations [*Vorstellungen*], categories or concepts—and one would not be dealing with a simple beginning. One would then also have to ask oneself which of the two concepts that are not yet concepts (but rather only opinions or names) would have the logical primacy over the other and would thus also precede it" (Eidam, "Der Anfang der Logik," 52). We are not dealing here with concepts, categories, or representations. His alternative—being and nothing are either opinions or names—can only be decided (again a decision!) in one way: they have to be names, as opinions necessarily have to have some content (even the content of having no content), names do not.

85. Gilles Deleuze, "He Stuttered," in *Essays Critical and Clinical* (London: Verso, 1998), 110.

86. One might go as far as to claim that this is the most fundamental structure of a name.

87. Cf. Mladen Dolar, *What's in a Name?* (Ljublana: Aksioma, 2014).

88. Henrich, *Hegel im Kontext*, 89–90.

89. Alain Badiou, Joel Bellassen, and Louis Mossot, *The Rational Kernel of the Hegelian Dialectic* (Melbourne: re.press, 2011), 51.

90. Badiou introduces this terminology (space of placement, etc.) in his *Theory of the Subject*. Although he treats Hegel as a materialist, Badiou criticizes him for having succumbed to an idealist reading of his own position. One of the key issues in this discussion is the distinction between circularity and periodization of dialectical sequences. One could state here that any idealist reading insists on the necessary circularity (and continuity) between the *Phenomenology* and the *Logic*, whereas a materialist reading emphasizes their differences.

91. Badiou, *Theory of the Subject*, 20.

92. Ibid., 6.

93. After acknowledging that we have some sort of Borromean knot as soon as we start thinking about how to properly begin, the Hegelian decision cuts this knot apart (k—not). What then emerges is a "not" cut off from the "knot." Hamacher states: "The sentence is exthesis. ... Hegel's logic of the sentence ... proves to be ... alogic" (cf. Werner Hamacher, "Das Nicht im Satz der Identität," unpublished typescript).

94. Hamacher speaks of a "Not-Nothing that is the Surplus [*Mehr*] of the proposition" (ibid.).

95. Deleuze, "He Stuttered," 113.

96. Adorno, "Punctuation Marks," 300.

97. Ibid.

98. Ibid., 301.

99. After "Being Comma Pure Being Comma Dash," Hegel continues in the next section: "Nothing Comma the Pure Nothing Semicolon." There is weak phrasing between "being" and "pure being" and strong phrasing between "nothing" and "the pure nothing."

100. Ibid.

101. With the concept of difference we do not simply gain another concept, we gain a concept that can be applied to itself: we thereby move from the *concept of difference* to the *difference to the concept*(*ual*).

102. SL1, 83; WL1, 84.

103. SL1, 103; WL1, 84.

104. For this term, again see Badiou, *Theory of the Subject*, 3–12.

105. Taking only the italicized words in the first sections (Being, Nothing, Becoming), one reads the following: "Being, pure being—nothing—Nothing" (in the section on Being); "Nothing, the pure nothing—nothing—is—Being" (in the section on Nothing); "The pure Being and the pure Nothing is thus the same—not the same—absolutely distinguished—each disappears in its contrary—movement—the Becoming." All first moves are contained in the italicized parts of the text. Yet, no verb, no article in the whole first section.

106. Hegel himself indicates this in stating that "being … is, in fact, not *nothing*, and neither more nor less than *nothing*" (SL1, 82; WL1, 83). There can be not only more but also less than nothing.

107. Deleuze, "He Stuttered," 112.

108. Badiou, *The Rational Kernel*, 54; Badiou, *Theory of the Subject*, 27.

109. Dolar, "Reading Notes." It has to be a form before form, because the content-form distinction is still suspended, since "content and form are reflexive determinations, pertaining again to the logic of essence."

110. There is a close link between Hegel's formalization and what Badiou develops concerning the presentation of being qua being on its most elementary level. See Badiou, *Being and Event*.

111. The idea that repetition precedes time originated in a conversation with Alenka Zupančič. If the repetition also concerns the decision, this means that the decision is itself not within time (this is why it is impossible to determine *when* the *Logic* begins) but grounds it.

112. Badiou, *Theory of the Subject*, 22.

113. We are in the section on "quality" and not "quantity": Two here is not a quantitative (Two as reflection of the One), but a qualitative term.

114. Badiou, *Being and Event*, 86.

115. This is another proximity between Hegel and psychoanalysis. The whole beginning of the *Logic* and its relation to the *Phenomenology* comes close to the Freudian slogan of "Remembering, Repeating, Working Through." First we need to remember

what the *Phenomenology* achieved (subtracting determinations, etc.), then we need to repeat (subtracting all presuppositions about how to begin and inscribe the very form of repetition into the beginning), and then we come to work through (repeating repetition in the sense of repeatability) that which can only be indexed and not be presented (as it never will have been present). See Sigmund Freud, "Remembering, Repeating, Working Through (Further Recommendations on the Technique of Psycho-Analysis II)," in *The Standard Edition of the Complete Psychological Works of Sigmund Freud*, vol. 12 (New York: Norton, 2001), 145–156.

116. The idealist reading does insist only on iteration and differentiation, whereas the materialist reading insists on the iterability and the infinitization of infinite series as necessary preconditions for accessing what grounds these "forms."

117. In the beginning there is "only not," "nur nicht," or "nur—," "only—" (PH, §808, 493; PHÄ, 591).

118. Eidam, "Der Anfang der Logik," 61.

119. Noah Lukeman, *A Dash of Style: The Art and Mastery of Punctuation* (New York: Norton, 2006), 111.

120. Eidam, "Der Anfang der Logik," 56.

121. Quoted from Eric Santner, *On the Psychotheology of Everyday Life: Reflections on Freud and Rosenzweig* (Chicago: University of Chicago Press, 2001), 38ff.

122. Short for "decision in scission."

123. Here one can think of Hegel's own example of *Er-innerung* from the *Phenomenology* and of *abs-traction*, *in-determinate*, *im-mediate*, etc.

124. One should note that the dash does not end the sentence (can one end a sentence with a dash?), but only interrupts it; the end—as always in Hegel—is not the end.

125. Eidam, "Der Anfang der Logik," 55.

126. Cf. Jacques Lacan, *The Seminar of Jacques Lacan, Book XVII: The Other Side of Psychoanalysis*, trans. Russell Grigg (New York: Norton, 2007), 14.

127. Henrich, *Hegel im Kontext*, 93.

128. SL1, 69; WL1, 68.

129. Jacques Alain Miller, "Matrix," *Symptom* 13 (Summer 2012), http://www.lacan.com/symptom13/matrix.html.

130. Ibid.

131. Cf. Jacques-Alain Miller, "Matrice," in *Un début dans la vie*, 139. In this formulation addressing the very beginning: there is another dash.

132. SL1, 37; WL1, 27.

133. SL 1, 82; WL1, 22.

134. Cf. Henrich, *Hegel im Kontext*, 93.

1. G. W. F. Hegel, "Entschluss," in *Gesammelte Werke*, vol. 5, *Schriften und Entwürfe* (1799–1808) (Hamburg: Meiner, 1998), 51. Our translation. Hegel wrote this poem in 1801 and published it anonymously in 1803 in the *Vossische Zeitung*.

2. Eidam, "Der Anfang der Logik," 61.

3. SL, 48; WL1, 68.

4. Henrich, *Hegel im Kontext*, 92–93.

5. Ibid., 90.

6. As always, one must commit to a speculative attitude; we must undertake an *Entschluss* to discover the speculative riches of the word *Entschluss*. The word *resolve* demands for its comprehension the resolve it names.

7. "The idealism of philosophy consists in nothing else than in the recognition that the finite is not truly an existent" (SL, 124; WL1, 172).

8. That *Entlassen* (release, discharge) is an *Entschluss* Hegel states clearly: "The idea *freely discharges* itself, absolutely certain of itself and internally at rest. ... But what is posited by this next *resolve* of the pure idea to determine itself as external idea is only the mediation out of which the concept ... raises itself up" (SL, 753; WL2, 573; translation modified, our emphasis).

9. "Absolute spirit, at the end of the development, freely externalizes itself, letting itself go into the shape of an immediate being—resolving itself into the creation of a world which contains all that fell within the development preceding that result and which, through this reversal of position with its beginning, is converted into something dependent on the result as principle" (SL, 49; WL1, 70).

10. PH §806, 491; PHÄ, 589.

11. PH §806, 491; PHÄ, 589.

12. On why this is not a tragic insight, see Frank Ruda, *Abolishing Freedom. A Plea for a Contemporary Use of Fatalism* (Lincoln: Nebraska University Press, 2016).

13. PH §807, 492; PHÄ, 590. "Seine Grenze wissen heißt, sich aufzuopfern wissen."

14. SL, 48; WLI, 68. Our emphasis.

15. SL, 123; WL1, 109–111.

16. And, of course, motivated by Hegel's distinction between youth and old age in the life of an individual: the former opts for singularity and for the temporality of the future, whereas the old refers to the past and to the universal. See, inter alia, Robert Nola, "The Young Hegelians, Feuerbach, and Marx," in *The Age of German Idealism*, ed. Robert C. Solomon and Kathleen M. Higgins (London: Routledge, 1993), 290–329.

17. Cf. *Die Hegelsche Rechte*, ed. Hermann Lübbe (Stuttgart: Fromann, 1962).

18. See Karl Löwith, "Einleitung," in *Die Hegelsche Linke*, ed. Karl Löwith (Stuttgart: frommann, 1962), 9.

19. PhRi 287; RPh, 449.

20. Bruno Bauer, Russland und das Germanenthum (Charlottenburg: Verlag von Egbert Bauer, 1853), 74.

21. Cf. Frederick Engels, Ludwig Feuerbach and the End of Classical German Philosophy, 382.

22. Cf. Kierkegaard, Concluding Unscientific Postscript to "Philosophical Fragments" (Princeton, NJ: Princeton University Press, 1968).

23. Cf. Arnold Ruge, Unsere letzten zehn Jahre, in Sämmtliche Werke, vol. 5 (Mannheim: Verlag von J. P. Grohe, 1848), 1–135.

24. HPh 1, 52; VGP 1, 71.

25. To overcome the religiosity of philosophy, and thus to develop Hegel's own insights to their conclusion, Feuerbach argues that "politics must become our religion" (Ludwig Feuerbach, "Grundsätze der Philosophie, Notwendigkeit einer Veränderung," in Sämtliche Werke, vol. 2 [Stuttgart: frommann-holzboog, (1842–1843) 1903], 219).

26. David Riazanov, Karl Marx and Frederick Engels: An Introduction to Their Lives and Work (New York: Monthly Review Press, 1974), chap. 3.

27. This criticism anticipates Habermas's criticism of Hegel's reading of the French Revolution as celebrating a revolutionary event without revolutionaries (Jürgen Habermas, "Hegel's Critique of the French Revolution," in Theory and Practice [Boston: Beacon Press, 1973], 82).

28. Think of Lenin's transformative encounter with Hegel's Science of Logic in Switzerland from 1914 to 1915.

29. Of course Strauss, Bauer, and Feuerbach took direct inspiration from Hegel's Berlin lectures on religion (which Bauer even edited for publication), discovering the resources for a "destruction of religion." See Bruno Bauer, Die Posaune des jüngsten Gerichts über Hegel, den Atheisten und Antichristen (Leipzig: Wiegand, 1844).

30. Cf. Kant's early exploration of the noncognitive certainty, the "feeling," that orients the internal division of our body parts (left and right) within the universal continuum of space. Immanuel Kant, "On the Ultimate Ground of the Differentiation of Regions of the Body in Space" (1768), in Immanuel Kant, Theoretical Philosophy, 1755–1770 (Cambridge: Cambridge University Press, 1992), 361–372. Of course in the Conflict of the Faculties, the familiar parliamentary sense of the left/right opposition will become prominent. Immanuel Kant, Conflict of the Faculties (1798), in Immanuel Kant, Religion and Rational Theology (Cambridge: Cambridge University Press, 1996).

31. SL, 45; WL 1, 65.

32. "Consciousness supplies its own criterion," PH §84, 53; PHÄ, 75.

33. SL, 47; WL 1, 68.

BIBLIOGRAPHY

Abraham, Nicolas, and Maria Torok. *The Shell and the Kernel*. Vol. 1. Ed. and trans. Nicholas T. Rand. Chicago: University of Chicago Press, 1994.

Adorno, Theodor W. *Einführung in die Dialektik*. Berlin: Suhrkamp, [1958] 2015.

Adorno, Theodor W. *Hegel: Three Studies*. Cambridge, MA: MIT Press, 1993.

Adorno, Theodor W. *Kant's "Critique of Pure Reason."* Ed. Rolf Tiedemann, trans. Rodney Livingstone. Stanford, CA: Stanford University Press, [1959] 2001.

Adorno, Theodor W. *Minima Moralia: Reflections on a Damaged Life*. Trans. E. F. N. Jephcott. London: Verso, 2005.

Adorno, Theodor W. *Negative Dialectics*. Trans. E. B. Ashton. London: Routledge, 1974.

Adorno, Theodor W. "Punctuation Marks." In *Notes to Literature*, vol. 1, trans. S. W. Nicholson. New York: Columbia University Press, 1991.

Adorno, Theodor W. "Zur gegenwärtigen Stellung der empirischen Sozialforschung in Deutschland." In *Gesammelte Schriften*, vol. 8, *Soziologische Schriften I*, ed. Rolf Tiedemann. Frankfurt am Main: Suhrkamp, 1997.

Agamben, Giorgio. *Language and Death: The Place of Negativity*. Minneapolis: University of Minnesota Press, 2006.

Ainslie, Douglas. "Translator's Introduction" to Benedetto Croce, *What Is Living and What Is Dead of the Philosophy of Hegel*. New York: Russell & Russell, 1969.

Altizer, Thomas J. J. *The Genesis of God: A Theological Genealogy*. Louisville, KY: Westminster John Knox Press, 1993.

Aristotle. "On Generation and Corruption." In *The Complete Works of Aristotle*, vol. 2, ed. J Barnes. Princeton, NJ: Princeton University Press, 1984.

Aristotle. "Problems." In *The Complete Works of Aristotle*, vol. 2, ed. J. Barnes. Princeton, NJ: Princeton University Press, 1984.

Badiou, Alain. *Being and Event*. London: Continuum, 2007.

Badiou, Alain. *Le Séminaire—L'infini: Aristote, Spinoza, Hegel, 1984–1985*. Paris: fayard, 2016.

Badiou, Alain. *Logic of Worlds: Being and Event 2*. London: Continuum, 2006.

Badiou, Alain. *Pour aujourd'hui: Platon! Séminaire d'Alain Badiou, 2007–2008*. http://www.entretemps.asso.fr/Badiou/07-08.htm.

Badiou, Alain. *Séminaire: L'image du temps présent II, 2002–2003*. Session from May 14, 2003. http://www.entretemps.asso.fr/Badiou/02-03.3.htm.

Badiou, Alain. *Theory of the Subject*. London: Continuum, 2009.

Badiou, Alain, Joel Bellassen, and Louis Mossot. *The Rational Kernel of the Hegelian Dialectic*. Melbourne: re.press, 2011.

Badiou, Alain, and Barbara Cassin. *Il n'y a pas de rapport sexuel*. Paris: fayard, 2010.

Bauer, Bruno. *Russland und das Germanenthum*. Charlottenburg: Verlag von Egbert Bauer, 1853.

Benjamin, Walter. "On Language as Such and the Language of Man." In *Selected Writings*, vol. 1, 1919–1923, ed. Marcus Bullock and Michael Jennings, 62–74. Cambridge, MA: Harvard University Press, 1996.

Benjamin, Walter. *The Origin of German Tragic Drama*. London: Verso, 1977.

Benjamin, Walter. "The Task of the Translator." In *Selected Writings*, vol. 1, 1919–1923, ed. Marcus Bullock and Michael Jennings, 253–263. Cambridge, MA: Harvard University Press, 1996.

Benjamin, Walter. *Understanding Brecht*. London: Verso, 2003.

Bernasconi, Robert. "'We Philosophers': *Barbaros medeis eisito*." In *Endings: Questions of Memory in Hegel and Heidegger*, ed. Rebecca Comay and John McCumber, 77–96. Evanston, IL: Northwestern University Press, 1999.

Beyer, Wilhelm Raimund. "Wie die Hegelsche Freundesvereinsausgabe entstand: Aus neu aufgefundenen Briefen der Witwe Hegels." *Deutsche Zeitschrift für Philosophie* 15, no. 5 (1967): 563–569.

Bloch, Ernst. "Gesprochene und geschriebene Syntax: Das Anakoluth." In *Literarische Aufsätze*. Frankfurt am Main: Suhrkamp, 1985.

Bloch, Ernst. *Leipziger Vorlesungen zur Geschichte der Philosophie: Neuzeitliche Philosophie II: Deutscher Idealismus, die Philosophie des 18. Jahrhunderts*. Vol. 4. Frankfurt am Main: Suhrkamp, 1985.

Bloch, Ernst. *Subjekt-Objekt: Erläuterungen zu Hegel*. Frankfurt am Main: Suhrkamp, 1971.

Blumenbach, Johann Friedrich. "Über den Bildungstrieb (Nisus formativus) und seinen Einfluß auf die Generation und Reproduktion." *Göttingisches Magazin der Wissenschaften und Literatur* 1, no. 5 (1780): 247–266.

Bonsiepen, Wolfgang, and Reinhard Heede. "Anhang." In G. W. F. Hegel, *Gesammelte Werke*, vol. 9, *Phänomenologie des Geistes*. Hamburg: Meiner, 1980.

Brandom, Robert B. *A Spirit of Trust*. Unpublished MS. http://www.pitt.edu/~brandom/spirit_of_trust_2014.html.

Chiesa, Lorenzo. *The Not-Two: Logic and God in Lacan*. Cambridge, MA: MIT Press, 2016.

Cicero. *Tusculan Disputations*. Cambridge, MA: Harvard University Press, 1927.

Comay, Rebecca. *Mourning Sickness: Hegel and the French Revolution*. Stanford, CA: Stanford University Press, 2011.

Comay, Rebecca. "Resistance and Repetition: Hegel and Freud." *Research in Phenomenology* 45 (2015): 237–266.

Croce, Benedetto. *What Is Living and What Is Dead of the Philosophy of Hegel*. New York: Russell & Russell, 1969.

Deleuze, Gilles. "He Stuttered." In *Essays Critical and Clinical*. London: Verso, 1998.

Derrida, Jacques. *Adieu to Emmanuel Levinas*. Stanford, CA: Stanford University Press, 1999.

Derrida, Jacques. *The Gift of Death*. Chicago: University of Chicago Press, 2008.

Derrida, Jacques. *Of Grammatology*. Trans. Gayatri Chakravorty Spivak. Baltimore: Johns Hopkins University Press, 1988.

Derrida, Jacques. "The Pit and the Pyramid: Introduction to Hegel's Semiology." In *Margins of Philosophy*, trans. Alan Bass, 69–108. Chicago: University of Chicago Press, 1982.

Derrida, Jacques. *Politics of Friendship*. London: Verso, 2006.

Di Giovanni, George, and H. S. Harris, eds. *Between Kant and Hegel: Texts in the Development of Post-Kantian Idealism*. Albany: SUNY Press, 1985.

Dolar, Mladen. "One Divides into Two." http://www.e-flux.com/journal/one-divides-into-two/.

Dolar, Mladen. "The Atom and the Void—from Democritus to Lacan." *Filozofski Vestnik* 44, no. 2 (2013): 11–26.

Dolar, Mladen. "Being and MacGuffin." *Crisis and Critique: "Hegel's Today"* 4, no. 1 (2017): 82–101.

Dolar, Mladen. "Reading Notes on Hegel's *Logic*." Unpublished typescript.

Dolar, Mladen. "Si fractus illabatur orbis, impavidum ferient ruinae." https://www.youtube.com/watch?v=liDeHZh4qJg&t=3271s.

Dolar, Mladen. "Two Shades of Grey." Unpublished typescript.

Dolar, Mladen. *What's in a Name?* Ljubljana: Aksioma, 2014.

Eidam, Heinz. "Der Anfang der Logik." In *Anfänge bei Hegel*, ed. Wolfdietrich Schmied-Kowarzik and Heinz Eidam, 51–62. Kassel: Kassel University Press, 2009.

Engels, Frederick. *Ludwig Feuerbach and the End of Classical German Philosophy.* In Karl Marx and Frederick Engels, *Collected Works*, vol. 26: *Engels, 1882–89.* London: International Publishers, 1991.

Feuerbach, Ludwig. "Grundsätze der Philosophie, Notwendigkeit einer Veränderung." In *Sämtliche Werke*, vol. 2. Stuttgart: frommann-holzboog, [1842–1843] 1903.

Feuerbach, Ludwig. "Towards a Critique of Hegel's Philosophy." In *The Fiery Brook: Selected Writings of Ludwig Feuerbach*. London: Verso, 2013.

Fink, Bruce. *The Lacanian Subject: Between Language and Jouissance.* Princeton, NJ: Princeton University Press, 1995.

Förster, Eckart. *The Twenty-Five Years of Philosophy.* Cambridge, MA: Harvard University Press, 2012.

Foster, John Bellamy. *Marx's Ecology: Materialism and Nature.* London: Monthly Review Press, 2000.

Foucault, Michel. "The Order of Discourse." In *Untying the Text: A Post-Structuralist Reader*, ed. Robert Young. Boston: Routledge, 1981.

Freud, Sigmund. "The Antithetical Meaning of Primal Words." In *The Standard Edition of the Complete Psychological Works of Sigmund Freud*, vol. 11, ed. James Strachey, 155–161. London: Hogarth Press, [1910] 1957.

Freud, Sigmund. "Fetishism." In *The Standard Edition of the Complete Psychological Works of Sigmund Freud*, vol. 21, ed. James Strachey, 147–158. London: Hogarth Press, [1927] 1975.

Freud, Sigmund. "Introductory Lectures on Psycho-Analysis." In *The Standard Edition of the Complete Psychological Works of Sigmund Freud*, ed. James Strachey. New York: Norton, 1966.

Freud, Sigmund. "Mourning and Melancholia." In *The Standard Edition of the Complete Psychological Works of Sigmund Freud*, vol. 18, ed. James Strachey. London: Hogarth Press, 1960.

Freud, Sigmund. "New Introductory Lectures on Psycho-Analysis." In *The Standard Edition of the Complete Psychological Works of Sigmund Freud*, vol. 16, ed. James Strachey. New York: Norton, 1990.

Freud, Sigmund. "The Psychopathology of Everyday Life." In *The Standard Edition of the Complete Psychological Works of Sigmund Freud*, vol. 6, ed. James Strachey. London: Hogarth Press, [1901] 1960.

Freud, Sigmund. "Remembering, Repeating, Working Through (Further Recommendations on the Technique of Psycho-Analysis II)." In *The Standard Edition of the Complete Psychological Works of Sigmund Freud*, vol. 12, ed. James Strachey, 145–156. New York: Norton, 2001.

Gadamer, Hans-Georg. "Hegel und die antike Dialektik." In *Hegels Dialektik: Sechs hermeneutische Studien*. Tübingen: Mohr, 1980.

Gethmann-Siefert, Annemarie. *Einführung in Hegels Ästhetik*. Stuttgart: UTB, 2005.

Givsan, Hassan. "Hegels Logik—die Frage des Anfangs: Kritik und Affirmation." In *Anfänge bei Hegel*, ed. Wolfdietrich Schmied-Kowarzik and Heinz Eidam, 63–81. Kassel: Kassel University Press, 2009.

Glockner, Hermann. *Beiträge zum Verständnis und zur Kritik Hegels sowie zur Umgestaltung seiner Geisteswelt*. Bonn: Bouvier, 1965.

Glockner, Hermann. "Georg Wilhelm Friedrich Hegel: Entwicklung und Schicksal der Hegelschen Philosophie." In G. W. F. Hegel, *Sämtliche Werke*, vol. 22, ed. Hermann Glockner. Stuttgart–Bad Cannstatt: frommann-holzboog, 1964.

Gödel, Kurt. "On Completeness and Consistency." In *Collected Works, vol. 1, Publications 1929–1936*, 235–238. New York: Oxford University Press, 1986.

Goethe, Johann Wolfgang von. *Faust*. Munich: Beck, 1984.

Goethe, Johann Wolfgang von. *The Metamorphosis of Plants*. Cambridge, MA: MIT Press, 2009.

Grondin, Jean. *Introduction to Metaphysics: From Parmenides to Levinas*. New York: Columbia University Press, 2012.

Gulyga, Arsen. *Georg Wilhelm Friedrich Hegel*. Leipzig: Reclam, 1974.

Gurvitch, Georges. "Hyper-Empirisme dialectique." *Cahiers Internationale de Sociologie* 15 (1953): 3–33.

Haas, Andrew. *Hegel and the Problem of Multiplicity*. Evanston, IL: Northwestern University Press, 2000.

Habermas, Jürgen. "Hegel's Critique of the French Revolution." In *Theory and Practice*. Boston: Beacon Press, 1973.

Habermas, Jürgen. *Knowledge and Human Interest*. London: Heinemann, 1981.

Habermas, Jürgen. *The Theory of Communicative Action, vol. 1, Reason and the Rationalization of Society*. Trans. Thomas McCarthy. Boston: Beacon Press, 1984.

Haering, Theodor. "Die Entstehungsgeschichte der Phänomenologie des Geistes." In *Verhandlungen des dritten Hegelkongresses*. Tübingen: J. C. B. Mohr, 1934.

Hamacher, Werner. "Afformative, Strike." In *Walter Benjamin's Philosophy: Destruction and Experience*, ed. Andrew Benjamin and Peter Osborne, 155–182. London: Routledge, 1994.

Hamacher, Werner. "Das Nicht im Satz der Identität." Unpublished typescript.

Hamacher, Werner. *Pleroma—Reading in Hegel*. Stanford, CA: Stanford University Press, 1998.

Hamacher, Werner. "The Promise of Interpretation: Remarks on the Hermeneutic Imperative in Kant and Nietzsche." In *Premises: Essays on Philosophy and Literature from Kant to Celan*, trans. Peter Fenves, 81–142. Cambridge, MA: Harvard University Press, 1996.

Hartmann, Eduard von. *Die dialektische Methode*. Berlin: Carl Duncker Verlag, 1868.

Haym, Rudolf. *Hegel und seine Zeit*. Hildesheim: Olms, 1962.

Hegel, G. W. F. "Aphorismen aus Hegels Wastebook." In *Werke*, vol. 2. Frankfurt am Main: Suhrkamp, [1803–1806] 1986.

Hegel, G. W. F. *Berliner Schriften (1818–1831)*. In *Werke*, vol. 11. Ed. Eva Moldenhauer and Karl Markus Michel. Frankfurt am Main: Suhrkamp, 1970.

Hegel, G. W. F. *Briefe von und an Hegel: Dokumente und Materialien zur Bibliographie*. Ed. Friedhelm Nicolin and Johannes Hoffmeister. Hamburg: Meiner, 1977.

Hegel, G. W. F. "Der Geist des Christentums und sein Schicksal." In *Frühe Schriften*. Frankfurt am Main: Suhrkamp, 1971.

Hegel, G. W. F. "Die Idee des absoluten Wesens ..." In *Gesammelte Werke*, vol. 5, 262–266. Hamburg: Meiner, 1988.

Hegel, G. W. F. "Diese Vorlesungen ..." Fragment. In *Gesammelte Werke*, vol. 5, 259–261. Hamburg: Meiner, 1998.

Hegel, G. W. F. *The Difference between Fichte's and Schelling's System of Philosophy*. Albany: SUNY Press, 1977.

Hegel, G. W. F. "Differenz des Fichteschen und Schellingschen Systems der Philosophie" (1801). In *Werke*, vol. 2, 9–140. Frankfurt am Main: Suhrkamp, 1986.

Hegel, G. W. F. *Encyclopaedia of the Philosophical Sciences in Basic Outline: Part 1, Science of Logic*. Cambridge: Cambridge University Press, 2015.

Hegel, G. W. F. *The Encyclopaedia Logic (with the Zusätze): Part 1 of the Encyclopaedia of Philosophical Sciences with the Zusätze*. Trans. T. F. Geraets, W. A. Suchting, and H. S. Harris. Indianapolis: Hackett, 1991.

Hegel, G. W. F. "Entschluss." In *Gesammelte Werke*, vol. 5, Schriften und Entwürfe (1799–1808). Hamburg: Meiner, 1998.

Hegel, G. W. F. *Enzyklopädie der philosophischen Wissenschaften im Grundrisse*, vol. 2. In *Werke*, vol. 9. Frankfurt am Main: Suhrkamp, 1982.

Hegel, G. W. F. *Enzyklopädie der philosophischen Wissenschaften im Grundrisse*, vol. 3. In *Werke*, vol. 10. Frankfurt am Main: Suhrkamp, 1982.

Hegel, G. W. F. *Faith and Knowledge*. Trans. Walter Cerf and H. S. Harris. Albany: SUNY Press, 1977.

Hegel, G. W. F. "Fragment of a System." In *On Christianity: Early Theological Writings*, trans. T. M. Knox, 309–320. New York: Harper & Brothers, [1800] 1948.

Hegel, G. W. F. "Glaube und Wissen." In *Werke*, vol. 2, 287–433 . Frankfurt am Main: Suhrkamp, 1986.

Hegel, G. W. F. "Habilitationsthesen." In *Werke*, vol. 2. Frankfurt am Main: Suhrkamp, 1986.

Hegel, G. W. F. *Hegel's Aesthetics: Lectures on Fine Art*. 2 vols. Trans. T. M. Knox. Oxford: Clarendon Press, 1975.

Hegel, G. W. F. *Hegel's Philosophy of Nature*. 3 vols. Trans. M. J. Petry. London: Allen and Unwin, 1970.

Hegel, G. W. F. *Hegel's Science of Logic*. Trans. George di Giovanni. Cambridge: Cambridge University Press, 2010.

Hegel, G. W. F. *Hegel's Science of Logic*. Trans. A. V. Miller. London: Allen and Unwin, 1967.

Hegel, G. W. F. *Jenaer Systementwürfe*. Vol. 1. Ed. Klaus Düsing and Klaus Kimmerle. Hamburg: Meiner, 1986.

Hegel, G. W. F. *Lectures on the History of Philosophy, vol. 1, Greek Philosophy to Plato*. Trans. E. S. Haldane. Lincoln: University of Nebraska Press, 1995.

Hegel, G. W. F. *Lectures on Logic: Berlin, 1831*. Bloomington: Indiana University Press, 2008.

Hegel, G. W. F. *Lectures on the History of Philosophy, vol. 3, Medieval and Modern Philosophy*. Trans. E. S. Haldane and F. H. Simson. Lincoln: University of Nebraska Press, 1995.

Hegel, G. W. F. *Lectures on the Philosophy of Religion: The Lectures of 1827*. Trans. P. Hodgson. Berkeley: University of California Press, 1988.

Hegel, G. W. F. *The Letters*. Bloomington: Indiana University Press, 1984.

Hegel, G. W. F. "Logica et Metaphysica." In *Gesammelte Werke*, vol. 5, 267–276. Hamburg: Meiner, 1988.

Hegel, G. W. F. *The Logic of Hegel*. Trans. William Wallace. Oxford: Clarendon Press, 1873.

Hegel, G. W. F. "Love." In *On Christianity: Early Theological Writings*, trans. T. M. Knox, 302–308. New York: Harper & Brothers, 1948.

Hegel, G. W. F. Natural Law: The Scientific Ways of Treating Natural Law, Its Place in Moral Philosophy, and Its Relation to the Positive Sciences of Law. Trans. T. M. Knox. Philadelphia: University of Pennsylvania Press, 1975.

Hegel, G. W. F. "Notiz zur Überarbeitung des Werks von 1807." In Gesammelte Werke, vol. 9, Phänomenologie des Geistes, ed. Wolfgang Bonsiepen and Reinhard Heede. Hamburg: Meiner, 1980.

Hegel, G. W. F. Outlines of the Philosophy of Right. Trans. T. M. Knox, ed. Stephen Houlgate. Oxford: Oxford University Press, 2008.

Hegel, G. W. F. Phänomenologie des Geistes. In Gesammelte Werke, vol. 9. Hamburg: Meiner, 1980.

Hegel, G. W. F. Phenomenology of Spirit. Trans. A. V. Miller. Oxford: Oxford University Press, 1970.

Hegel, G. W. F. The Philosophy of History. Mineola, NY: Dover, 2004.

Hegel, G. W. F. Philosophy of Mind. Trans. W. Wallace. Oxford: Oxford University Press, 1971.

Hegel, G. W. F. Prolegomena to the Study of Hegel's Philosophy and Especially His Logic. Trans. William Wallace. Oxford: Clarendon Press, 1894.

Hegel, G. W. F. Selbstanzeige. In Werke, vol. 3, Phänomenologie des Geistes. Frankfurt am Main: Suhrkamp, 1986.

Hegel, G. W. F. "Solgers nachgelassene Schriften und Briefwechsel." In Werke, vol. 11, 205–274. Frankfurt am Main: Suhrkamp, 1985.

Hegel, G. W. F. "The Spirit of Christianity and Its Fate." In On Christianity: Early Theological Writings, trans. T. M. Knox, 182–302. New York: Harper & Brothers, 1948.

Hegel, G. W. F. "Systemfragment von 1800." In Werke, vol. 1, 419–427. Frankfurt am Main: Suhrkamp, 1986.

Hegel, G. W. F. "[Über] Friedrich Heinrich Jacobis Werke. Dritter Band." In Werke, vol. 4, 429–461. Frankfurt am Main: Suhrkamp, 1982.

Hegel, G. W. F. "Vorlesungen über die Philosophie der Religion II." In Werke, vol. 17. Frankfurt am Main: Suhrkamp, 1982.

Hegel, G. W. F. Vorlesungen über Logik und Metaphysik: Heidelberg 1817. Hamburg: Meiner, 1992.

Hegel, G. W. F. Vorlesungen über Rechtsphilosophie 1818–1831, vol. 4, ed. Karl-Heinz Ilting. Stuttgart: frommann-holzboog, 1974.

Hegel, G. W. F. "Vorlesungsmanuskripte: 1816–1831." In Gesammelte Werke, vol. 17. Hamburg: Meiner, 1987.

Hegel, G. W. F. *Vorlesungen über die Ästhetik III*. In *Werke*, vol. 15. Frankfurt am Main: Suhrkamp, 1986.

Hegel, G. W. F. *Wissenschaft der Logik*. Vol. 1. Nuremberg: Schrag, 1812.

Hegel, G. W. F. *Wissenschaft der Logik*. 2 vols. In *Werke*, vols. 5–6. Frankfurt am Main: Suhrkamp, [1812] 1986.

Heidegger, Martin. "Aristoteles-Hegel-Seminar." In *Gesamtausgabe* 4, no. 86: *Seminare: Hegel-Schelling*. Tübingen: Klostermann, 2011.

Heidegger, Martin. *Being and Time*. New York: Harper & Row, 2008.

Heidegger, Martin. *Gesamtausgabe, vol. 68, Hegel*. Ed. Ingrid Schussler. Frankfurt am Main: Klostermann, 1993.

Heidegger, Martin. "Hegel's Concept of Experience." In *Off the Beaten Track*, ed. and trans. Julian Young and Kenneth Haynes, 86–156. Cambridge: Cambridge University Press, 2002.

Heidegger, Martin. *Hegel's Phenomenology of Spirit*. Bloomington: Indiana University Press, 1994.

Heidegger, Martin. "What Is Metaphysics?" In *Pathmarks*, ed. William McNeill, 82–96. Cambridge: Cambridge University Press, 1998.

Heinrich, Michael. "Capital after MEGA: Discontinuities, Interruptions, and New Beginnings." *Crisis and Critique* 3, no. 3 (2016): 93–138.

Heinrich, Michael. *Die Wissenschaft vom Wert: Die Marxsche Kritik der politischen Ökonomie zwischen wissenschaftlicher Revolution und klassischer Tradition*. Münster: Westfälisches Dampfboot, 2011.

Hello, Ernest. *L'homme*. Paris: Perrin, [1872] 1921.

Henrich, Dieter. *Hegel im Kontext*. Frankfurt am Main: Suhrkamp, 1975.

Hölderlin, Friedrich. "Remarks on Antigone." In *Essays and Letters on Theory*. Ed. and trans. Thomas Pfau. Albany: SUNY Press, 1988.

Hösle, Vittorio. *Hegels System: Der Idealismus der Subjektivität und das Problem der Intersubjektivität*. Hamburg: Meiner, 1998.

Houlgate, Stephen. *The Opening of Hegel's Logic: From Being to Infinity*. West Lafayette, IN: Purdue University Press, 2006.

Hyppolite, Jean. *Genesis and Structure of Hegel's "Phenomenology of Spirit."* Evanston, IL: Northwestern University Press, 1974.

Hyppolite, Jean. *Logic and Existence*. New York: SUNY Press, 1997.

Jaeschke, Walter. *Hegel-Handbuch: Leben—Werk—Schule*. Stuttgart: Metzler, 2010.

Jameson, Fredric. *The Hegel Variations: On the Phenomenology of Spirit*. London: Verso, 2010.

Jung, C. G. "On the Nature of the Psyche." In *Collected Works*, vol. 8. Princeton, NJ: Princeton University Press, 1969.

Kant, Immanuel. "An Answer to the Question: What Is Enlightenment?" In *Practical Philosophy*, ed. Mary J. Gregor. Cambridge: Cambridge University Press, 1999, 11-22.

Kant, Immanuel. *Critique of Judgment*. Trans. James Creed Meredith. Oxford: Oxford University Press, 2007.

Kant, Immanuel. *Critique of Pure Reason*. Trans. and ed. Paul Guyer and Allen W. Wood. Cambridge: Cambridge University Press, 1998.

Kant, Immanuel. "The Jäsche Logic." In *Lectures on Logic*, trans. J. Michael Young. Cambridge: Cambridge University Press, 1992.

Kant, Immanuel. *Lectures on Logic*. Cambridge: Cambridge University Press, 1992.

Kant, Immanuel. "On the Miscarriage of All Philosophical Attempts in Theodicy." In *Immanuel Kant, Religion and Rational Theology*, 24–37. Cambridge: Cambridge University Press, 2001.

Kant, Immanuel. "On the Ultimate Ground of the Differentiation of Regions of the Body in Space" (1768). In *Theoretical Philosophy, 1755–1770*, 361–372. Cambridge: Cambridge University Press, 1992.

Kaufmann, Walter. *Hegel: A Reinterpretation*. Garden City, NY: Doubleday, 1965.

Kierkegaard, Søren. *Concluding Unscientific Postscript to "Philosophical Fragments."* Princeton, NJ: Princeton University Press, 1968.

Kittler, Friedrich. *Discourse Networks 1800/1900*. Stanford, CA: Stanford University Press, 1990.

Kleist, Heinrich von. "On the Gradual Production of Thoughts Whilst Speaking." In *Kleist: Selected Writings*, ed. and trans. David Constantine, 405–410. Indianapolis: Hackett, 2004.

Kleist, Heinrich von. *Über die allmählige Verfertigung der Gedanken beim Reden*. Frankfurt am Main: Dielmann, 1999.

Klibansky, Raymond, Erwin Panofsky, and Fritz Saxl. *Saturn and Melancholy: Studies in the History of Natural Philosophy, Religion, and Art*. New York: Basic Books, 1964.

Koyré, Alexandre. "Note sur la langue et la terminologie hégéliennes." In *Études d'histoire de la pensée philosophique*. Paris: Gallimard, 1971.

Kroner, Richard. "Hegel heute." *Hegel-Studien* 1 (1961): 135–153.

Lacan, Jacques. *Encore: The Seminar of Jacques Lacan, Book XX: On Feminine Sexuality: The Limits of Love and Knowledge, 1972–1973*. Ed. Jacques-Alain Miller, trans. Bruce Fink. New York: Norton, 1988.

Lacan, Jacques. "Kant avec Sade." In Écrits, trans. Bruce Fink, 645–670. New York: Norton, 2002.

Lacan, Jacques. Le moment de conclure: Séminaire XXV. http://staferla.free.fr/S25/S25.pdf.

Lacan, Jacques. The Seminar of Jacques Lacan, Book X, Anxiety. Ed. Jacques-Alain Miller, trans. A. R. Price. Cambridge: Polity Press, 2014.

Lacan, Jacques. The Seminar of Jacques Lacan, Book XI, The Four Fundamental Concepts of Psychoanalysis. Ed. Jacques-Alain Miller, trans. Alan Sheridan. New York: Norton, 1981.

Lacan, Jacques. The Seminar of Jacques Lacan, Book XVII, The Other Side of Psychoanalysis. Trans. Russell Grigg. New York: Norton, 2007.

Lacoue-Labarthe, Philippe, and Jean-Luc Nancy. The Literary Absolute: The Theory of Literature in German Romanticism. Albany: SUNY Press, 1988.

Landmann, Michael. "Gespräch mit Ernst Bloch (Tübingen, 22. December 1967)." Bloch-Almanach 4 (1984): 15–40.

Lebrun, Gérard. La patience du Concept: Essai sur le discours hégélien. Paris: Gallimard, 1972.

Lebrun, Gérard. L'envers de la dialectique: Hegel à la lumière de Nietzsche. Paris: Seuil, 2004.

Lenin, V. I. "Conspectus of Hegel's Book 'The Science of Logic.'" In Lenin's Collected Works, vol. 38, 85–241. Moscow: Progress Publishers, 1976.

Lenin, V. I. "On the Significance of Militant Materialism." In Lenin's Collected Works, vol. 33. Moscow: Progress Publishers, 1965.

Lenin, V. I. What Is to Be Done? Burning Questions of Our Movement. New York: International Publishers, 1978.

Levinas, Emmanuel. New Talmudic Readings. Pittsburgh: Duquesne University Press, 2007.

Longuenesse, Beatrice. Hegel's Critique of Metaphysics. Cambridge: Cambridge University Press, 2007.

Löwith, Karl. "Einleitung." In Die Hegelsche Linke, ed. Karl Löwith. Stuttgart: Frommann, 1962.

Lübbe, Hermann, ed. Die Hegelsche Rechte. Stuttgart: Frommann, 1962.

Lukács, Georg. The Young Hegel: Studies in the Relation between Dialectics and Economics. London: Merlin Press, 1975.

Lukeman, Noah. A Dash of Style: The Art and Mastery of Punctuation. New York: Norton, 2006.

Magee, Glenn A. *Hegel and the Hermetic Tradition.* Ithaca, NY: Cornell University Press, 2001.

Maker, William. *Philosophy without Foundation: Rethinking Hegel.* Albany: SUNY Press, 1994.

Marcuse, Herbert. *Reason and Revolution: Hegel and the Rise of Social Theory.* London: Routledge, 1955.

Marx, Karl. "A Contribution to the Critique of Hegel's 'Philosophy of Right': Introduction." In *Critique of Hegel's Philosophy of Right,* ed. Karl Marx, 129–142. Cambridge: Cambridge University Press, 1970.

Marx, Karl. *A Contribution to the Critique of Political Economy.* Moscow: Progress Publishers, 1977.

Marx, Karl. "The Poverty of Philosophy: Answer to the 'Philosophy of Poverty' by M. Proudhon." In Karl Marx and Frederick Engels, *Collected Works,* vol. 6, 1845–1848, 105–212. New York: International Publishers, 1976.

McCumber, John. "Writing Down (Up) the Truth: Hegel and Schiller at the End of the *Phenomenology of Spirit.*" In *The Spirit of Poesy: Essays on Jewish and German Literature and Thought in Honor of Géza von Molnár,* ed. Richard Block and Peter Fenves. Evanston, IL: Northwestern University Press, 2000, 47-59.

Meillassoux, Quentin. *After Finitude: An Essay on the Necessity of Contingency.* London: Bloomsbury, 2010.

Menke, Christoph. *Force: A Fundamental Concept of Aesthetic Anthropology.* New York: Fordham University Press, 2013.

Miller, Jacques-Alain. "Matrice." In *Un début dans la vie,* 135–144. Paris: Gallimard, 2002.

Miller, Jacques-Alain. "Matrix." *Symptom* 13 (Summer 2012). http://www.lacan.com/symptom13/matrix.html.

Nancy, Jean-Luc. *Hegel: The Restlessness of the Negative.* Minneapolis: University of Minnesota Press, 2002.

Nancy, Jean-Luc. *The Speculative Remark: One of Hegel's Bons Mots.* Palo Alto, CA: Stanford University Press, 2001.

Ng, Karen. "Life, Self-Consciousness, Negativity: Understanding Hegel's Speculative Identity Thesis." In *The Freedom of Life: Hegelian Perspectives,* ed. Thomas Khurana. Frankfurt: August Verlag, 2013.

Nicolin, Friedhelm. "Zum Titelproblem der 'Phänomenologie des Geistes.'" *Hegel-Studien* 4 (1967): 113–123.

Nicolin, Günther, ed. *Hegel in Berichten seiner Zeitgenossen.* Hamburg: Meiner, 1970.

Nietzsche, Friedrich. *Anti-Education: On the Future of Our Educational Institutions.* Ed. Paul Reitter and Chad Wellmon. New York: New York Review of Books, 2016.

Nietzsche, Friedrich. *Genealogy of Morals*. Trans. Walter Kaufmann. New York: Vintage, 1989.

Nietzsche, Friedrich. *The Will to Power*. Ed. Walter Kaufmann, trans. Walter Kaufmann and R. J. Hollingdale. New York: Random House, 1967.

Pahl, Katrin. *Tropes of Transport: Hegel on Emotion*. Evanston: Northwestern University Press, 2012.

Peden, Knox. "Introduction to Volume Two: 'The Fate of the Concept.'" In *Concept and Form*, vol. 2, *Interviews and Essays on the "Cahiers pour l'Analyse,"* ed. Peter Hallward and Knox Peden, 1–14. London: Verso, 2012.

Pinkard, Terry. *Hegel: A Biography*. Cambridge: Cambridge University Press, 2000.

Pöggeler, Otto. "Die Komposition der Phänomenologie des Geistes." In *Materialien zu Hegels "Phänomenologie des Geistes,"* ed. Hans Friedrich Fulda and Dieter Henrich, 329–390. Frankfurt am Main: Suhrkamp, 1973.

Pugh, David. *Dialectic of Love: Platonism in Schiller's Aesthetics*. Montreal: McGill–Queen's University Press, 1997.

Riazanov, David. *Karl Marx and Frederick Engels: An Introduction to Their Lives and Work*. New York: Monthly Review Press, 1974.

Rosenkranz, Karl. *Georg Wilhelm Friedrich Hegels Leben*. Darmstadt: WBG, 1991.

Rosenzweig, Franz. *Hegel und der Staat*. Berlin: Suhrkamp, 2010.

Ruda, Frank. *Abolishing Freedom: A Plea for a Contemporary Use of Fatalism*. Lincoln: University of Nebraska Press, 2016.

Ruda, Frank. *For Badiou: Idealism without Idealism*. Evanston, IL: Northwestern University Press, 2015.

Ruge, Arnold. *Unsere letzten zehn Jahre*. In *Sämmtliche Werke*, vol. 5, 2, 1–135. Mannheim: Verlag von J. P. Grohe, 1848.

Santner, Eric. *On the Psychotheology of Everyday Life: Reflections on Freud and Rosenzweig*. Chicago: University of Chicago Press, 2001.

Schiller, Friedrich. *On the Aesthetic Education of Man*. Mineola, NY: Dover, 2004.

Schiller, Friedrich. *Schillers Werke, Nationalausgabe*. Vol. 1. Ed. J. Petersen and F. Beißner. Weimar: Hermann Böhlaus Nachfolger, 1962.

Schiller, Friedrich. *Schillers Werke, Nationalausgabe*, vol. 20, *Philosophische Schriften*. Ed. Benno von Wiese and Helmut Koopman. Weimar: Hermann Böhlaus Nachfolger, 1963.

Schlegel, Friedrich. *Philosophische Vorlesungen aus den Jahren 1804 bis 1806: Nebst Fragmenten vorzüglich philosophischen Inhalts*. Vol. 2. Berlin: E. Weber, 1837.

Schmidt, James. "Cabbage Heads and Gulps of Water." *Political Theory* 26, no. 1 (Feb. 1998), 4–32.

Sell, Annette. *Der lebendige Begriff: Leben und Logik bei G. W. F. Hegel*. Freiburg: Karl Alber, 2013.

Sellars, Wilfrid. *Empiricism and Philosophy of Mind*. Cambridge, MA: Harvard University Press, 1997.

Semm, Markus. *Der springende Punkt in Hegels System*. Munich: Boer, 1994.

Solomon, R. C. *In the Spirit of Hegel*. Oxford: Oxford University Press, 1983.

Spaventa, Bertrando. *Scritti filosofici*. Vol. 1. Naples: Pierro, 1900.

Stewart, Jon, ed. *The Hegel Myths and Legends*. Evanston, IL: Northwestern University Press, 1996.

Theunissen, Michael. *Sein und Schein: Die kritische Funktion der Hegelschen Logik*. Frankfurt am Main: Suhrkamp, 1978.

Trendelenburg, Friedrich Adolf von. *Logische Untersuchen*. Leipzig: Hirzel, 1840.

Tugendhat, Ernst. "Das Sein und das Nichts." In *Durchblicke: Martin Heidegger zum 80. Geburtstag*, 132–171. Frankfurt am Main: Klostermann, 1970.

Vollrath, Ernst. "Die Gliederung der Metaphysik in eine Metaphysica generalis und eine Metaphysica specialis." *Zeitschrift für philosophische Forschung* 16 (1962): 258–281.

Weber, Samuel. *Benjamin's -abilities*. Cambridge, MA: Harvard University Press, 2009.

Wismann, Heinz. *Les avatars du vide: Démocrite et les fondements du atomisme*. Paris: Hermann Editeurs, 2010.

Wittgenstein, Ludwig. *Tractatus Logico-Philosophicus*. London: Routledge, 2001.

Wohlfart, Günter. *Der Punkt: Ästhetische Meditationen*. Freiburg: Karl Alber, 1986.

Wohlfart, Günter. *Der spekulative Satz: Bemerkungen zum Begriff der Spekulation bei Hegel*. Berlin: De Gruyter, 1981.

Žižek, Slavoj. *Absolute Recoil: Towards a New Foundation of Dialectical Materialism*. London: Verso, 2015.

Žižek, Slavoj. "An Ethical Plea for Lies and Masochism." In *Lacan and Contemporary Film*, ed. T. McGowan and S. Kunkle, 173–186. New York: Other Press, 2004.

Žižek, Slavoj. *The Fragile Absolute, or Why the Christian Legacy Is Worth Fighting For*. London: Verso, 2000.

Žižek, Slavoj. *Less Than Nothing: Hegel and the Shadow of Dialectical Materialism*. London: Verso, 2012.

Žižek, Slavoj. "A Modest Plea for a Hegelian Reading of Christianity." In Slavoj Žižek and John Milbank, *The Monstrosity of Christ: Paradox or Dialectic?*, 24–110. Cambridge, MA: MIT Press, 2009.

Žižek, Slavoj. *The Most Sublime Hysteric: Hegel with Lacan*. Cambridge: Polity Press, 2014.

Žižek, Slavoj. *The Parallax View*. Cambridge, MA: MIT Press, 2009.

Žižek, Slavoj. "Philosophy, the 'Unknown Knowns,' and the Public Use of Reason." *Topoi* 25, no. 1–2 (2006): 137–142.

Žižek, Slavoj. *The Sublime Object of Ideology*. London: Verso, 1989.

Zupančič, Alenka. *The Odd One In: On Comedy*. Cambridge, MA: MIT Press, 2008.

The Dash—

THE OTHER SIDE OF ABSOLUTE KNOWING
REBECCA COMAY AND FRANK RUDA

This book sets out from a counterintuitive premise: the "mystical shell" of Hegel's system proves to be its most "rational kernel." Hegel's radicalism is located precisely at the point where his thought seems to regress most. Most current readings try to update Hegel's thought by pruning back his grandiose claims to "absolute knowing." Comay and Ruda invert this deflationary gesture by inflating what seems to be most trivial: the absolute is grasped only in the minutiae of its most mundane appearances. Reading Hegel without presupposition, without eliminating anything in advance or making any decision about what is essential and what is inessential, what is living and what is dead, they explore his presentation of the absolute to the letter.

The Dash is organized around a pair of seemingly innocuous details. Hegel punctuates strangely. He ends The Phenomenology of Spirit with a dash, and he begins Science of Logic with a dash. This distinctive punctuation reveals an ambiguity at the heart of absolute knowing. The dash combines hesitation and acceleration. Its orientation is simultaneously retrospective and prospective. It both holds back and propels. It severs and connects. It demurs and insists. It interrupts and prolongs. It generates non sequiturs and produces explanations. It leads in all directions: continuation, deviation, meaningless termination. This challenges every cliché about the Hegelian dialectic as a machine of uninterrupted teleological progress. The dialectical movement is, rather, structured by intermittency, interruption, hesitation, blockage, abruption, and random, unpredictable change—a rhythm that displays all the vicissitudes of the Freudian drive.

Rebecca Comay is Professor of Philosophy and Comparative Literature at the University of Toronto. **Frank Ruda** is Senior Lecturer in Philosophy at the University of Dundee.